APPROACHING THE END

Approaching the End

Eschatological Reflections on
Church, Politics, and Life

Stanley Hauerwas

William B. Eerdmans Publishing Company
Grand Rapids, Michigan / Cambridge, U.K.

Published 2013 by
Wm. B. Eerdmans Publishing Co.
2140 Oak Industrial Drive N.E., Grand Rapids, Michigan 49505 /
P.O. Box 163, Cambridge CB3 9PU U.K.

Printed in the United States of America

19 18 17 16 15 14 13   7 6 5 4 3 2 1

Library of Congress Cataloging-in-Publication Data

Hauerwas, Stanley, 1940-
Approaching the end: eschatological reflections on church, politics, and life /
    Stanley Hauerwas.
        pages   cm
    Includes bibliographical references and index.
    ISBN 978-0-8028-6959-3 (pbk.: alk. paper)
    1. Hauerwas, Stanley, 1940- 2. Christianity and politics. 3. Christian life.
    I. Title.

BX4827.H34A5   2013b
236 — dc23
                                                          2013031430

www.eerdmans.com

Contents

Preface

I have been teaching for forty-five years. That is what I understand myself to be — a teacher. I suspect that is not how those external to Notre Dame and Duke think of me. I suspect I am thought of as a person who "writes a lot" and/or holds views about what it means to be a Christian that are not widely shared. Given my track record, that I am so regarded by many is quite understandable, but I hope that is not who I am. I hope I am first and foremost a teacher.

I am soon to retire. If I have any regret about retirement it is that I will miss interaction with graduate students. I am not sure how many dissertations I have directed. I am sure I do not want to know how many dissertations I have directed. To know how many would only make me tired. What I do know is that the trust students have put in me has been a gift. I have learned from every dissertation I have directed. It would, I suspect, be a fascinating investigation to show the difference students have made for how I think and what I have written over time.

To teach means you must be taught. I have never liked sentiments that suggest teachers learn more from their students than students learn from their teachers. Of course, everything depends on what you think you are "learning." I think teachers should know more than students about the subject they are teaching. The "more" they should know is not necessarily "information," but rather judgments that depend on years of close reading. Teachers can and certainly do learn from students, but that does not mean they cease being teachers.

That I will soon retire, moreover, does not mean I will stop being a teacher. As I think my students will testify, I have never limited my teaching to giving lectures, leading seminars, or directing dissertations. A teacher understands that every interaction with students in one way or another involves exchanges that are formative. This is particularly true when the interactions are about baseball. After all, baseball is a game with clear eschatological significance because it is a game that is never "over."

All of this is but an attempt to say "thank you" to all the good people who have made me a teacher. I am particularly grateful to those who have entrusted me to direct their dissertations. To all who claim me to be their teacher I dedicate this book.

Introduction

The title, *Approaching the End*, is deliberately ambiguous in order to re-flect the different but interrelated subjects I address in this book. Any reference to the "end" in a book on theology usually indicates that the eschatological character of the Christian faith will be a central consider-ation. I hope *Approaching the End* meets that expectation. To the best of my ability I try to show the significance of eschatology for understanding how Christians are to negotiate the world. By doing so I hope to make clear why I have maintained that the church does not have a social ethic but is a social ethic.[1]

Accordingly this is also a book about the church and, in particular, the end of the church. In *The State of the University: Academic Knowledges and the Knowledge of God* I suggested there are two questions you cannot ask about the contemporary university.[2] Those questions are, "What is it for?" and "Who does it serve?" You cannot ask those questions because many of us who count ourselves among those who represent the univer-sity know we do not know how to answer those questions or we do not

1. I am not particularly happy with the very idea that you need to talk about some-thing called "social ethics." The ethical presumptions that would tempt anyone to dis-tinguish between social ethics and whatever is thought to constitute ethics that is not social must be mistaken. I have the same reaction to the phrase "social justice." Justice by its very nature is social just as any ethic by its nature is social. I use "social ethics" only because of its widespread use.

2. Stanley Hauerwas, *The State of the University: Academic Knowledges and the Knowledge of God* (Oxford: Blackwell, 2007).

like the answers we know we should give. The same questions need to be asked about the church. But they have not been asked for reasons I suspect are very similar to why they are not asked about universities.

It may be, however, that these questions are not asked about the church because many assume that the church is in a survival mode. The end that the church is approaching, or at least some churches may be approaching, is quite literally death. So the end to which the church is moving is not a purposive end that gives order to the practices that make the church the church. Rather, the end some churches face, particularly churches for which the Reformation is their legitimating narrative, is demise.[3] We may have already seen the end of many churches that bear the name Christian while failing to recognize that we have done so because those churches still seem to be in business. But the business they are in may have only a very accidental relation with Christianity.

There are, of course, many different kinds of churches. Not all churches seem to be experiencing the same fate as mainstream Protestantism. It is my judgment, however, a judgment I defend in "Church Matters: On Faith and Politics," that churches that may currently seem to be flourishing — and that includes churches in the Roman Catholic tradition as well as Protestant evangelicals — are fated to endure the same end as churches in the Protestant mainstream. The church is in a buyer's market that makes any attempt to form a disciplined congregational life very difficult.

There is another end that may be approaching that has implications for the church — that is, we may be nearing the end of Christendom. Of course "Christendom" is the name used to describe quite diverse forms of societal organization, but what seems to be occurring is that the general societal approval and support the church has enjoyed particularly in America is coming to an end. Of course one of the costs Christians have paid for the social and political status they have enjoyed is not to take their Christian identity so seriously that they might destabilize the social order by, for example, challenging the presumption that war is a neces-

---

3. For a set of reflections concerning this possibility see *Postliberal Theology and the Church Catholic: Conversations with George Lindbeck, David Burrell, and Stanley Hauerwas*, ed. John Wright (Grand Rapids: Baker Academic, 2012).

sity if democracies are to survive. Thus I am long on record as thinking the loss of Christendom to be a "good thing."[4]

One of the reasons I think the waning days of Christendom to be a good thing has everything to do with the recovery of the eschatological character of the gospel. When Christians begin to think we are at home in the world our sense that we live "between the times" is not only muted but close to being unintelligible. The recovery of the eschatological vision is crucial for how the church understands her relation to the world.

My oft-made claim, a claim that many find offensive, that the first task of the church is not to make the world just but to make the world the world, is rightly understood only in light of these eschatological convictions. Dualities such as faith and reason, grace and nature, creation and redemption are properly to be understood in the light of the church/world alternative. The church/world alternative, moreover, must be under constant reconfiguration because what it means to be church must always be open to the work of the Holy Spirit. Rightly understood, however, the presumption that the church exists so that the world might recognize itself as world is in fact good news.[5]

From this perspective the loss of the social and political status of the

---

4. It is hard to believe *Resident Aliens* (Nashville: Abingdon, 1989), the book Will Willimon and I wrote announcing this reality, will soon be twenty-five years old.

5. This way of putting the matter obviously owes much to John Howard Yoder's *The Christian Witness to the State* (Newton, KS: Faith and Life, 1970). The Kingdom of God is the central image that expresses the New Testament eschatological vision, but it is crucial to recognize, as Yoder does, that time is at the heart of that vision. Thus Yoder's suggestion that from a New Testament perspective we live in two times (aeons) simultaneously. The difference between the ages is not temporal — that is, one does not follow after the other, but rather they represent two different directions. The old age is characterized by sin. The coming aeon, made present by Christ through the Holy Spirit, is redemptive. It is therefore possible, Yoder maintains, to rationally believe as the New Testament believes that "Christ has triumphed and is reigning (which is true for the church through the Holy Spirit, and for the world by anticipation) and that the powers are still rampant" (p. 9). For Yoder's extended reflections on eschatology see his chapter, "Christ the King: Last Things," in *Preface to Theology: Christology and Theological Method*, ed. with an introduction by Stanley Hauerwas and Alex Sider (Grand Rapids: Brazos, 2002), pp. 240-80. In *Preface to Theology* Yoder makes explicit what is implied in *The Christian Witness to the State*, that is, that "the preaching of the gospel is why time does not stop. This then is the meaning and content of his [Jesus'] kingship. Kingship is the ruling over history so that this can happen" (p. 249).

church may have made it possible for Yoder's account of the "politics of Jesus" to at least be understood and perhaps even be thought to have the ring of truth.[6] As long as the church has to act in a "politically responsible" manner she will find it hard to take her own existence as a political reality seriously. Given the eschatological presumptions that shape this book, however, the church does not so much have a political mission as her very existence is a political mission; it provides an alternative to the politics of the world. Such a view may seem counterintuitive, but I think it nonetheless true. In most matters we discover what makes us who we are or should be when we have nothing to lose.

It would serve little purpose for me to say in this introduction what I have said throughout the chapters of this book. But I hope I have said enough to alert and prepare the reader for the eschatological position developed in quite diverse ways throughout this book.[7] The chapters in Part One address directly my understanding of the eschatological character of the Christian faith. There is much more that needs to be said about eschatology than I say in these essays, but I hope what I have said is at least the beginning of such conversations. Rightly understood, every loci of the Christian faith has an eschatological dimension, making impossible any isolated account of eschatology. So the "more" that needs to be said about eschatology is the "more" that gestures toward the necessary unfinished character of Christian theology.

As is often the case in the books I put together, the ordering of the chapters is arbitrary. That is a little strong. Better put, there is no clear logical development from one chapter to the next. All the essays are, I think, interrelated in interesting ways, making it possible for readers to begin anywhere. What is only a suggestion in one essay will be developed

---

6. John Howard Yoder, *The Politics of Jesus: Vicit Agnus Noster* (Grand Rapids: Eerdmans, 1995).

7. For a short but quite useful overview of what is meant by eschatology see Thomas Finger's article "Eschatology and Ethics," in the *Dictionary of Scripture and Ethics*, ed. Joel Green (Grand Rapids: Baker Academic, 2011), pp. 276-79. Finger suggests that through my work I have expanded many of Yoder's points about eschatology by emphasizing that Christian ethics is taught and practiced in the church. Finger says this means I think ethics is developed and transmitted by traditions and narratives rather than by rational arguments. I hope Finger is wrong about that because I think tradition and narrative constitute the possibility of making rational arguments.

more fully in another. I have always thought what I have to say, which admittedly many find "hard to take," might be given a second thought if the reader is trusted to make connections I may well miss myself. I hope that trust is evident in this book.

I could, for example, have begun the book with the essays in Part Two. I chose to begin with the more theological essays not only because they more directly engage Scripture but also because they make explicit the fundamental concepts that shape the book. In particular the first chapter, "The End Is in the Beginning: Creation and Apocalyptic," can be understood as my attempt to engage the fundamental "methodological" issues at the heart of all the subsequent chapters. In that chapter, for example, I consider the status of natural law for Christian practical reason.[8]

I am, of course, hesitant to describe that essay as "methodological" because I am quite suspicious of "method." I hope I have never had a "method" if by method it is meant that one must begin with a theory to determine what can be said. I have always assumed it best to "dive in at the deep end" so that one must sink or swim. But the essays in Part One do deal with fundamental questions concerning the apocalyptic character of Christian eschatological convictions. The third chapter, "Witness," is important not only because in it Pinches and I explore the witness of the New Testament but also because we draw on recent work concerning the significance of martyrdom for understanding the eschatological politics of the church.

The chapters that make up Part Two deal directly with the political reality of the church. Some readers may find it odd that several of these essays deal not only with the church's relation with the world but also with issues surrounding the divided character of the church and the imperative of Christian unity. Again I make no claim to have dealt adequately with the ecumenical challenge before us as Christians, but I am sure that the divided character of the church makes Christians far too ready to go

---

8. I have also recently discussed the nature of practical reason in the "Afterword" to the new edition of *With the Grain of the Universe* soon to be published by Brazos Press. In particular I discuss Eugene Garver's very important book, *For the Sake of Argument: Practical Reasoning, Character, and the Ethics of Belief* (Chicago: University of Chicago Press, 2004).

to war. That is why the chapter "War and Peace" hopefully serves as an appropriate "summing up" of the first two sections of this book.

There is one theme running through the first two sections to which I feel I need to call attention. I have become convinced that if we are to understand our politics, and in particular the politics of war, we must attend to sacrifice as a crucial practice determining our lives. I have obviously been influenced in this respect by René Girard and Paul Kahn, but even before I had read them Yoder had alerted me to sacrifice as a crucial category. I began exploration of the significance of sacrifice in *War and the American Difference*, but I think my response in "The End of Sacrifice: An Apocalyptic Politics" to Peter Leithart's defense of Constantine for prohibiting "pagan" sacrifices helps make the connection between sacrifice and politics clearer.[9]

There is yet another "end" that some may associate with the title of this book, namely, they may well think, given my retirement, that "the end" that is approaching is my own. Some might even be led to think the title suggests that I might intend for this book to be my "swan song." Am I trying in *Approaching the End* to have the last word? That is certainly not how I understand what I am about in this book. Rather than trying to have the last word, I am trying in *Approaching the End* to write in a different voice.

I do not want to be misunderstood. Those familiar with my work will find arguments and positions in *Approaching the End* that I have used or taken in the past. But I also hope the reader will find some surprises in this book. At least I know there are some surprises for me in this book. For example, I was surprised, though I suspect I should not have been, to see how important it is for me to continue to draw on Barth's work if I am to say what I think needs to be said. Of course Yoder also remains a necessary resource, but my reliance on Yoder has been constant in a way my reliance on Barth has not been.

I have written much, but I have tried to avoid saying the same thing

---

9. For my reflections on war as sacrifice see Stanley Hauerwas, *War and the American Difference: Theological Reflections on Violence and National Identity* (Grand Rapids: Baker Academic, 2011), pp. 53-70. For an excellent book of essays on Leithart's *Defending Constantine* (Downers Grove: InterVarsity, 2010) see *Constantine Revisited*, ed. Jon Roth (Eugene, OR: Wipf and Stock, forthcoming).

time after time. It is not always a bad idea to say the same thing again if saying the same thing requires us to say what we had not anticipated we needed to say given what we had said in the past. What I have tried to do by what I write is show how I am forced to have thoughts I did not know I had until I tried to think through the implications of what I have thought. So I am sure readers of my past work will find familiar themes in *Approaching the End*, but I think they may also be surprised by the tone if not the substance of some of the essays in this book.

In the preface to volume IV/2 of the *Church Dogmatics*, Barth observes that some of his former friends and fellows wonder if in his attempt to better understand more sympathetically Roman Catholics, Pietists, and "Evangelical groups" he had gone too far in what he had ascribed to man. Had he not become "an old lion who has finally learned to eat straw"? Barth answers by observing that "perspicuous readers" will notice that his more sympathetic attitude toward those with whom he has disagreed with in the past signals no qualification of the basic view he has adopted since his break with Liberalism. He continues to maintain that Jesus alone is the basis and power of any exaltation of our humanity. Barth observes, however, that he is a continual learner, making every aspect of the *Church Dogmatics* exhibit a quiet but persistent movement that testifies to his content with the broad lines of the Christian tradition.[10]

I am, of course, no Karl Barth, but I call attention to Barth's observations because they express exactly how I think about my own work. I am well aware that I am identified as one whose theological voice tends to overwhelm an appropriate acknowledgment of what it means to be human. The centrality of Christ in my work leaves some with the impres-

---

10. Karl Barth, *Church Dogmatics*, IV/2 (Edinburgh: T&T Clark, 1958), pp. vii-xiii. In one of his last interviews before he died Barth confessed, "I am not ultimately at home in theology, in the political world, or even in the church. These are all preparatory matters. They are serious but preparatory. We have to learn to stand in them, to do so fully, and I want to do this quite cheerfully, but we have also to learn to look beyond them." He then observed in answer to a question about grace: "Grace itself is only a provisional word. The last word that I have to say as a theologian or politician is not a concept like grace but a name: Jesus Christ. He is the grace and he is the ultimate one beyond world and church and even theology. . . . In him is grace. In him is the spur to work, warfare, and fellowship. In him is all that I have attempted in my life in weakness and folly." *Final Testimonies* (Grand Rapids: Eerdmans, 1977), pp. 29-30.

sion that I have no place for reflection on what it means to be human. Yet I should like to think that the Christological center of my work has been an attempt to help us see what it would mean for us to be what we were created to be — that is, no more or no less than human. If I have been a critic of "humanism" I have been so because I find so much that passes as "humanism" to be impoverished.

The first essay in Part Three, "Bearing Reality," is my attempt to show how and why the Christological center of my work as well as my focus on the church do not mean that I lack the intellectual resources to address the difficulties of being human. Some may interpret that chapter as an indication that I have in fact "learned to eat straw." Such a reading I believe, as Barth believed about his work, to be a profound mistake. Rather, I should hope that, like Barth, I am a "continual learner" ready to have "movement" in my work by discovering conversation partners I did not know I had.

In particular, "Bearing Reality" draws on J. M. Coetzee's great novel *Elizabeth Costello*, and the philosophical reflections on the novel by Cora Diamond, Stephen Mulhall, and Stanley Cavell. I have engaged that novel and their reflections on that novel, not because I am trying to show my critics that I am not as theologically reactionary as they assume I must be, but because Coetzee and these philosophers rightly see that the challenge is how to be human in a world of cruelty.

"Bearing Reality" was written to be the presidential address to the Society of Christian Ethics in 2012.[11] I mention the context I had for writing this lecture because it may help explain my use of Yoder's great presidential address to the Society of Christian Ethics, "To Serve Our God and to Rule the World." In truth, I wanted to use the opportunity given me at the Society to hopefully make many of my colleagues in the Society of Christian Ethics think twice about how they had learned to think about how I think. I make no apologies for the strong theological voice I think necessary if Christian ethics is to be done well, but I hope "Bearing Reality" makes clear that a strong theological voice does not make reality any less difficult.

11. In my memoir, *Hannah's Child: A Theologian's Memoir* (Grand Rapids: Eerdmans, 2010), I report that as far as I know I am the only person to be defeated for the presidency of the Society of Christian Ethics — twice. But I was elected on the third go-around. So much for making a virtue out of not winning.

Moreover, I hope "Bearing Reality," as well as the other essays in this book, suggests (contrary to some characterizations of my work) that I do not think that for the church to be the church it must be "pure." I am quite well aware that too often the desire and the attempt to make the church "pure" — no matter how well intentioned — can be quite coercive. There is no way to make the church safe from the world. When the church seeks that kind of place in the world, too often the result is an inverted Christendom. I have little use for purity, but I do pray for a more faithful church. A more faithful church, moreover, would, I suspect, make being a Christian more difficult but also more interesting.

And that is how I hope the reader will find the essays in Part Three, that is, interesting explorations in what it means to be human. They also revisit subjects I have addressed in the past. I am particularly grateful for being given the opportunity to reconsider and expand on what I once thought. Although I am a continual learner, I am also at the age when death becomes a more present reality. It turns out, therefore, that eschatology can and does have quite immediate implications.

We are bodily creatures whose bodies make life rich and vital, but embodiment also means we are destined to endure pain, illness, and death. That medicine is the subject of several of these essays is therefore not surprising, given the role medicine has for the care of the body. Medicine is but one way we express our care of one another by our willingness to be *with* those who are suffering and dying. We dare not forget, moreover, that we must be present to ourselves even as we are forced by our bodily nature to acknowledge that we too are destined to die.

If we are to be human, we are in the business of learning to die. That, in short, is what this book is about. That is what Christianity is about. It is my hope, therefore, that those who are not Christian might find some of the reflections in this book "useful." For it is my deepest conviction that Christianity is training in how to be human. What Christians have to say should therefore be interesting to those who do not share our faith. But it is equally true that we Christians will have much to learn from those who are not so identified.

PART ONE

Theological Matters

The End Is in the Beginning:
Creation and Apocalyptic

Why No Method Is a Method

When I began to think about what I should say about creation, the title "The End Is in the Beginning" immediately came to mind. That it did so I suspect is due to my long-held conviction that creation, at least creation as understood by Christians, must be understood from an eschatological perspective. We only know there was a beginning because we have seen the end in Christ. Indeed, as I argued in the Brazos Commentary on Matthew, I think Matthew wrote his Gospel with the conviction that the story he has to tell is a story of a new creation. Thus Matthew begins the Gospel with the declaration that this is "the book of the genesis of Jesus Christ."[1]

I confess I was pleased with the title "The End Is in the Beginning." But I also thought, given that I originally wrote this for the Wilken Lecture, I should see if Robert Wilken might have said something I could use in support of my argument that creation must be rendered through the eschatological imagination shaped by the gospel. You can imagine my chagrin as well as my joy to discover Robert's chapter in *The Spirit of Early Christian Thought: Seeking the Face of God* on Basil and Gregory of Nyssa entitled "The End Given in the Beginning."[2] I had, as so often is the case,

---

1. Stanley Hauerwas, *Matthew*, Brazos Theological Commentary on the Bible (Grand Rapids: Brazos, 2006), pp. 23-25.
2. Robert Wilken, *The Spirit of Early Christian Thought: Seeking the Face of God* (New Haven: Yale University Press, 2003), pp. 136-61.

forgotten where I had learned that the end is in the beginning. As Robert puts it, commenting on Gregory's development of Basil's thought: "Creation is promise as well as gift, and it is only in seeing Christ that we know what was made in the first creation."[3]

Calling attention to Robert's great book, moreover, allows me to make some comments to clarify my "method," or what many think to be my lack of method, for doing theology. I am rightly well known for disavowing any attempt to do theology as a system.[4] My work is occasional if not haphazard. I admire and learn from Robert Jenson's *Systematic Theology*, but I do not have Jenson's erudition or metaphysical imagination to do theology as "system."[5] Perhaps another way to put the matter is that I should like to think my work is closer in style and substance to the second volume of Jenson's *Systematic Theology*, which deals with "The Works of God" and, in particular, creation.[6] There, for example, Jenson asserts that "the story told in the Gospels states the meaning of creation."[7]

That "the story told in the Gospels states the meaning of creation" is, of course, a systematic remark, but it is also a remark that begs for practical display. My worry about theology done as "system" is how that way of doing theology may give the impression that, as I observe in *Sanctify Them in the Truth: Holiness Exemplified*, "Christianity is a set of ideas that

---

3. Wilken, *The Spirit of Early Christian Thought*, p. 155.

4. John Webster suggests systematic theology names the attempt "to present Christian teaching as a unified whole; even though particular exercises in the genre may restrict themselves to only one or other element of Christian doctrine, they have their place in the entire corpus." "Introduction: Systematic Theology," in *The Oxford Handbook of Systematic Theology*, ed. John Webster, Kathryn Tanner, and Iain Torrance (Oxford: Oxford University Press, 2007), p. 2. I, of course, have no reason to call into question systematic theology so understood, though I worry that theology so understood tempts theologians to present what Webster identifies as "Christian reality claims" as "symbolic" representations of some anterior experience. Webster is, of course, a representative of the alternative view, that is, that Christian reality claims are irreducible, which means they cannot be translated into other conceptual schemes without loss. Webster provides an exceptionally clear account of these alternatives on pp. 10-11.

5. Robert Jenson, *Systematic Theology*, vol. 1: *The Triune God* (New York: Oxford University Press, 1997).

6. Robert Jenson, *Systematic Theology*, vol. 2: *The Works of God* (New York: Oxford University Press, 1999).

7. Jenson, *Systematic Theology*, vol. 2, p. 27.

need to be made consistent with one another."[8] I go on to argue in *Sanctify Them in the Truth* (yet another of my books that, as far as I can tell, fell stillborn from the press) that theology is an intricate web of *loci* that requires ongoing exploration and repair. Exploration and repair are required because we are tempted to overemphasize one "doctrine" or *locus* in a manner that distorts what we believe and how we live.[9] All of which is to say that the occasional character of my work is at least partly due to my conviction that theology is best understood as an exercise in practical reason.

I should like to think this way of understanding the theological task to be consistent with the way Wilken tells the story of the development of early Christian thought. He observes that the early Christian thinkers were not in the business of "establishing something." Rather, they understood their task to plumb "the facts of revelation" by employing "the language and imagery of the Bible, and how the life and worship of the Christian community gave Christian thinking a social dimension that was absent from ancient philosophy."[10] Accordingly, Wilken observes by way of commentary on Justin's conversion that in contrast to the philosophers, who rely on demonstrations, "the Word of God makes its way not by argument but as men and women bear witness to what has happened."[11]

Of course, Wilken would be quick to deny that argument is not an essential aspect of Christian witness. Rather, I take his point to be that argument without witness is empty. Even worse, argument without witness threatens to become a coercive ideology. Put even more strongly, witness is a form of argument if we remember — as Wilken, drawing on Origen, argues — that in the Scriptures seeing is never simply a beholding some-

---

8. Stanley Hauerwas, *Sanctify Them in the Truth: Holiness Exemplified* (Nashville: Abingdon, 1998), p. 2.

9. For example, the stress on so-called doctrines of atonement in some Protestant traditions often betrays an attenuated Christology and an ecclesiology in which the church is but a collection of individuals. As a result "the politics of Jesus" is lost.

10. Wilken, *The Spirit of Early Christian Thought*, p. 3.

11. Wilken, *The Spirit of Early Christian Thought*, p. 6. Wilken makes clear, however, that the contrast between philosophy and theology in the ancient world is not as clear as the current divisions suggest because to become a philosopher in the ancient world entailed becoming an apprentice to a master.

thing that makes no difference for how we live, but rather seeing is a "discernment and identification with what is known. What one sees reflects back on the one who sees and transforms the beholder. As Gregory the Great will put it centuries later, 'We are changed into the one we see.' "[12]

I hope my "method" has been an attempt to display the difference Christian convictions make for how we see the world, and how we see the world shapes how we rightly live. Some may well suspect that makes me a pragmatist. I have no objections to being so labeled as long as pragmatism is properly understood to be an attempt to show the differences necessary for what we claim to be true.[13] Interestingly enough, I find myself in deep agreement with Austin Farrer's way of putting the matter, that is, the necessity of theologians to do their work in such a manner that "the inseparability of real knowledge from activity" is maintained. Farrer elaborates this claim by observing "that to know real beings we must exercise our actual relation with them. No physical science without physical interference; no personal knowledge without personal intercourse; no thought about any reality about which we can do nothing but think."[14]

You may well begin to wonder if I have forgotten this is supposed to be an essay on creation. I have not forgotten. Before I am through I hope to make clear how these remarks about method are interrelated with an understanding of creation as an eschatological reality. The methodolog-

12. Wilken, *The Spirit of Early Christian Thought*, p. 21.

13. Charles Sanders Peirce may well exemplify this understanding of pragmatism better than William James, though I continue to find, as I tried to suggest in *With the Grain of the Universe: The Church's Witness and Natural Theology* (Grand Rapids: Brazos, 2001), that James's "empiricism" is best understood as an attempt to help us see the "differences." I do not think it accidental that James was one of Ludwig Wittgenstein's favorite authors.

14. Austin Farrer, *Faith and Speculation* (New York: New York University Press, 1967), p. 22. I am indebted to Professor Robert MacSwain for his work on Farrer. It is far too easy to forget those who have shaped how one has come to think. See also Jeffrey Vogel, "A Little While in the Son of God: Austin Farrer on the Trinitarian Nature of Prayer," *Scottish Journal of Theology* 64, no. 4 (2011): 410-24. Vogel quotes Farrer's wonderful claim that "Prayer and dogma are inseparable. They alone can explain each other. Either without the other is meaningless and dead. If he hears a dogma of faith discussed as a cool speculation, about which theories can be held and arguments propounded, the Christian cannot escape disquiet. 'What are these people doing?' he will ask. 'Do not they know what they are discussing? How can they make it an open question what the country is like, which they enter when they pray?'" (p. 413).

ical remarks, moreover, I hope also help explain why I have seldom written about creation as a topic in and of itself. Rather, I have tried to find contexts to illumine the work an account of creation can and should do to help us understand the way things are.[15] For example, I wrote, with Jeff Powell, an article on William Stringfellow's use of the Book of Revelation to illumine the role of the principalities and powers as perversions of their role in creation.[16] I was attracted to Stringfellow because I thought he helps us see how creation understood apocalyptically helps us read our world in a manner not unlike how John of Patmos read his.[17]

My most extended account of creation, however, was in an article on Iris Murdoch's work. As someone who had learned much from Ms. Murdoch, I was taken aback by her defense of Plato's myth of the Demiurge in her book *Metaphysics as a Guide to Morals*. She defended Plato's understanding of the Demiurge because she thought it a perfect metaphor for how she would have us understand the moral life, that is, as the art of making necessity beautiful. I thought her position to be profoundly wrong in a manner that makes clear why Christians have rightly thought that our understanding of creation necessarily has at its center creation *ex nihilo*. For if God did not create from nothing, Murdoch is right to suggest that our existence is pointless; but because Christians believe all that is exists by the grace of God, we can have hope that life is not without

15. I should like to think this puts me in deep agreement with David Kelsey's great book *Eccentric Existence: A Theological Anthropology*, vols. 1 and 2 (Louisville: Westminster John Knox, 2009). Kelsey observes that in modern systematic theology " 'doctrines of creation' do remarkably little work." He suggests that this is due partly to the abstract character of talk about creation, which results in creation making little difference in the broader project of Christian theology. His project is to clarify not only what it means to say we are creatures of God but also what theological and practical difference it makes to say so (vol. 1, p. 160).

16. See "Creation as Apocalyptic: A Tribute to William Stringfellow," in my *Dispatches from the Front: Theological Engagements with the Secular* (Durham, NC: Duke University Press, 1994), pp. 107-15.

17. Not only does Joe Mangina use Stringfellow's work to great effect in his commentary on the Book of Revelation, but he also carries through more consistently than Stringfellow the idea that, although the church can and must rely on God, such a reliance "does not exclude the possibility of its receiving all manner of help from creaturely sources, providing it does not confuse the latter with the help it receives from the Creator himself." *Revelation*, Brazos Theological Commentary on the Bible (Grand Rapids: Brazos, 2010), p. 157.

purpose. This summary does not do justice to Murdoch's position, but I hope it is sufficient to show how I try to display the work an account of creation does for how we understand the moral life.[18]

I call attention to how I have tried to position how I think about creation in the past to prepare you for the argument I now want to make. The claim that creation is an eschatological doctrine may seem to have little practical import, but by juxtaposing Barth's account of the doctrine of creation with Jean Porter's use of creation to sustain a natural law ethic I hope to show why these matters matter for how we understand how Christians should live and, in particular, how we reason morally. Porter argues with great clarity that the scholastic understanding of natural law is misunderstood if it is divorced, as it often is, from the theological context that makes natural law intelligible. That theological context she identifies with the doctrine of creation. I will argue, however, that her account of creation is insufficiently eschatological, which results in a deficient account of practical reason. Before engaging Porter, I need first to outline Barth's account of the doctrine of creation.

Barth on Creation

Barth's most developed account of creation is to be found in volume III of the *Church Dogmatics*.[19] I obviously cannot provide an overview of the thick account of creation in the four volumes. What I can do, however, is direct our attention to his concentrated discussion of creation in *Dogmatics in Outline*. In *Dogmatics in Outline* Barth begins to develop his account of creation as the external basis for covenant and the covenant as the internal basis of creation.[20] I hope to show how creation so understood re-

18. My chapter on Murdoch entitled "Murdochian Muddles: Can We Get through Them If God Does Not Exist?" is in my book *Wilderness Wanderings: Probing Twentieth-Century Theology and Philosophy* (Boulder: Westview, 1997), pp. 155-70. For Murdoch's reflections on the Demiurge see *Metaphysics as a Guide to Morals* (New York: Penguin, 1992), pp. 477-78.

19. Karl Barth, *Church Dogmatics*, III/1: *Doctrine of Creation*, trans. G. W. Bromiley and T. F. Torrance (Edinburgh: T&T Clark, 1957; repr. Peabody, MA: Hendrickson, 2004).

20. Karl Barth, *Dogmatics in Outline* (New York: Harper Torchbook, 1959). In the

quires an eschatological account of creation that makes unavoidable an account of the contingent, that is, the historical character of existence.

In *Dogmatics in Outline* Barth begins his account of creation, noting that when Christians confess that God is creator they do so only on the basis of God's revelation. So creation is not a speculative judgment about "the beginning."[21] According to Barth, we are not asked by the Confession, the Apostles' Creed, to believe in the created world, nor even the work of creation, but we are asked to believe in God the creator. Creation, therefore, is no less a matter of faith than is our belief in the redemption of the world in Christ — a claim that obviously reflects Barth's fundamental theological method, but that does not mean that the faith necessary to acknowledge God's creation has no purchase in the world as we know it. We are, after all, creatures bound in space and time. Barth, with characteristic dramatic prose, puts it this way:

> What the meaning of God the Creator is and what is involved in the work of creation, is in itself not less hidden from us men than everything else that is contained in the Confession. We are not nearer to believing in God the Creator, than we are to believing that Jesus Christ was conceived by the Holy Spirit and born of the Virgin Mary. It is not the case that the truth about God the Creator is directly accessible to us and that only the truth of the second article needs a revelation. Both in

---

foreword to the Torchbook edition of *Dogmatics in Outline* Barth comments on the term "systematic theology," suggesting it to be equivalent to "wooden iron." Accordingly he confesses he could never, as Tillich has done, write a book entitled "systematic theology." He could not write a book under that title because a "system" is an edifice of thought constructed on fundamental conceptions selected on the basis of a philosophy by methods that correspond to those conceptions (p. 5). Page references to *Dogmatics in Outline* will appear in parentheses in the text.

21. David Fergusson in his article in *The Oxford Handbook of Systematic Theology* puts the matter in a straightforward way when he says, "The account of creation is not primarily hypothesis about how the world got started" (p. 77). He is, moreover, certainly right to suggest that the theological and scientific accounts of the origin of the universe are different "levels" of explanation (p. 74). According to Fergusson, the former is an account of "why" and the latter asks "how." I am not as convinced as Fergusson that the difference is so easily characterized. For theological reasons I suspect it is important to hold out the possibility that it is at least possible in principle for the "levels" to be in conflict.

the same sense in both cases we are faced with the mystery of God and His work, and the approach to it can only be one and the same. (p. 50)

Accordingly, Barth argues that it is impossible to separate knowledge of God as Creator from God's work of redemption. "Only when we keep before us what the triune God has done for us as men in Jesus Christ can we realize what is involved in God the creator and his work" (p. 52). Therefore Barth argues that what God does as the Creator can only be understood as a reflection of the inner life of the Trinity. That is why the work of creation is ascribed to the Father: because there is an intrinsic relation between the work of creation and the relation of the Father to the Son. That relation makes clear that God does not exist for himself; rather, through the love that the persons of the Trinity share is willed a reality distinct from God. God, who has no need for us, no need for heaven and earth, who is sufficient to himself, has willed that the created order exist (pp. 53-54).[22]

Creation is, therefore, grace. That there is a world is a miracle. The question, therefore, is never, "Does God exist?" Rather, what should astonish us is that we exist. That we exist, according to Barth, implies the good news that all that exists cannot be confused with God's existence. Any attempt to understand creation as an emanation from God, a view that threatens pantheism, cannot express what Christians mean by creation. For Christians creation is a creaturely reality that cannot be understood as a manifestation of God; rather, as God's creature the world exists to glorify God.

---

22. Interestingly enough, Barth's understanding of the relation of Trinity and creation is quite similar to Thomas's argument that "knowledge of the divine persons" is necessary "for the right idea of creation. The fact of saying that God made all things by His Word excludes the error of those who say that God produced things by necessity. When we say that in Him there is a procession of love, we show that God produced creatures not because he needed them, not because of any other extrinsic reason, but on account of the love of His own goodness. So Moses, when he said, 'In the beginning God created heaven and earth,' subjoined, God said, 'Let there be light,' to manifest the divine Word; and then said, 'God saw the light that it was good,' to show the proof of the divine love. The same is also found in the other works of creation. In another way, and chiefly, that we may think rightly concerning salvation of the human race, accomplished by the Incarnate Son, and by the gift of the Holy Ghost." *Summa Theologica*, trans. Fathers of the English Dominican Province (Westminster, MD: Christian Classics, 1948), I, 32, 1, 3. I am indebted to Matthew Whelan for directing me to this text.

Creation so understood is an expression of divine grace. *Creatio ex nihilo* rightly indicates that all that is was created out of nothing, but because "there is now something, since we exist by divine grace, we must never forget that, as the basis of our existence and of the existence of the whole world, there is in the background that divine — not just *facere*, but — *creation*. Everything outside God is held constant by God over nothingness" (p. 55). That such is the case means that all the things we call evil — death, sin, the Devil, and hell — are, therefore, not God's creation. They in fact are nothing (p. 57).

That we exist means we do so as creatures of time and space. Once we were not and soon we will no longer be, which means that there was a once and that there is a now. God is eternal, but we exist in time. That does not mean that there is no time in God, but it is a different time from ours. "God's time and space are free from the limitations in which alone time and space are thinkable for us. God is Lord of time and the Lord of space. As He is the origin of these forms too, nothing in Him has any limitations or imperfections, such as pertain to creaturely existence" (p. 56).[23]

Yet we have agency befitting our status as creatures. We have the freedom to decide and act one way rather than another. Our freedom is, however, the freedom appropriate to our creaturely existence in time and space. We are subject to law as well as our fellow creatures. "For if we are free, it is only because our Creator is infinitely free. All human freedom is but an imperfect mirroring of divine freedom" (p. 56).

Barth concludes his exposition of the first article of the Confession with the affirmation that "what exists *exists*, because it exists not of itself, but by God's Word, for His Word's sake, in the sense and in the purpose of His Word. . . . The whole was made by Him for its own sake. The Word which is attested for us in Holy Scripture, the story of Israel, of Jesus Christ and His Church, is the first thing, and the whole world with its

---

23. Barth puts this extremely important point this way in *Church Dogmatics*, III/1: "As in Jesus Christ God and man, eternity and time, converge and overlap in a temporal and time-transcending perfect willed and achieved by God, so it is in the act of creation. As God *has* accepted man in His Son, He *has* created him once and for all with heaven and earth. The fact and the way that God has acted historically cannot be mistaken in creation when we have learned to know it, as we must, in the light of the atonement, and therefore of the person and work of Jesus Christ" (p. 27).

light and shadow, its depths and its heights is the second. By the Word the world exists. A marvelous reversal of our whole thinking!" (p. 57).

In *Church Dogmatics* III/1, Barth makes explicit the eschatological character of creation by asserting that "the aim of creation is history."[24] God has willed and created the creature for the sake of the Son and for the glorification of the Son by the Holy Spirit. The very meaning of history is to be found in this covenant between God and us, known through the events that constitute a narrative in which God's patience with the creature is manifest by his willingness to give creation time — "time which acquires content through these events and which is finally to be 'fulfilled' and made ripe for its end by their conclusion."[25]

Creation is therefore not a timeless truth, but rather we know there was a beginning because we have seen the end. The end we have seen in Christ was in the beginning, and the beginning Christ has inaugurated is the end of the beginning. Real time, eschatological time, is the life-time of Jesus Christ. His life is "the turning point, the transition, the decision which was accomplished in His death and resurrection; together with the time preceding and following this event in the history of Israel and the existence of the Christian Church."[26] The very existence of the church, therefore, is a witness to the created character of our existence.

Such an understanding of creation obviously has profound implications for how ethics is understood and done. Barth develops his account of the ethics of creation in *Church Dogmatics* III/4. There he seeks to show how the command of the one God who is gracious to us in Jesus Christ is also the command of the Creator.[27] He therefore insists that "the God who meets man as Creator in His commandment is the God 'who is gracious to him in Jesus Christ.' He is not, then, a new and strange God who could require

24. Barth, *Church Dogmatics*, III/1, p. 59.
25. Barth, *Church Dogmatics*, III/1, p. 59.
26. Barth, *Church Dogmatics*, III/1, p. 76.
27. Gerald McKenny observes that Barth struggled in his ethical thought leading up to the *Church Dogmatics* to find a place for substantive moral guidance while preserving the critical eschatological thrust of his ethics. I am sure McKenny would not suggest that Barth ever resolved that tension, but I suspect it is a tension not peculiar to Barth but to Christian theological ethics. McKenny, *The Analogy of Grace: Karl Barth's Moral Theology* (New York: Oxford University Press, 2010), p. 252. McKenny's book is the best account of Barth's ethics we have.

of man as his Commander something new and strange."[28] Rather, he is the same God who is gracious to us in Christ, being no different from the Creator by whom all things were made and who is Lord over all. The significance of Barth's understanding of these matters I think will be readily apparent in contrast to Porter's use of creation to sustain a natural law ethic.

Porter on Creation and Natural Law

Jean Porter's argument that natural law is inadequately understood if it is divorced from the doctrine of creation might seem to make her an ally of Barth. But she explicitly distinguishes her understanding of the relation of creation to natural law from Barth. She notes that Barth rejects all versions of natural law theory because he does not think we can draw ethical conclusions from our flawed knowledge of creation; but even more significant, Barth argues that we can know creation and the demands of God as Creator only through our knowledge of Christ.[29]

Porter responds to Barth's objections by observing that Barth's critique of natural law must be seen as but a subtheme of his wider critique of moral philosophy as a self-contained enterprise. According to Porter, Barth's rejection of natural law is due to his confusion of a natural law ethic with the general conception of ethics, a conception based on the alleged autonomy of reason, which Barth identifies with our sinful attempt to be our own creator. Porter, however, finds Barth's position problematic because Barth fails to appreciate the fact that we are heirs to a very different understanding of morality, that is, an understanding of morality that is "intrinsically transcendent and a locus of human contact with the divine."[30] In contrast to Barth's critique of autonomous ethics, Porter argues that the scholastic

---

28. Karl Barth, *Church Dogmatics*, III/4, trans. G. W. Bromiley and T. F. Torrance (Edinburgh: T&T Clark, 1961), p. 35.

29. Jean Porter, *Natural and Divine Law: Reclaiming the Tradition for Christian Ethics* (Grand Rapids: Eerdmans, 1999), p. 169.

30. Porter, *Natural and Divine Law*, p. 169. Porter uses the phrase "to us" to indicate who represents the different idea of morality, but she does not tell us who the "us" is that will find Barth's view so problematic. The same problem is indicated by her use of "we."

13

concept of natural law was not the deliverance of pure reason, but rather itself a theological concept grounded in Scripture.[31]

Porter argues that Barth's theological worries about natural law can be met by recognizing that the scholastic concept of natural law in fact is a theological construal of the moral significance of human nature based on the doctrine of creation. She recognizes, however, that this is only a partial response to Barth's worries, because his concern is not that an account of natural law might not need a theological basis; instead, the issue is what kind of theological basis it would need. She acknowledges that for Barth the question is not only theological but Christological.[32]

Porter observes that the scholastics did situate natural theology in an overall theology in which the person and work of Christ were central; but they did not think, as Barth does, that Christology is directly relevant for shaping a natural law ethic. Porter, moreover, thinks it a very good thing that the scholastics thought the claim that the world is the good creation of God, without referencing Christ, is theologically appropriate.[33] She does so because she thinks it important to recognize that Christians are not alone in affirming the doctrine of creation. According to Porter, the belief in creation may be a central belief for Christians, but that does not mean the Christian understanding of creation is unique.[34]

31. Porter, *Natural and Divine Law*, p. 170.

32. Porter, *Natural and Divine Law*, p. 171. I confess I find this way of putting the matter confusing — that is, to suggest that the question is "not only theological but Christological." What could Christology be if it is not theological?

33. In her recent book, *Ministers of the Law: A Natural Law Theory of Legal Authority* (Grand Rapids: Eerdmans, 2010), Porter references Oliver O'Donovan's claim that the creation of the world and the redemption in Jesus Christ are poles in relation to which Christians narrate the moral history of the world. Accordingly, Porter affirms O'Donovan's presumption that the God who creates and the God who elects are one and the same God, but she insists that we experience the one God in diverse ways. So it is appropriate to develop an account of God from creation, that is, from "the natural forces which both sustain us and bear down and ultimately destroy us" (p. 57). The last phrase Porter explicitly borrows from Jim Gustafson. How she can at once express agreement with O'Donovan and Gustafson is not clear to me. Moreover, the appeal to "experience" to sustain a sense of creation begs for further elaboration and defense.

34. I find it odd that Porter does not engage David Burrell's comparison of creation in the Jewish, Christian, and Islamic traditions. Burrell helps us see that creation is understood in each of those traditions as the free origination of all from the one God and that this means creation so understood is not unique to Christianity. Burrell

Porter's way of putting this matter reflects her concern that Christian ethics not be thought to be distinctive or unique given the reality of, as well as need for, a common morality. She thinks it quite likely that our common secular morality is in fact more Christian than its critics suggest. Such critics confuse the question of a distinctive Christian account of morality with the question of what constitutes an adequate account of morality. Those, like Barth, who refuse to acknowledge an overlap between Christian morality and different forms of secular morality cannot help but fall into the theological error of "failing to take the doctrine of the creation with full seriousness and truncating the scriptural witness to God as the one who creates and sustains the natural world."[35]

Accordingly, Porter challenges Barth to think what it would mean to have a Christology without a doctrine of creation. "Taken to its extreme, an emphasis on Christ without some reference to the doctrine of creation risks a view according to which Christ is a wholly unexpected emissary from an utterly unknowable God — in other words, risks becoming a version of Catharism."[36] That is why Christian theology stands in need of the category of natural goodness: because without such a category it is impossible to preserve the doctrine of creation, making it impossible to hold on to the idea of Christ as Redeemer.[37]

Porter returns to these themes in her later book, *Nature as Reason: A Thomistic Theory of the Natural Law*, in which she worries about how the tendencies in Christianity associated with asceticism and perfectionism

---

notes, however, that this common conviction does not mean that there are no differences among these traditions about creation. See David Burrell, C.S.C., *Freedom and Creation in Three Traditions* (Notre Dame: University of Notre Dame Press, 1993), pp. 7-26. Burrell, moreover, argues that Barth makes explicit what Aquinas presumes, that is, that "the scriptures supply a personal language with which to speak of God the creator, and this reinforces the point that the covenant is the inherent goal of the creative activity of God. What the biblical accounts presume (and the Qur'an makes explicit) is that the goal of bringing the universe into being is to relate that world, via its human microcosm, to the One who creates it. So those narratives are not concerned to detail a *natural* level of divine activity and human response accessible to philosophy, but rather to offer an account of the origin of all which makes covenantal relationships possible" (pp. 21-22).

35. Porter, *Natural and Divine Law*, p. 166.
36. Porter, *Natural and Divine Law*, pp. 171-72.
37. Porter, *Natural and Divine Law*, p. 177.

can too easily develop into some forms of dualism that imply a denial of the fundamental doctrine that God is the Creator of the world. As a result, the continuity between God's goodness and wisdom and the goodness and intelligibility of the world "as we experience it" can be lost.[38]

I should be candid and acknowledge that Porter's critique of Barth is also a critique directed at me and, in particular, my pacifism. According to Porter, it is a mistake to think the difference between the scholastics and pacifists is that the former derive their ethics from reason and the latter derive their ethics from the Bible. Rather, what is at stake is two ways of interpreting the moral significance of Scripture. The scholastics interpret Scripture on the basis of natural law, but the concept of natural law is grounded in scripturally informed texts of creation.

So the fundamental difference is not scriptural but doctrinal. Pacifists can base Christian ethics only on Jesus Christ, whether Jesus is seen in more or less orthodox terms or considered as a central figure in the foundational narratives of the Gospels. Pacifists, therefore, reflect the influence of Karl Barth, even though they break with Barth in terms of the ethics of pacifism. "In contrast," according to Porter, "the scholastics give priority to preserving the integrity of Christian doctrine taken as a whole, and given the context within which they wrote, they give particular weight to the doctrine of creation. As a consequence, they have no theological stake in the uniqueness or distinctiveness of Christian morality."[39]

Porter acknowledges that positions such as Barth's rightly caution against too easy accommodations with secular orders; yet the witness comes at too high a price just to the extent that whatever does not fit neatly into a Christian framework must be rejected as alien or evil. Porter is not suggesting that Christians are called to embrace uncritically every aspect of secular culture, but her position does mean that there should be a willingness by Christians to accept the ambiguities that are present in every society. The scholastics' willingness to acknowledge such ambiguities, Porter suggests, makes them surprisingly similar to Reinhold Niebuhr's understanding of Christian realism.[40]

---

38. Porter, *Nature as Reason: A Thomistic Theory of the Natural Law* (Grand Rapids: Eerdmans, 2005), p. 137.

39. Porter, *Natural and Divine Law*, p. 287.

40. Porter, *Natural and Divine Law*, pp. 289-90. In *Ministers of the Law* Porter ar-

Porter justifies her appeal to Niebuhr as an ally of the scholastic understanding of natural law by calling attention to William of Auxerre's argument, an argument based on natural law, for the legitimacy of resisting force by force. According to Porter, William acknowledges that this is in tension with the Lord's command to turn the other cheek, but to turn the other cheek, according to William, is not always possible. To turn the other cheek in certain circumstances may be a way to draw men and women to God by unaccustomed mildness, but such a stance cannot always be required. Retaliation and vindication, reactions that draw on our naturally given anger and self-protective instincts, when subject to rational reflection, serve to sustain the purposes of the preservation of just societies.[41]

Porter concludes this line of reflection by observing that "our inclinations toward self-defense and retaliation can be understood in terms of human goods they serve. Given the scholastic concept of the natural law, this implies that they reflect the goodness of human nature and the wisdom and love of its Creator."[42] God as Creator and our status as creatures are therefore used by Porter to underwrite knowledge of moral norms that seem to be in some tension with the demands of discipleship.

Though I have reservations about Porter's account of natural law in scholastic theology, my concerns in this essay are not historical but theological. In spite of Porter's claim that her account of natural law presupposes a doctrine of creation, I do not see the difference an appeal to creation makes for how natural law is understood. I may have missed it, but I have been unable to discover in what Porter has written how her claims about creation as a necessary presumption for sustaining natural-law reasoning might result in judgments that are at odds with those who do not share her views about creation.[43]

---

gues against Niebuhr's defense of the nation-state as a manifestation of human sinfulness. She argues that the state, while often corrupted by sin, is nonetheless part of God's good creation and ordained to enable human cooperative life. Interestingly enough, I think she is right to so criticize Niebuhr.

41. Porter, *Natural and Divine Law*, pp. 291-92.

42. Porter, *Natural and Divine Law*, p. 293.

43. In her most recent book, *Ministers of the Law*, there are few references to creation as necessary for understanding how natural law is necessary to establish the authority of the law. I find myself, however, in agreement with her defense of how

With admirable candor, in *Ministers of the Law* Porter acknowledges that her defense of natural rights as an expression of her account of natural law has a great deal in common with leading secular theories such as those represented by Ronald Dworkin, Neil MacCormick, John Rawls, and Martha Nussbaum. Indeed, she suggests that the convergence is sufficient for some to suspect that her account of natural law and rights is "essentially a baptized version of secular liberalism." She acknowledges that there is some truth to that charge, but she defends the result, noting that she is "a twenty-first-century woman with strong liberal sensibilities, and it would be very strange if her theology were not shaped by this context to some degree."[44]

Yet the question must then be asked, What difference does her appeal to creation as a necessary theological presumption to sustain natural-law reasoning make for moral reflection? As far as I can see, in spite of her strong claims concerning the necessity of creation to justify a natural law ethic, her theological convictions do no work for her.

I can illustrate what it means for the appeal to creation to do work by calling attention to Barth's way of introducing his account of ethics in *Church Dogmatics* III/4. Barth begins his ethics with the Sabbath command. He does so by observing that the command to keep the Sabbath makes clear that we are creatures of time.[45] The command to observe the Sabbath therefore expresses the eschatological character of creation, indicating "the special history of the covenant and salvation in some sense embedded in the course of the general history of nature and the world, hidden but revealed in it, decisively determining its basis and its goal and secretly its way also. The omnipotent grace of God rules all world-occurrence as providence. But it does so from this starting point. It is at work here, in this particular, central sphere of history."[46]

Accordingly, Barth argues that the command to keep the Sabbath is

---

authority can and should be grounded in the political process. In particular, I am in sympathy with her contention that social life is not the result of sin but rather constitutive of what it means to be human.

44. Porter, *Ministers of the Law*, pp. 337-38. She argues, however, that such a judgment reflects the result of Christian ideals and practices that have shaped Western liberal ideals of equality and rights.

45. Barth, *Church Dogmatics*, III/4, p. 55.

46. Barth, *Church Dogmatics*, III/4, p. 55.

the command that explains all the other commandments. It does so because the command to observe the Sabbath is the *telos* for all God's commands. For the purpose of all we do is nothing less than the glorification of God. Such an understanding of the commandment to observe the Sabbath might be understood as an expression of natural law, but one must remember that the Sabbath has been reconstituted by the resurrection.[47]

Given the identification of the Decalogue with natural law in many of the scholastic theologians Porter admires, one might have thought she might have developed an account of our obligation to worship God.[48] That no such account is forthcoming I think reflects what I take to be the formal character of her understanding of natural law. Ironically, Porter's account of creation and correlative understanding of natural law in comparison to Barth is surprisingly a-historical. Porter insists that creation is a theological necessity for the intelligibility of a natural law ethic, but I remain unconvinced that she has shown that to be the case. I take that, moreover, to be the result of a deficient account of creation.

One Last Attempt to Say What Is at Stake

As a way to make as concrete as I can the significance of the eschatological account of creation, I think it is useful to call attention to the other Niebuhr, and in particular his influential book *Christ and Culture*. H. Richard Niebuhr argued in *Christ and Culture* that the great problem with the "Christ against culture" type was how advocates of that type understood the "relation of Jesus Christ to the Creator of nature and Gov-

47. Barth, *Church Dogmatics*, III/4, p. 53. For my account of the Decalogue see *Sanctify Them in the Truth: Holiness Exemplified* (Nashville: Abingdon, 1998), pp. 37-60, and *The Truth about God: The Ten Commandments in the Christian Life*, with William Willimon (Nashville: Abingdon, 1999).

48. Porter discusses the Decalogue in *Nature as Reason* (pp. 268-78), but there she is primarily concerned to show how the analysis of the precepts of the Decalogue by Aquinas clarifies the fundamental ideal of justice, which is to render each his due. She also briefly refers to the Decalogue in *Ministers of the Law*, noting that the scholastics did not think the precepts of the Decalogue to be, as much of the law in the Old Testament was regarded, provisional; but neither did they think the Decalogue to be a fully articulated moral code (p. 67).

ernor of history as well as to the Spirit immanent in creation and in the Christian community."[49] According to Niebuhr, the over-concentration of radical Christians (Tolstoy is his primary example) on the lordship of Christ results in an ontological bifurcation of reality. Their rejection of culture is joined to a suspicion of nature and nature's God in a manner that obscures the goodness of God's creation.

Niebuhr observes that, for Tolstoy, the Trinity had no ethical meaning, with the result that the God who creates cannot be identified with the God who redeems. Niebuhr's appeal to the Trinity, however, as John Howard Yoder points out, is odd, because Niebuhr's understanding of the Trinity is arguably modalist. In particular, Niebuhr used an appeal to the Trinity to underwrite an affirmative attitude toward nature and culture as manifestations of God the Father. Yoder argues that this emphasis results in creating a tension between God the Father and God the Son just to the extent that the former is used to underwrite moral knowledge that may contradict that determined by the teaching and example of Christ.[50]

Yet, according to Yoder, the intention of the post-Nicene doctrine of the Trinity was to deny that different revelations come to us through the Father, Son, and Holy Spirit. "The entire point of the debate around the nature of the Trinity was the concern of the church to say just the opposite, namely that in the Incarnation and in the continuing life of the church under the Spirit there is but one God."[51] Niebuhr's very presumption that a balance must be maintained between the doctrines of creation and redemption reflects an understanding of creation not unlike that of Porter.

I have introduced Niebuhr into this discussion not only because his habits of thought are replicated in how many today think about these matters but also because an engagement with his position helps us see the interrelation of the doctrine of the Trinity and an eschatological understanding of creation.[52] I may not do systematic theology, but I do

49. H. Richard Niebuhr, *Christ and Culture* (New York: HarperCollins, 1996), p. 80.

50. Glen H. Stassen, D. M. Yeager, and John Howard Yoder, *Authentic Transformation: A New Vision of Christ and Culture* (Nashville: Abingdon, 1996), p. 61.

51. Yoder, in *Authentic Transformation*, p. 62.

52. In what may seem counterintuitive to some, David Kelsey draws on Wisdom

understand that, theologically, everything we believe is interconnected with everything we believe. That is why theology can never be finished, requiring as it does constant reconnections.

I want to end, therefore, by making candid one agenda I hope this essay serves. I hope many of those who read this essay will be in sympathy with the emphasis on the eschatological character of the doctrine of creation. They will not, I suspect, be sympathetic with the kind of Christological pacifism I represent. An eschatological account of creation does not necessarily commit one to nonviolence, but it at least puts one in that ballpark. It does so because creation was, after all, God's determinative act of peace.[53] If, therefore, the end is in the beginning, at the very least Christians who justify the Christian participation in war bear the burden of proof.

---

literature to illumine the relation between an eschatological understanding of creation and a trinitarian understanding of God. He notes that how Wisdom's creation theology bears on a trinitarian understanding of the Creator's relation to creation can be displayed in the following fashion: "*The Father creates.* This phrase gets its force entirely from its Trinitarian context and is not open to any direct nuancing by Wisdom's creation theology. Classically, the Trinitarian formula tells of the triune God's creating in a certain pattern: It is not the 'Father' who creates as YHWH, or instead of or on behalf of the triune God. Rather, it is the triune God who creates. However, God creates by actively relating in a certain way that is told most aptly in a particular quasi-narrative pattern: the Father creates through the Son in the power of the Holy Spirit" (*Eccentric Existence,* vol. 1, p. 167).

53. John Milbank famously argues that "Christianity recognizes no original violence. It construes the infinite not as chaos, but as a harmonic peace which is yet beyond the circumscribing power of any totalizing reason. Peace no longer depends upon the reduction to the self-identical, but the *sociality* of harmonious difference. Violence, by contrast, is always a secondary willed intrusion upon this possible infinite order (which is actual for God)." Accordingly, Milbank argues that Christianity exposes the postmodern understanding of difference as violence as a false "encoding" of reality. In contrast, Christianity is the "coding of transcendental difference as peace." Milbank, *Theology and Social Theory: Beyond Secular Reason,* 2nd ed. (Oxford: Blackwell, 2006), pp. 5-6.

The End of Sacrifice: An Apocalyptic Politics

Martyn and Yoder on Apocalyptic

John Howard Yoder, as Douglas Harink has suggested, would have found Lou Martyn's account of Paul's apocalyptic gospel supportive of his reading of Paul.[1] Like Martyn, Yoder did not think Paul's "gospel" to be first and foremost about us. Rather, as Martyn suggests, Paul's gospel is centered on "God's liberating invasion of the cosmos. Christ's love enacted in the cross has the power to change the world because it is embodied in the new community of mutual service."[2] Thus Yoder and Martyn, in quite similar ways, contend that Paul understood that in the cross and resurrection of Christ a new creation has been enacted, bringing an end to the old age and inaugurating a new time characterized by the reign of God as King.[3]

Sometimes when I am reading Martyn I almost forget I am reading him and think instead that I am reading Yoder. Many of Martyn's sentences could have just as easily come from Yoder. For example, com-

---

1. Douglas Harink, *Paul among the Postliberals: Pauline Theology beyond Christendom and Modernity* (Grand Rapids: Brazos, 2003), p. 147.

2. J. Louis Martyn, "The Apocalyptic Gospel in Galatians," *Interpretation* 54, no. 3 (July 2000): 246.

3. J. Louis Martyn, *Galatians* (New Haven: Yale University Press, 2010), p. 22.

menting on Paul's view that God had dispatched the Spirit of Christ into the believers' hearts to make them soldiers for Christ, Martyn writes: "The martial, cosmic dimension of Paul's apocalyptic applies, then, to the church and for that reason Paul can speak of the church itself both as God's new creation and as the apocalyptic community called to the front trenches in God's apocalyptic war against the powers of the present evil age."[4] Yoder, who emphasized the significance of the principalities and powers for understanding what it means to live at the same time in two times, could have easily written that sentence.[5]

More, much more, could be done to show how Yoder anticipated Martyn's apocalyptic reading of Paul (and John), but, as interesting as that exercise would be, it is not the main purpose of this essay. I only call attention to their similar views on apocalyptic to suggest that Yoder can provide a politics that Martyn's account lacks. Douglas Harink observes that the focal concern of Martyn's later work has been that of divine and human agency. As a result, Martyn has not given attention to the political aspects of Paul's thought.[6] By contrast, Yoder's thought is political all the way down, and so it is my contention that Martyn's case would be stronger if he had read Yoder.[7] But such a statement is hardly helpful, so to move from a more constructive place I will reframe my argument by suggesting that for contemporary readers Martyn's work can be tested and complemented by reading him in conversation with Yoder.

Before turning to Yoder, however, I want to call attention to Harink's suggestions about how Martyn's work might be developed politically. For Harink quite rightly observes that there is a politics, a politics that is perhaps underdeveloped, in Martyn's understanding of the three-actor moral drama that constitutes Paul's understanding of the human situation. Besides divine and human agency, there also exist anti-God powers whose agency is apparent in their ability to deceive and enslave. Harink suggests that in most accounts of Christian ethics the role of these pow-

---

4. Martyn, *Galatians*, p. 102.

5. John Howard Yoder, *The Christian Witness to the State* (Scottdale, PA: Herald, 2002), pp. 8-9.

6. Douglas Harink, "Partakers of the Divine Apocalypse: Hermeneutics, History, and Human Agency after Martyn" (unpublished paper, 2010), p. 24.

7. As far as I can tell, Martyn never enters into conversation with Yoder's work.

ers, particularly as corporate agents, is ignored, which often means that the church as a political entity and agent is also lost.

Harink argues that, just to the extent that Martyn develops an account of the church as a corporate agent capable of countering the powers by fulfilling the law of Christ, he has begun to make explicit the politics inherent in Paul's apocalyptic gospel. What Martyn has not done, according to Harink, is suggest how this newly created agent called the church enacts this political witness among the nations. Harink thinks the way forward is to develop an account of how the messianic community even now participates in the Kingdom of God in a manner that avoids the "wreckage of worldly political history." Accordingly, this cruciform community will not be caught up in "locating those points of worldly-political leverage from which it might launch the next 'conservative' effort to keep things as they are, or the next 'progressive' movement in order to 'advance toward' or 'bring about' the Kingdom of God or at least a 'higher' stage of history."[8]

That certainly seems right to me, but surely more needs to be said about what *kind* of politics the church represents amid the "wreckage of worldly political history." In an attempt to develop the "more," I want to direct attention to the significance of sacrifice as a central political reality. I may well test the patience of my readers in the development of this theme because I cannot deny that the argument I try to make is anything but straightforward. I begin by suggesting that Yoder's account of apocalyptic that emphasizes the lordship of Christ is different from Martyn's account in important ways. The significance of Yoder's understanding of the crucified one as Lord, I will suggest, is best seen in light of Peter Leithart's criticism of Yoder in *Defending Constantine: The Twilight of an Empire and the Dawn of Christendom.*[9] For Leithart rightly contends that the heart of the political revolution that the church represented was to be "the end of sacrifice." In what follows I will try to show how the issue of sacrifice remains relevant to our current political realities.

---

8. Harink, "Partakers of the Divine Apocalypse," p. 29.

9. Peter Leithart, *Defending Constantine: The Twilight of an Empire and the Dawn of Christendom* (Downers Grove: InterVarsity, 2010).

Yoder on Christ the King

In his presidential address to the Society of Christian Ethics in 1988, "To Serve Our God and to Rule the World," John Howard Yoder took as his text Revelation 5:7-10. He explained that the Apocalypse was not his theme for that occasion, but the text from Revelation was crucial for what Yoder argued to be the main task of Christian ethics, that is, "to see history doxologically." To see history doxologically, according to Yoder, does not mean that Christians should try to usurp the emperor's throne or to pastor Caesar prophetically, but rather "to persevere in celebrating the Lamb's lordship and in building the community shaped by that celebration."[10] Christians see history doxologically because they are convinced that they participate in God's rule of the cosmos.

Yoder observes, however, that apocalypse is only one of many modes of discourse the believing community uses to discern what such a rule entails. But apocalyptic language is particularly appropriate to express what it means for God to be praised as the ruler of the world. That Yoder associates apocalyptic discourse with claims of God's rule of God's creation suggests a subtle but quite important difference from Martyn's account of apocalyptic. For in spite of the similarities between Martyn's and Yoder's accounts of apocalyptic, Yoder's stress on the lordship of Jesus Christ means that the political character of the Kingdom of God is evident from the beginning. To see Jesus "sitting at the right hand of the Father" not only indicates Jesus' role in the cosmic victory, in which he is put in charge of history by becoming sovereign over the principalities and powers; that Jesus sits at the right hand of the Father is also a declaration of his rule of the world.[11]

This way of stating the significance of apocalyptic allows Yoder to avoid Martyn's language of "invasion" and intervention. Of course, Yoder does not disavow God's agency, but he observes that what was novel about the Christian understanding of God's "intervention" was that the God who "intervenes" in Christ is the one God whose "intervention" is

10. John Howard Yoder, "To Serve Our God and to Rule the World," in *The Royal Priesthood: Essays Ecclesiological and Ecumenical*, ed. Michael Cartwright (Grand Rapids: Eerdmans, 1994), p. 130.

11. Yoder, "To Serve Our God and to Rule the World," pp. 132-33.

not unusual because that is the way God works. According to Yoder, what was unique about New Testament eschatology is that, instead of several gods using the world as their playground, the Christians maintained that there is one God who uses the world as the theater of divinely purposeful action. The God who is the Father of Jesus Christ has always wanted to gather a people to operate in fellowship with God and with one another. History has an end, and we are it.[12]

Everything Yoder writes is informed by his conviction that Jesus is "sitting at the right hand of the Father," but perhaps his most concentrated account of what it means for Jesus to be so enthroned he developed in his course in Christian doctrine, which was published after his death as *Preface to Theology: Christology and Theological Method*. In *Preface to Theology* Yoder develops his Christology in terms of the threefold office of prophet, priest, and king. I suspect he thought that by doing so he was staying closer to the language of the Bible and, just as important, the people of Israel. Yoder suggests, therefore, that when Jesus says, "I am the king, but the servant kind of king," he fulfills the hope of the Jews who had learned through bitter experience that earthly kings are, to say the least, a mixed blessing.[13]

If, as Yoder maintains, the lordship of Christ is at the heart of apocalyptic, then the political implications are immediate. Indeed, that way of putting the matter is misleading. It is not a matter of working out the "implications"; rather, the politics of apocalyptic simply *is* the existence of a people who refuse to acknowledge the claims of worldly rulers to be kings.[14] Moreover, because the one who is Lord has triumphed on the

12. John Howard Yoder, *Preface to Theology: Christology and Theological Method*, with an introduction by Stanley Hauerwas and Alex Sider (Grand Rapids: Brazos, 2002), p. 256.

13. Yoder, *Preface to Theology*, p. 245.

14. Anathea Portier-Young's account of the beginnings of apocalyptic literature supports Yoder's claim that the kingship of God necessitates a literature of resistance to empire. For empires exercise power over the world not only by force but also through propaganda and ideology. "Empire manipulated and co-opted hegemonic social institutions to express and reinforce its values and cosmologies. Resisting imperial domination required challenging not only the physical means of coercion, but also empire's claims about knowledge and the world. The first apocalypses did precisely this." *Apocalypse against Empire: Theologies of Resistance in Early Judaism* (Grand Rapids: Eerdmans, 2011), p. xxii.

cross, his followers refuse to use the violence of earthly rulers to achieve what are allegedly good ends.

Nonviolence is obviously a central commitment defining the kind of politics Yoder thinks is required to acknowledge the lordship of Christ, but it is equally important that nonviolence not be isolated as the defining feature of apocalyptic politics. Nonviolence is but one aspect of the conviction that history is determined not by kings and empires, but by the church. Nonviolence is therefore but an expression of a more determinative ecclesiology. The church's first duty to the societies in which she finds herself is, therefore, the same duty she has to her Lord. That means the church's witness to the lordship of the Crucified One cannot let "local obligations" to one state lead her to treat those in another state as an enemy. Any attempt, for example, "to justify war for the individual Christian citizen, after it has been judged incompatible with the ministry of the church, is a refusal to be honest with the absolute priority of church over state in the plan of God."[15]

Though often accused of being apolitical, Yoder makes the extraordinary claim that the church knows better than the state what the state is to be and do. The church may well be a moral stimulus to help a society and state to be better, but the church does not exist to enable the work of the alleged "wider" society. Rather, "it is for the sake of the church's own work that society continues to function."[16] The meaning of history is to be found in the existence of the church.

Apocalyptic politics is based on the confidence that God uses the power structures of this world in spite of themselves for God's purposes. Christ carries out the purposes of the One who is sovereign by ruling over the rebellious structures of the universe.[17] That rule is hidden but made visible through the servant church. The place of the church in the history of the universe is the place where Christ's lordship is operative. This is where it is clear that he rules, as well as the kind of rule he exercises. He is the suffering servant whose rule is decisively revealed on a cross. The

15. John Howard Yoder, *The Christian Witness to the State* (Scottdale, PA: Herald, 1992), p. 17.
16. Yoder, *The Christian Witness to the State*, p. 13.
17. Yoder, *Preface to Theology*, p. 247.

church makes history not through domination but through being the servant of a crucified Lord.[18]

That the gospel is to be preached to the ends of the world is why time does not stop. What it means for Christ to be King is that he rules over history to give the church time to preach the gospel. Yoder is quite well aware that strong metaphysical claims are correlative of this understanding of the role of the church. That God gives the church time to witness to the lordship of Christ means that God is not timeless. That does not mean God is not eternal, but rather eternity is not *not* temporal; eternity is atemporal. Put differently, God is "more temporal than we are, who is ahead of us and behind us, before us and after us, above us in several directions, and who has more of the character of timeliness and meaningfulness in movement rather than less."[19]

Metaphysics is often thought to be apolitical, but for Yoder these claims about the way the world is are constitutive of the position he takes in *The Politics of Jesus.* Yoder's view of God's timefulness expresses his contention that "the cross and not the sword, suffering and not brute power determine the meaning of history. The key to the obedience of God's people is not their effectiveness but their patience (John 13:10). The triumph of the right is assured not by the might that comes to the aid of the right, which is of course the justification of the use of violence and other kinds of power in every human conflict. The relationship between the obedience of God's people and the triumph of God's cause is not a relationship of cause and effect but cross and resurrection."[20] This relation between cross and resurrection, moreover, is the most determinative mode of seeing history doxologically.

Yoder's well-known criticisms of the Constantinian settlement are but the expression of this understanding of the eschatological character of the gospel. The fundamental problem that beset the church when Constantine became a member, a problem Yoder recognizes was beginning well before Constantine, was how becoming established changed the self-understanding of the church. Under the influence of Constantin-

---

18. Yoder, *Preface to Theology,* p. 248.

19. Yoder, *Preface to Theology,* p. 276.

20. John Howard Yoder, *The Politics of Jesus: Vicit Agnus Noster* (Grand Rapids: Eerdmans, 1994), p. 232.

ianism the church no longer understood herself to live simultaneously in two times. Eschatology had now become an ideal relegated to the future rather than a reality that transforms the character of time.

As a result, the church no longer thinks she is standing in the obedient line of the true prophets, witnessing to the reality of God's kingdom. Rather, the church now has a vested interest in the present order, tempting her to use cultic means to legitimize that order.[21] Consequently, it is now assumed that everyone is Christian, so that Christian ethics no longer is the exploration of what makes us faithful disciples, but rather is an attempt to develop an ethic that is workable for all of society. For it is now assumed that the church exists to serve society, and as a result the apocalyptic presumption that society exists to serve the church is lost.

Yoder's understanding of Constantinianism is nuanced and complex, but hopefully I have said enough to suggest how Yoder's emphasis on the lordship of Christ for determining the apocalyptic imagination is a politics.[22] It is a politics, moreover, that I should like to think is compatible with Martyn's understanding of Paul's apocalyptic gospel in Galatians. For Martyn, like Yoder, thinks no questions are more important for determining the politics of apocalyptic than "What time is it?" and "In what cosmos do we actually live?"[23] The answer to those questions is revealed by the sacrifices of a people who think it necessary to legitimate their existence.

Leithart on Sacrifice

In his book *Defending Constantine: The Twilight of an Empire and the Dawn of Christendom*, Peter Leithart develops a helpful critique of Yoder's politics. His critique is helpful because Leithart's criticisms, I hope to show, help us better appreciate the significance of Yoder's eschatology. I need to

---

21. John Howard Yoder, *The Original Revolution: Essays on Christian Pacifism*, with a foreword by Mark Thiessen Nation (Scottdale, PA: Herald, 2003), p. 65.

22. For both the best analysis and the best criticism of Yoder's account of Constantianism see Alex Sider, *To See History Doxologically: History and Holiness in John Howard Yoder's Ecclesiology* (Grand Rapids: Eerdmans, 2011), pp. 97-132.

23. Martyn, *Galatians*, p. 104.

be clear. I am not particularly concerned with Leithart's defense of Constantine's integrity as a Christian. As Leithart recognizes, Yoder's critique of Constantinianism has little stake in questions surrounding the authenticity of Constantine's "conversion." Much more interesting is Leithart's suggestion that Yoder failed to appreciate how Christianity fundamentally transformed Rome by Constantine's outlawing of sacrifice.

That Constantine outlawed sacrifice, a law he enforced haphazardly according to Leithart, was significant because sacrifice was thought to be essential to Roman social and political life. That sacrifice was considered essential to a good politics was an unquestioned assumption in the ancient world. For example, Leithart calls attention to Celsus's contention that religion had to do with culture and political traditions, with support of the city or state, and was expressed primarily through the act of offering sacrifices.[24]

Leithart develops a strong case that sacrifice was at the center of Roman life. It was so because Romans assumed sacrifice was the chief religious act that allowed them to communicate with the gods and to keep the gods happy. Moreover, sacrifice disclosed the secrets of the future when the entrails of slaughtered animals were read. Political decisions by the senate were determined by sacrifices, as were imperial decrees. Soldiers sacrificed to the gods prior to battle with the hope of insuring their success. Particularly important were the sacrifices made to or for the emperor to acknowledge him as Lord, Savior, or Deliverer. Because Christians believed there was another King, they refused to sacrifice to the emperor, which invited the Romans to sacrifice Christians not only for entertainment but also for the good of the Empire.[25]

One of the reasons Christianity proved to be so offensive to Romans, according to Leithart, was that it could not be a civic religion in the Roman sense because it was a religion without sacrifice.[26] That is why,

24. Leithart, *Defending Constantine*, p. 40.
25. Leithart, *Defending Constantine*, pp. 327-28.
26. Leithart, *Defending Constantine*, p. 40. Leithart's assertion that Christianity is a religion without sacrifice is overstated. Later in the book he qualifies that claim. He may be right that Christianity could not supply the kind of sacrifice that sustained the civic culture of Rome, but sacrifice remained at the heart of Christian worship. Leithart refers a number of times to Guy Stroumsa, *The End of Sacrifice: Religious Transformations in Later Antiquity*, trans. Susan Emanuel (Chicago: University of Chicago Press, 2009). I think Stroumsa gets it right when he observes that in some aspects

Leithart argues, we should not miss the significance that after Constantine's triumph and establishing himself as Caesar, he refused to enter the Capitolium and sacrifice, as was required, to Jupiter. After his defeat of Maxentius, Constantine made clear that a new political theology was being established, that is, one without sacrifice.[27]

Through his refusal to sacrifice to the pagan gods Constantine gave political expression to Christ's triumph over the "elementary things of this world." History is not a tale told by idiots, because we see how our freedom from bondage, liberation from structures determined by distinctions between the holy and profane, clean and unclean, Jew and Gentile, has now gained political expression through Constantine's renunciation of sacrifice. Constantine "secularized" political life by showing that the state would no longer be the agent of salvation (pp. 325-27). By bringing an end to sacrifice, Constantine brought an end to Rome, because now Rome depended on a more determinative civic polity, that is, the church.

By recognizing the church's superiority to Rome, Constantine acknowledged that the sacrifice of Christ, the blood of Jesus, is the end of bloodshed. "The church too was a sacrificial city, the true city of final sacrifice, which in the Eucharistic liturgy of sacrifice announced the end of animal sacrifice and the initiation of a new sacrificial order" (p. 329). The rest, so to speak, is history. Constantine's refusal to sacrifice, his welcoming of the church as the true polis, created a non-sacrificial politics that became the norm even after the demise of Rome. Leithart celebrates this achievement, noting that "for millennia every empire, every city, every nation and tribe was organized around sacrifice. Every polity has been a sacrificial polity. We are not, and we have Constantine to thank for that" (p. 329).

"early Christianity represents a transformation of Judaism that opens new horizons, but it seems in other ways to mark a conservative return to Israel's sacrificial system. While the rabbis gathered in Yavneh in 70 succeeded in transforming Judaism — without admitting doing so, and perhaps also without admitting it completely to themselves — into a non-sacrificial religion, Christianity defined itself precisely as a religion centered on sacrifice, even if it was a reinterpreted sacrifice. The Christian *anamnesis* was the reactivation of the sacrifice of the Son of God, performed by the priests" (p. 72). Stroumsa argues that the Christian sacrifice was not a blood sacrifice as were the sacrifices of Rome.

27. Leithart, *Defending Constantine*, pp. 66-67. Hereafter, page references to *Defending Constantine* will appear in parentheses in the text.

It is not clear who Leithart thinks the "we" refers to in the last sentence. He has a brief account of Augustine's understanding of Christ's sacrifice now embodied in the Eucharist to suggest that any polity that acknowledges the church at least has the potential to be more just. So the church did not "fall" with the Constantinian settlement; rather, with that settlement a politics was begun that in all its variety can be thought to be Christian. The Middle Ages, in particular, are a model of the kind of political arrangement between church and state that Constantine made possible.

But, according to Leithart, Constantine's achievement has been lost in modernity. Modern states do not welcome the church as the true city because they are willing to recognize only a church that reduces itself to a religion or private piety. This is as true of totalitarian states as it is of democratic ones, for both forms of the modern state are "secretly united in their anti-Constantinianism" (p. 340). As a result, the modern state has reasserted its status as a sacrificial state so that it might be resacralized through the shedding of blood. Interestingly, this resacralization of the state is an expression of a nihilistic politics just to the extent that such states become ends in themselves, because there are no gods to receive the sacrifices the state asks of its members (pp. 340-41).

Therefore the modern state in its refusal to welcome the church as teacher and judge has reasserted its status as a sacrificial state. It has done so, moreover, with a vengeance. The medieval world was bloody, but the "Eucharistic blood of Jesus founded the true city," which meant there was a brake on bloodshed. Modern nations know no limits, attempting as they must to be resacralized. That states now can "demand the 'ultimate sacrifice'" means, according to Leithart, that in modernity "the 'Constantinianism' Yoder deplores becomes a horrific reality, as the church has too often wedded itself to power" (pp. 340-41).

This last remark, suggesting as it does how similar Leithart's position is to Yoder's ecclesiology, is why I find Leithart's criticism of Yoder so interesting. Like Yoder, Leithart thinks the church is the only true polity. Leithart, for example, seems to think Augustine is right to maintain that the church displays for the world what true justice is because true justice is first and foremost giving back to God what God has given us through the sacrifice of the Son. Leithart recognizes that Yoder is quite close to Augustine in that he assumes that the justice of a social order begins in the recognition that the church is a more determinative reality than the state. That the church is so, moreover, means that the church betrays herself and the world when she identifies with the power structures of the world.

Leithart is a Calvinist. He therefore says that "if there is going to be a Christian politics, it is going to have to be an evangelical Christian politics, one that places Jesus, his cross and his resurrection at the center" (p. 332). Yoder would not disagree as long as we remember that such a politics can only be found in the church. Leithart, I suspect, thinks that to be a mistake because he assumes that theocracy should always, at least in principle, be thought to be a possibility.

He also thinks Yoder is wrong about nonviolence. He acknowledges, however, that the most powerful argument for nonviolence is Yoder's contention that the cross makes nonviolence an unavoidable stance for Christians. For it was at the cross that Jesus' lordship was established, making clear that the one who is King refuses to save coercively. Leithart acknowledges the power of this reading of Jesus' death but suggests that more "detailed exegesis" is required — although finally the matter cannot be determined by examination of specific texts but only by "attention to the full sweep of biblical history" (p. 333). Yet "a full sweep of biblical history" is exactly what Yoder has given with his reading of the apocalyptic character of the gospel.

Leithart, like Yoder, wants to read history doxologically, but I am not convinced that he is right to suggest that all politics after Constantine were non-sacrificial. That, however, is a topic for another time. More helpful for the argument I am trying to make is Leithart's contention that there has been an attempt to resacralize the state in modernity. By exploring that contention I hope to show that Yoder's understanding of what it means for Christ to be Lord is no less a challenge to the world in which we find ourselves than it was to Rome.

The End of Sacrifice

These last remarks indicate that I think Yoder, though often criticized for tempting Christians to withdraw from politics, is the most political of theologians. For as Leithart suggests, Yoder challenges some of the deepest presuppositions of modern political reality, that is, that only the state has the right to ask that we make sacrifices that are life-changing. The problem with that presupposition is that the state that is legitimated by such sacrifices is not and cannot be acknowledged to be one that requires sacrifice. The sacrifices called for to legitimate the state are hidden even from those who sacrifice and are sacrificed, because it is assumed that whatever anyone does they are acting as free individuals.

Paul Kahn, for example, argues in his book *Putting Liberalism in Its Place* that the liberal story of the birth of the modern state as an act of reason and free choice in which sacrifice is no longer necessary is a profound illusion.[28] It is an illusion of great power, however, because the presumption that a politics can be founded in reason between self-interested free individuals has become such a determinative story that it creates its own reality. But Kahn argues that a politics so conceived cannot give an account of the body and, in particular, the experience of love that constitutes any politics. As a result, how liberal societies determine life and death remains out of sight in liberal theory.[29]

Kahn, however, observes that the political only properly begins at the point where anyone can imagine sacrificing one's life or killing others to maintain the state. Thus the general presumption that "the modern state has fully arrived not when it defends me against violence, but when it conscripts me into the armed force."[30] The legitimacy of claims to authority by the modern state depends, therefore, on the sacrifices we are asked to make on its behalf. Kahn argues that such sacrifices are best understood as acts of love. Sacrifice is an act of love constituting the very character of politics just to the extent that sacrifice is "linked to the reciprocal possibility of infliction of injury."[31]

That is why war is so crucial for the legitimization of the modern state. The capacity of the nation-state to sacrifice its citizens in war was the great discovery, Kahn argues, of the nineteenth century. That dis-

28. Paul Kahn, *Putting Liberalism in Its Place* (Princeton: Princeton University Press, 2005), pp. 93-94.
29. Kahn, *Putting Liberalism in Its Place*, p. 21.
30. Kahn, *Putting Liberalism in Its Place*, p. 240.
31. Kahn, *Putting Liberalism in Its Place*, p. 234.

covery began with Napoleon's armies, shaped as they were by the popular enthusiasm of the Revolution. The fullest expression of that development is to be found in the American Civil War, in which democratic armies, based on mass conscription, confronted one another. As the result of these developments, the conception of citizenship and political participation broadened, which meant so did the conception of the reach of military service. "The people's state is supported by people's armies."[32]

A liberal state is therefore no less dependent on sacrifice for legitimacy than the states of the past. In this respect, Western politics is but the expression of the faith of Western religious practices — that is, only by being willing to die does one participate in the sacred. Liberal societies are therefore exemplifications of sacrificial politics just to the extent that the violent destruction of the self is "necessary for the realization of the transcendent character of the sovereign."[33]

Sacrifice and sovereignty are therefore linked in the politics of the state. For sacrifice transforms the finite self in order to express the infinite value of the sovereign. Sovereignty is brought into existence through the sacrificial destruction of the body. "The subject, or bearer, of sovereignty in the West has moved from God to monarch to the people. The point, however, is always the same. The sovereign is the source of meaning: it is not a means to any end apart from itself. It reveals itself in the act of sacrifice."[34]

Kahn's account of the relation of sovereignty and the state, a relation that depends on a memorialization of a chain of martyrs to the founding moment in which the state was born, is controversial, drawing as it does on the work of Carl Schmitt.[35] However, I cannot help but think Kahn's analysis of the relation of sovereignty and sacrifice helps to illumine, and is illuminated by, Leithart's engagement of Yoder's apocalyptic politics. Kahn confirms Leithart's contention that the modern state has recovered

32. Kahn, *Putting Liberalism in Its Place*, p. 263.

33. Paul Kahn, *Sacred Violence: Torture, Terror, and Sovereignty* (Ann Arbor: University of Michigan Press, 2011), p. 184.

34. Kahn, *Sacred Violence*, p. 144.

35. Kahn discusses Schmitt's views in his recent book *Political Theology: Four New Chapters on the Concept of Sovereignty* (New York: Columbia University Press, 2011). Kahn is quite critical of some aspects of Schmitt's work, but his fundamental understanding of modern political life owes much to Schmitt.

the centrality of sacrifice for sustaining its legitimacy. What is new about such states, however, is the inability to make those sacrifices constitutive of the theory that informs their self-understanding.

By appealing to Yoder in order to illumine Martyn's understanding of apocalyptic, I hope I have shown how Martyn's reading of Galatians should be understood to be an instance of insightful exegesis. Martyn's reading has immediate political implications, calling into question all sacrifices whose end is not determined by the one sacrifice that is the end of all worldly sacrifices. From such a perspective, the question of Christian participation in war turns out to be a question not restricted to "the ethics of war"; instead, it is a question of how Christians can at once say "Jesus is Lord," the end of all sacrifices, and yet continue to participate in the sacrifice of war.[36]

36. For the development of this way of putting the matter see my *War and the American Difference: Theological Reflections on Violence and National Identity* (Grand Rapids: Brazos, 2011).

Witness

With Charles Pinches

Beginning Explorations

Christians are people expected to bear witness to what makes them Christian. Indeed, to connect witness to Christianity is commonplace. But as with many theological commonplaces, we can miss the significance of the grammar of a faith that demands that Christians witness to what they believe. The complexity of these matters is evident by the way the grammar of the last sentence betrays our contention about witness. Christians do not witness to what they believe, but what they believe must be a witness. Why should the God Christians worship require witnesses?

In fact, believer and non-believer alike often assume that any god worth believing in should *not* depend on witnesses to be made known. So if the God of Israel who raised Jesus from the dead requires witnesses, then this suggests that what Christians believe about this God must be false. Yet we will argue that if the God we worship as Trinity, and worship is the right word, could be known *without* witnesses, that would indicate that such a God, the Christian one, actually does not exist. No doubt this is a strong claim to which we cannot do full justice in what follows; yet we hope to say enough to suggest why the claim matters and what might be some of its important theological implications.

One robust metaphysical point that relates to the connection between witness and truth is simply that all that is, the vast expanse of creation in all its complexities and intricacies, did not have to be. And of course, we are part of this "all." We are created, contingent beings that did not have to be. Only God exists by necessity, as Christians (along with certain others) claim. But Christians believe further that the God that exists by necessity is known only through contingent creatures. "Witness" names the truth that the only way we can know the character of the world, the only way we know ourselves, the only way we know God is by one person telling another.[1]

We believe an exploration of the relation between God, truth, and witness[2] is appropriate in an essay that seeks to honor Fergus Kerr. We hope it helps illumine his work, in particular his understanding of Thomas. As Kerr observes in *After Aquinas: Versions of Thomism*, Thomas thought arguments for God's existence were necessary not so as to convince hypothetically open-minded atheists, or even to persuade "fools," but rather "to deepen and enhance the mystery of the hidden God. . . . Far from being an exercise in rationalistic apologetics, the purpose of arguing for God's existence is to protect God's transcendence."[3]

Kerr develops this extremely important point by noting that Thomas's arguments for God's existence are expressions of his understanding of God's simplicity. Divine simplicity makes clear that we cannot know what God is; rather, we can only reason to God from the existence of the world that did not have to be. Indeed, from this perspective, arguments for God's existence are actually a way to resist idolatry, presuming as they do that those things about which we do have knowledge — that is, that which exists but requires no explanation — are best known as "effects." According to Kerr, the notion that all that is testifies as "effect" expresses that all that is is created. In short, all that is witnesses to God by acknowledging that all that is is created.

Kerr thinks rightly that his understanding of the character of Thom-

---

1. Stanley Hauerwas, *With the Grain of the Universe: The Church's Witness and Natural Theology* (Grand Rapids: Brazos, 2001).

2. This is the title of a collection of essays on Hauerwas's work. We do not mean to mimic the title; rather, we simply agree with the editors of the volume that this is indeed a crucial confluence of words. L. Gregory Jones, Reinhard Hütter, and C. Rosalee Velloso Ewell, eds., *God, Truth, and Witness: Engaging Stanley Hauerwas* (Grand Rapids: Brazos, 2005).

3. Fergus Kerr, *After Aquinas: Versions of Thomism* (Oxford: Blackwell, 2002), p. 58.

as's "proofs" expresses his affinity with Alasdair MacIntyre's arguments in *Three Rival Versions of Moral Enquiry: Encyclopaedia, Genealogy, and Tradition* against the epistemological turn in modern philosophy.[4] With MacIntyre, Kerr argues that the epistemological turn skewed readings of Thomas after *Aeterni Patris*.[5] Joseph Kleutgen[6] and other Thomists misread Thomas as responding to the Cartesian problematic to defeat skepticism. But this fundamentally distorts his position. It assumes that the *Summa* exemplifies a great system wherein the arguments are so tightly interrelated there can be no "externality."[7]

Quite to the contrary, what Thomas meant to do was truthfully describe God's world, in all its contingency. Indeed, one of the fundamental callings of the theologian is to read the world as God's creation. As one of us has suggested, a suitable image for Aquinas at work in the *Summa* is that of an expert forester whose eye is trained to mark leaf and branch, bark and span.[8] He draws distinctions, notes likenesses, groups in one way, then the other, all so as to draw toward a fuller and more truthful vision of what the forest is.

The image of Thomas as a forester, moreover, suggests how important is contingency in his work.[9] Aquinas saw quite clearly that "accidents which are altogether accidental are neglected by every art, by reason of their uncertainty and infinity."[10] We need to know which accidents not to neglect. Put another way, if all that is bears the character of "accident," in order to find your way through a forest of such contingent truths you will have to know which ones count to tell you what you need to know.

---

4. Alasdair MacIntyre, *Three Rival Versions of Moral Enquiry: Encyclopaedia, Genealogy, and Tradition* (South Bend: University of Notre Dame Press, 1990).

5. Kerr, *After Aquinas*, pp. 17-22.

6. See Kerr, *After Aquinas*, chapter 2, note 3, p. 216.

7. Besides MacIntyre, Kerr may well be reflecting the influence of Stanley Cavell for his reading of Thomas. Kerr thinks, rightly we think, that Cavell is right that it is a mistake to try to defeat skepticism. See Kerr's chapter on Cavell in Kerr's *Immortal Longings: Versions of Transcending Humanity* (London: SPCK, 1997), pp. 113-35.

8. For the development of this understanding of Thomas Aquinas see Charles R. Pinches, *Theology and Action: After Theory in Christian Ethics* (Grand Rapids: Eerdmans, 2002), pp. 5-9.

9. See John Bowlin, *Contingency and Fortune in Aquinas's Ethics* (New York: Cambridge University Press, 1999).

10. *Summa Theologiae*, I-II, 7, 2.

The *Summa* is Thomas's attempt not only to display the forest but also to negotiate a path through it without getting lost in the details.

This is how the whole of the *Summa*, not only its second part, can count as ethics — just to the extent, that is, that Thomas means to show throughout what it means that we are human beings who are the "principle of our actions."[11] We are beings capable of truth because we are capable of actions that require that we say what we have done — which we cannot do truthfully unless we know the world we act within. The repertoire of descriptions as well as their interrelation is complicated, requiring care and attention if we are not to be self-deceived. And this means we must describe all that is properly, namely, as God's creative and redemptive work.

This is a tall order, for what could be more vast and varied than the contingencies of the created world? Yet, as Kerr notes, Thomas believed (and showed) that we can proceed with a certain confidence. Unencumbered by Cartesian doubt, "for Thomas, human beings are created in God's image and likeness, and, more particularly, are born such that our own minds are connaturally open to the world that reveals itself to us and even reveals itself as created."[12] Since the created world includes us, knowing it means knowing ourselves — as created, as in God's image, and as sinners.

A key point for Kerr is that modern philosophers have become entangled in the "Enlightenment's mechanistic conception of causation."[13] Read back into Thomas, "first cause" is assumed to be something other than the personal God Thomas worshiped. But as Kerr notes, Thomas's view about cause was much more subtle and supple, rooted in Aristotle

11. *Summa Theologiae*, I-II, Prologue. Servais Pinckaers, O.P., has consistently shown this fundamental unity in his reading of the *Summa*. Regarding the text quoted here he says: "The famous Prologue of the *prima secundae* is not simply a threshold. It shows God laying a foundation, free will, which will support all that follows: morality viewed as man's return to God. Nor should we forget that finally, in the *tertia pars*, St. Thomas will study Christ who, in his humanity, is the necessary way to God, while in his divine personality Christ is the Word of God, the perfect Image of the Father." *The Pinckaers Reader*, ed. John Berkman and Craig Steven Titus (Washington: Catholic University Press, 2005), pp. 132-33.

12. Kerr, *After Aquinas*, p. 33.

13. Kerr, *After Aquinas*, p. 48.

and, in fact, in the quite sensible pre-modern notion that "cause" was carried in its meaning by what it is for us human beings to cause something. Summing up, Kerr notes that "God as First Cause is already [for Thomas] God as freely self-communicating goodness, and as final cause attracting created agents to their proper end or *telos*."[14]

Cause and agency, then, are fundamentally related notions, both in God and in us. Here we find ourselves once again at the beginning of the *prima secundae*, where ethics "officially" begins and where Thomas launches his inquiry into the truth about human actions. Such inquiry is a kind of "science," although different from what we usually call by that name, since it is not only about the so-called "natural world" but also about us as we live in it. Indeed, this is why it is rightly about all of "creation," since it does not assume that "natural" and "human" world are radically different entities.[15] But as just implied, the "science" becomes decidedly more complicated with the inclusion of human actions.

For instance, as Elizabeth Anscombe argued in *Intention*, human actions fall under a variety of descriptions, which means truthful inquiry can proceed in a variety of directions.[16] Moreover, often it is not possible to give *the* description of an action, because to know what is the case or what has been done requires that the action be placed in a narrative that is still ongoing. This means the process through which we discover what has happened or what we have done requires that we reason practically — which of course we cannot do well without all the virtues.

We hope these points display our deep sympathy with Kerr's attempt to "overcome epistemology" — just to the extent that the epistemological project was an attempt to escape contingency by supposing theoret-

---

14. Kerr, *After Aquinas*, p. 50.

15. As Pinckaers notes, "For us, 'nature' stands for the physical or biological universe, or again the ontological world, that is to say, one dimension, one part of things, radically distinct from freedom and conscience, and belonging to the order of the necessary and irrational. In our minds, nature and freedom are necessarily opposed. This was not the concept of nature held by the ancients, among them Christian authors. St. Thomas does not hesitate to place nature at the origin and source of freedom. For him, we are free not in spite of but because of our natural inclinations." *The Pinckaers Reader*, pp. 132-33.

16. Elizabeth Anscombe, *Intention*, 2nd ed. (Cambridge: Harvard University Press, 2009).

ical reason could entirely substitute for the work of practical reason. We also share his use of Ludwig Wittgenstein to "overcome epistemology." Though we do not make extensive use of Wittgenstein in the account of witness that follows, it owes much to his work. Indeed, much of what we say is a sort of commentary on Wittgenstein's remark that "a language-game must 'show' the facts that make it possible. (But that's not how it is.)"[17] Put differently, we think it is crucial for understanding the grammar of theology that we recognize that language is not one thing and the world another.

"Witness," then, as we believe, is required by the Christian faith, does not sit atop the world as if it is an epiphenomenal layer of words that help us cope "morally" or "spiritually" in a reality otherwise ruled by the endless bump and grind of "cause" and "effect." To witness is to speak the truth about the world as God's, that is, the God of Israel, the same God who raised Christ from the dead — of which we are witnesses. This may make witness seem like a simple, formulaic thing that simply rehearses one alleged truth. Yet, to the contrary, we hold that proper attention to witness is essential if we are to avoid the sort of reductionism that assumes that some deeper account of "meaning" is necessary to support what we say as Christians. By rejecting such "deeper accounts" we do not mean to imply that Christians cannot be wrong in what they say; indeed, we invite objections to how we speak about the world — without supposing that fielding them demands that we speak a language more determinative than that we have learned as Christians.

In this way, witness requires the faithful display of Christian speech sufficient to test what is said in the light of how it is said. Such a testing, moreover, cannot be separated from the character of those who speak. Indeed, to speak Christianly means that the speakers' lives must correspond with what they say. The very grammar of Christian speech presumes that those who use the language have a character commensurate with it.

This is a key reason why theology and ethics cannot be separated; indeed, theology is first and foremost an exercise in practical reason.[18]

17. Ludwig Wittgenstein, *On Certainty* (New York: Harper Torchbooks, 1969), p. 618.

18. For an account of practical reason with which we are very sympathetic see Charles Taylor, "Iris Murdoch and Moral Philosophy," in his *Dilemmas and Connec-*

Again, this is not to say that theology is about anything else than the truth. But the truth it is about involves us as creatures of God, made in God's image, even if fallen. So we cannot speak this truth without it having worked truthfully in us. Speaker and what is spoken cannot be separated if Christians' claims about God and God's world have the purchase of truth. "Witness" is the crucial grammar that upholds and enfolds these claims.

Of course, such claims beg for further explication. Yet this cannot come merely at a theoretical level. Indeed, if witness is only spoken of theoretically, it empties out. More than explanation, the character of witness requires concrete display, as we hope to do as we retell the story of the witness of the first Christians. Such stories are not optional, not only because witness is always specifically given in place and time but also because the first witnesses display something about how Christian witness will go. Moreover, they give us means for practical judgments. This is doubly important since the ways in which Christians subvert their witness to Christ proliferate as they take up forms of "practical reason" that skew political prudence. To glimpse what we take as the ethical and political implications of our account of witness, such subversions will

---

tions: Selected Essays (Cambridge, MA: Harvard University Press, 2011), pp. 3-23. Taylor provides a compelling critique of the accounts of ethics that depict moral rationality as a disengaged commitment to a single term that is assumed to be basic. He refuses, however, to characterize such a view of morality as "foundational" because that "word is bad," implying as it does a philosophical view that is impossible. That is, "foundationalism" implies that you can argue someone who shares absolutely no moral sense into "morality." But that cannot be done, nor should we think it should be done. Taylor observes that some may interpret the line from Dostoyevsky, "If God does not exist, then everything is permitted," as implying a foundationalist view. Taylor argues, however, that Dostoyevsky's claim is rightly characterized as a statement of the constitutive good of a way of life (p. 13). That is why it is a mistake to assume that a choice must be made between foundationalism and anti-foundationalism. The problem with the latter is that it too often mirrors the foundational desire to give an account of morality in a singular term. In contrast, Taylor argues that practical reason works against a background of acquired habits and paradigms that can never be transcended or escaped. The articulacy we develop through the use of practical reason, therefore, helps us know not only what to do but also what we want to be by helping us love the good. Any account of practical reason that does not attend to the narratives that shape our understanding of morality as well as the exemplars that exhibit those narratives is impoverished (pp. 14-15).

need attention, which we give briefly in the final section of this essay. As we hold, such subversions almost always have to do with abandoning witness for some more apparently powerful way of speaking — a point Kerr's work has helpfully prepared us for. Here the political suppression of witnesses, that is, the attempt to make witnesses voiceless, will also be briefly considered. This is particularly important if we remember that the fundamental form of witness by Christians is called martyrdom.

Witness Exemplified: Explorations from the New Testament

Witness is required by those of us who would count ourselves Christians because the God we worship is not a general truth that can be known apart from those who worship him and have been called into his Kingdom. It is not accidental that Jesus calls disciples so that they might be witnesses to him. Discipleship and witness together constitute Christology; Jesus cannot be known without witnesses who follow him. Discipleship and witness together remind us that the Christ we follow and to whom we bear witness defies generalization.

The witness of the disciples, moreover, has a definite shape. In the tenth chapter of the Gospel of Matthew Jesus summons his disciples, gives them explicit instructions, and then sends them to the lost sheep of Israel.[19] They are to go as witnesses to Jesus in whom the Kingdom of Heaven has come near. And they have work to do: cure the sick, raise the dead, cleanse leapers, and cast out demons. Furthermore, they are to receive no compensation for their work, nor are they to travel weighed down by money or clothing. They should not be deterred by those who do not respond to their mission, but rather they should see such rejection as an invitation to go to others.

These instructions indicate the character of the witness given throughout the New Testament. The disciples of Jesus are sent out as bearers of news; they have received a message to spread, but they themselves are also the exemplification of what they have to say. However, this

19. For a fuller account of this "sending" see Hauerwas, *Matthew*, Brazos Theological Commentary on the Bible (Grand Rapids: Brazos, 2006), pp. 105-12.

is not really their doing. That is to say, whatever actions are theirs as faithful disciples, and to whatever degree their lives bear truthful witness, this is always also the result of a gift they have been given. This is why the news or story they have to tell turns out always to be inseparable from what has happened to them. The story they tell is about them insofar as they testify in the telling to what has happened to them. But it points past them, or through them, to the God they believe they have met in Christ Jesus.

To be sure, as they tell their story the disciples often provide inadequate witnesses to Jesus, but the inadequacy itself is also a kind of witness. They have been called to live lives that point to Christ — lives that are unintelligible if the one they follow is not the Son of God. Sometimes the pointing is off direction. But this is revealed precisely as the intelligible Christ is unveiled and their inadequacies are marked in relation to him. Like the sleeping disciples in the garden or Peter warming himself by the fire, even their failures are given focus in relation to Christ to whom they witness. The disciples' very identity is tied up in what they witness to. In this way Christian witnesses are unlike those "witnesses" who might appear in a court of law to testify dispassionately to events they may have seen or heard, like bits of facts that have no bearing on their own lives and that they pass over to judge or jury to do with as they please. Instead, they are more like people who have witnessed a horrible accident that cannot be forgotten; it lives with them daily, shaping the contours of their lives henceforth.[20]

Yet the witness of Christians does more than carry forward from what has happened; it also carries back from what *will* happen. The disciples of Jesus are called to be witnesses to the reality of a new age, a new time, constituted by his life, death, and resurrection. Apocalypse is the name given to describe the inauguration of this new beginning. The story of Jesus is the story of a new creation, the telling of which cannot but challenge the reigning stories that legitimate the practices of the old age. This is present not in overcoming force or power but rather precisely

---

20. See Hauerwas's and Brian Goldstone's chapter, "Disciplined Seeing: Forms of Christianity and Forms of Life," in Stanley Hauerwas, *Working with Words: On Learning to Speak Christian* (Eugene, OR: Cascade, 2011), pp. 49-52.

in witness. Indeed, that witness is the form in which the new age is revealed indicates why what has happened requires that a people exist who exemplify the new reality. The existence of the church is itself the determinative (although not the only)[21] witness to an alternative politics to that of the old age.[22]

The new politics is a politics of speech — and so also of act. But it begins in the speech of the church, which is a story we Christians believe is not just ours but everyone's. As such it cannot but be a complex story with many subplots. Nevertheless, it begins simply in a meeting with the Christ. This story is told in hope that it will be received, that those who hear it will be able to recognize how all that is exists as a witness to God. Spoken as witness, its purpose is not definitive; it does not end all arguments but rather opens space for them to appear. Here is the story — now what do you think? Indeed, witness is a first step in introducing arguments we need to have, ones that could not have been discovered until each particular witness was offered.[23]

While witnesses expect they will be heard, they also know that sometimes they will not. Genuine witnesses to the Christian gospel are fully aware that it can and might be rejected. Indeed, to be a "witness" in the New Testament is also to be a martyr — or, better put, the term "martyr" is the New Testament Greek term for witness. Of course, "martyr" subsequently came to mean that one died in the act of witnessing — although it was not so narrowly circumscribed for the first Christians.[24]

21. For an elaboration of this point regarding witness outside the church, see Hauerwas and Romand Coles, *Christianity, Democracy, and the Radical Ordinary* (Eugene, OR: Cascade, 2008), especially pp. 17-30.

22. In *With the Grain of the Universe* Hauerwas tries to show that Barth so understands the significance of the church; cf. pp. 199-200.

23. For a remarkable account of this process see Vincent J. Donavan, *Christianity Rediscovered*, 2nd ed. (Maryknoll, NY: Orbis, 2003). Fr. Donavan relates his witness to the Masai of Tanzania in the 1960s. The progression of his chapter titles bespeaks the progression: "A Time to Be Silent and a Time to Think"; "A Time to Speak and a Time to Act"; "What Do You Think of the Christ?"; and "The Response." The response, as Donavan says, was simply "church," but church in a new light, in the light of the Masai, who also needed to have new arguments about what Christian faith might mean if fully embraced in the Masai context.

24. For a discussion of the significance of μάρτυς and its first Christian uses in Acts, see C. Kavin Rowe, *World Upside Down: Reading Acts in the Graeco-Roman Age*

The Book of the Acts of the Apostles uses the term "witness" twenty-three times.[25] This frequent use is fitting since the book's task is to describe what the first followers of Christ told others about him. Yet the usage is not generalized; witness is not so much treated as a concept as it is displayed in a story. Moreover, the Book of Acts is a narrative that carries its story not principally, as the Gospels do, by following the story of one person, but rather by focusing on first one act and then another of a crowd of witnesses. Those who witness understand themselves to have been uniquely claimed by Christ. Indeed, the witnessing we hear in Acts frequently takes a highly personal form: this is what happened to me, or us, as we encountered the Christ. These encounters are then drawn up into the whole story, becoming pillars of support. Following on the Gospels, Christ remains the center of the narrative in Acts, yet now through these others who witness to him. As their stories are told, they point to his. However, and crucially, the details and particularities of the stories are not obliterated in the pointing, nor are the characters whose stories they are.

As Kavin Rowe suggests, "readers do not have to labor long in the book of Acts until they come across its programmatic thesis: after receiving the power of the Holy Spirit, says the risen Jesus, the disciples 'shall be my witnesses in Jerusalem and in all Judea and Samaria and to the end of the earth'" (Acts 1:8).[26] Such a program, however, depends on there being particular people who respond to the call to witness, each in his or her peculiar manner. Nearer the end of his narrative Luke dwells especially on St. Paul.

Intriguingly, Paul often witnesses by telling his own story. This is not only because it is interesting but also because it describes Paul's own call to be a witness. The story is well known, one of the most reported in the New Testament. We hear it first within the sequence of Luke's narrative in chapter 9 of Acts, and then it is retold twice in considerable detail by Paul himself (as Luke has it) in chapters 22 and 26. Finally, Paul alludes to the episode in his letters more than once, that is, in Galatians 1 and 1 Corinthians 9 and 15. So many references invite comparative study. Yet our

---

(New York: Oxford University Press, 2009), p. 121. We are indebted to Rowe's analysis of Acts in much of the account that follows.

25. Rowe, *World Upside Down*, p. 120.

26. Rowe, *World Upside Down*, p. 120.

interest here is focused on the two accounts Luke accredits to Paul when he retells the story of how he became a witness. These are especially interesting since they are also cases of witnessing, that is, Paul is witnessing about becoming a witness.

In the first case, in chapter 22 of Acts, Paul has just been arrested in Jerusalem amid a cloud of confusion. As they are about to take him into the barracks and away from the angry crowd, the arresting Roman soldiers are surprised to discover that Paul speaks Greek; they had been operating under the mistaken assumption that he was a notorious Egyptian revolutionary.[27] The surprise seems to help Paul, since the soldiers grant him his request to "speak to the people" (22:39) — namely, the Jews. He tells the interesting tale of his life, focusing on the road to Damascus experience. Here he accents the part of the story where, after the encounter, he is put under Ananias's wing in Damascus. It is Ananias who tells him: "The God of our ancestors has chosen you to know his will and to see the Righteous One and to hear words from his mouth. *You will be his witness to all men of what you have seen and heard.* Get up, be baptized and wash your sins away, calling on his name" (22:14-16, emphasis added).[28]

Ananias's role is important in this telling not only because it is from him that Paul gets his charge to be a witness, but also because he (Ananias) can perform something of a witnessing role for Paul's listeners. Paul's encounter on the road is not his to interpret; he needs others to place the strange event in a fruitful context of meaning. Indeed, Ananias speaks for the church, and so for the God who is calling it forth throughout the progression of Luke's narrative in Acts. Moreover, it is not by accident that Luke's Paul includes about Ananias that he is a "devout man according to the law and well spoken of by all the Jews living [in Damascus]" (22:12). In this role Paul clearly hopes his Jewish audience will hear Ananias as a kind of second source, a corroborating witness.

---

27. Rowe suggests that this mistake indicates Luke's view that the Christian witness includes a genuine challenge to the first-century Roman world, but it is importantly not a seditious challenge (*World Upside Down*, p. 147).

28. Stephen is called "witness" by Paul as he is worked into Paul's story a few verses later (22:20). This usage is often translated "martyr," although there is no linguistic distinction between the usage Paul applies to himself in the story and what he calls Stephen.

Perhaps this is the reason it is not surprising that Ananias is omitted in the subsequent retelling in chapter 26. Here Paul is speaking before the Roman Agrippa, who no doubt will be entirely unimpressed by the devout follower of the law in Damascus. This change in the story might seem disingenuous, as if Paul is playing to his audience. But of course he is — for he wants them to listen. He is, after all, witnessing.

Paul witnesses so as to win people over, which is not to say that he speaks falsehood to do so; that would be absurd, since he believes he is preaching the truth about all that is, which clearly cannot be held together with a lie. Yet the story can be both truthfully and differently told, which Luke's Paul is happy to do if the different telling will bring different people differently into the truth.

Witness in this regard is not merely passing over plain, unadorned truth. As mentioned earlier, it is *affecting* truth; if it is "believed" yet bears no active fruit in response, it has failed as witness. As Jesus says, you need ears to hear it — which implies that some listen but do not hear. If the gospel is to be "heard" it must penetrate into one's life. And this cannot happen if it remains foreign. As he witnesses, Paul means to bring his witness close. For some, the story of Ananias will help; for others it will not.

While Ananias disappears in the second story, the crucial point he speaks in the first story about Paul's call to be a witness remains. As Paul relates,

> "About noon, O king, as I was on the road, I saw a light from heaven, brighter than the sun, blazing around me and my companions. We all fell to the ground, and I heard a voice saying to me in Aramaic, 'Saul, Saul, why do you persecute me? It is hard for you to kick against the goads.' Then I asked, 'Who are you, Lord?' 'I am Jesus, whom you are persecuting,' the Lord replied. 'Now get up and stand on your feet. *I have appeared to you to appoint you as a servant and as a witness of what you have seen of me and what I will show you.* I will rescue you from your own people and from the Gentiles. I am sending you to them to open their eyes and turn them from darkness to light, and from the power of Satan to God, so that they may receive forgiveness of sins and a place among those who are sanctified by faith in me.'" (26:13-18 NIV, emphasis added)

These passages not only demonstrate how witness is crucial to the program of Acts but also focus our attention on the particular stories where witness is displayed. Especially in these cases, one telling builds on another. Luke here tells us what Paul told Agrippa or the crowd in Jerusalem about what Jesus or Ananias told him — and this is all about witnessing, which itself involves telling. Witness, then, is displayed as it is introduced; indeed, this is inevitable, for witness to the Christ always requires that the one who witnesses is him- or herself drawn up into the message.

One might fear that the layering, witness upon witness, would produce monotony. Yet, to the contrary, the stories are lively and bring strong reaction. This is partly because, as just noted, it is the prerogative, perhaps even the duty, of the teller to retell the story in such a way as to intrigue. But, more to the point, the nature of Christian witness brings the teller into the story and invites the listener to investigate her. Her life is opened by her speech as witness. In academic argument we typically protest when this occurs: the argument should stand on its own legs. Not so with witness; if the witness fails to instantiate that to which she witnesses, her listeners rightfully reject what she says. Put another way, with respect to Christian witness, *ad hominem* is entirely fair game. Since this is so, as opposed to "pure" argument, witness is dull only if the one witnessing is dull. And, indeed, if the Christian witness is a dull person, something is wrong — since there is no greater adventure than the Christian life.

This is not a throwaway point. Christian witness is about nothing more or less than how we were made to live, or, expressed more classically, what is our true end. With the story St. Paul tells we are presented with his encounter or "experience" with Christ, yes, but this means little if it does not take his life somewhere, indeed, in the direction it was meant to go. This is why both accounts of the Damascus road encounter take as their focus the new calling or "appointment" Paul receives in it. The calling is the message, but the message requires, as we have seen, both word and deed. This, in fact, is an essential component of the point, made earlier with respect to Kerr's work, that theology requires, indeed, is a form of practical reason. In this way, the life of Christian witness is linked inextricably to crucial questions of morality properly understood, namely, what is the good life for human persons.[29] The life of Christian witness is, as St. Paul has come to know both by hearing and also by doing, the truest and best way to live. To be sure, it can be lived differently, as Acts shows us by showing us so many different witnesses. But each is a full, profoundly interesting life, the life the particular witness was meant for, and which the witness now lives out as a gift received from Christ to whom he or she bears witness.

Evidently dullness was not a problem for Paul, although in another sense "interesting" came to be. For interesting living is also imaginative living, and this is not always well received. So it is that both accounts of Paul's witnessing about being appointed as a witness carry forward to a reaction. In the first we get the following report from Luke: "The crowd listened to Paul until he said this [that he was sent by God to the Gentiles]. Then they raised their voices and shouted 'Rid the earth of him! He's not fit to live'" (Acts 22:22). In the second, Luke tells us that Festus, who is listening with King Agrippa, "interrupted Paul's defense. 'You are out of your mind, Paul!' he shouted. 'Your great learning is driving you insane'" (26:24).

A commonality in the reaction is that suddenly what Paul is saying, and Paul himself, appears strange, even offensive, to his audience. Commenting especially on the second episode, Kavin Rowe notes that

> considered from a pagan point of view — that is, any Graeco-Roman perspective outside the specifically Christian rationale for mission — the Christian mission must inevitably appear strange. It is not simply that the death of one Jew at the hands of a Roman governor would not even make the news, or the idea that all of time should be thought in relation to this Jew rather than the emperor, or his followers' belief that the Jew was alive again, or the conviction that what was "wrong with the world" was directly related to humanity's worship of the god of Is-

---

29. In Thomas this is the question of beatitude. As Pinckaers notes, for Thomas "[t]he first principle is that morality, and even philosophy in its entirety, begins with the question of beatitude and is an attempt to answer this question." *The Pinckaers Reader*, p. 138. As he also notes, the loss of this question in modern "morality" has meant the loss of the sense of morality (and philosophy) that animated ancient and medieval thought.

rael, as strange as these things would doubtless appear. It is rather, to be conceptually more precise, that there was no preexistent category or tradition of inquiry within which the phenomenon of Christian mission could be rightly perceived. . . . Festus' perplexity . . . was the proper epistemological posture of someone who thinks the Christians are literally crazy.[30]

As Rowe's book title indicates, Christian witness in Acts turns the pagan world "upside down" — which also means that very often the witnesses and the Christ they carry will appear simply crazy to the likes of the Roman governor Festus. For Rowe, Festus's description of Paul as "crazy" is indicative of and integral to the pattern of Acts. Far from being an apologia for the Greco-Roman (as opposed to the Jewish) way — as some scholars have alleged — Luke's story repeatedly displays what Rowe calls the "collision" between Christian mission and the pagan world it encountered. Using Charles Taylor's notion of the "social imaginary," Rowe shows how the new Christian vision challenged the metaphysical order in which the typical practices of the Greco-Roman world made sense.

> Sacrificing to the gods, soothsaying, magic, the use of household shrines, and so forth all gain their intelligibility as practices within a moral or metaphysical order that underwrites the reality in which it makes sense to do these things. . . . [A]ccording to Acts, sacrificing to gods, soothsaying, magic, and so forth, do not "make sense" for the early Christians. The reason is not hard to find: the wider predicament in which these practices made sense has disappeared. Thus the collision between the Christian mission and the larger Mediterranean world is both extraordinarily deep and "thick" for the reason that it entails multiple layers of sense-making, that is, a social imaginary.[31]

The witness that is the Christian gospel is hardly harmless. Rowe calls it "a deep threat to preexisting foundational ways of life in the Mediterranean world." As Paul brings the news to Lystra or Philippi or Ath-

---

30. Rowe, *World Upside Down*, p. 125.
31. Rowe, *World Upside Down*, p. 145.

ens, his visits presage what Rowe calls "cultural collapse."[32] But the threat comes not in a swarm of military might, nor, for that matter, in a barrage of innovative political ideas. It comes rather as theology. "The possibility of cultural demise [of the pagan world] is rooted in the counter-cultural explication of the break between God and the world. . . . Because 'God' in Luke's sense corresponds not to a particular point within the widest of human horizons but to that which constitutes — makes possible and stands over against — the entirety of the human horizon, the call to (re) turn to God carries with it an entire pattern of life."[33]

The truth to which Paul and others witness in Acts is comprehensive: it renarrates the whole of human life, indeed, all that is, in the light of the God who is — now fully known through Christ. This requires a change in the way we live, according to Rowe a change in the "entire pattern of life." This also displays why the theology is embodied precisely in the ones who arrive with the news of it; they witness to the new vision and also inhabit it. So both what they say and who they are represent a potential threat. As such, it and they may be violently rejected, as the growing connection in the New Testament between witness and martyrdom reminds us. So those who arrive with the news may also be called to give their lives for it. Yet whether they live or die, for the gospel to take root and grow — and so challenge, even bring the demise of, the cultures it encounters — it must be brought by people who both speak and practice it. Christian faith is not a disembodied set of ideas or theories; it is not intuited or received by osmosis. The Kingdom grows person to person; it is brought through witness. Once again, the reason is theological: the God Christians worship is no general truth that can be known apart from those who have been called into his Kingdom. So if the Kingdom is to grow, these ones must travel, bearing witness.

This is why Paul thinks the feet of those who bring the gospel are so beautiful (Rom. 10:10). If they had not walked, the gospel would not have come. Moreover, they come not simply as carriers of a package they can leave on the doorsteps of cities and villages throughout the Mediterranean world, for the locals to unwrap on their own. Rather, as Luke's story

---

32. Rowe, *World Upside Down*, p. 141.
33. Rowe, *World Upside Down*, p. 142.

shows, we cannot know Jesus without those, like Paul, who were called by him. And the same remains today: there is no Christ without those who are still being called. To reiterate, the fact that such witnesses are required arises from the fact that the witness is to a life that defies generalization. It is a life that was and is seen, heard, even touched.

Rowe rightly accents the threat that Christianity posed to the "social imaginary" of the Mediterranean world. In this, he reminds us that the Christian gospel never can be fit within a preexisting culture, tamed and cordoned off in a protected space in that culture, as, for instance, modern Western culture hopes to cage Christian conviction within the "personal belief systems" of its members. The threat Christianity poses is, in fact, merely the "flip side of the reality that God's identity receives new cultural explication in the formation of a community whose moral or metaphysical order requires an alternative way of life."[34]

The source of life for the new community is none other than the resurrected Christ, to which it bears witness. As Rowe comments,

> it would not be too much, in fact, to say that the resurrection of Jesus is the reason for mission. . . . [T]he connection between the resurrection of Jesus and the witness to the end of the earth is essential and runs much deeper than a purely formal analysis might suggest. Briefly put, the former generates the latter. It is not only the case that, literally speaking, Acts narrates explicitly that what the disciples witness to is the resurrection, it is also the case that the resurrection is the fount of new reality out of which the *novum* that is Christian mission emerges.[35]

As Rowe notes, it is the risen Christ who in the opening scene of Acts anchors the universal mission of witness "to the ends of the earth" that the apostles set out upon. And it is the risen Christ whom Paul meets on the road — indeed, who also speaks through Ananias, commissioning Paul to carry the news to the Gentiles. The universal mission arises from the new reality that is the risen Christ for the world; yet, again, this is to be carried to the world by a people whose pattern of communal life is the very form of the good news.

34. Rowe, *World Upside Down*, p. 146.
35. Rowe, *World Upside Down*, p. 122.

This brings us to an important point less accented by Rowe. The gospel is indeed universal, but it is particularly carried. Moreover, because the gospel is carried as witness rather than simply by courier, the new life that is Christ's resurrection can take up various forms in the various places it comes to reside. What Paul sees and hears on the road explodes into a world of words, a language. The explosion is also a witness.

Of course, the shape of the witness is not unbounded; indeed, it remains tethered to the first witnesses and, as noted at the beginning of this section, to the specific work Jesus gives to his disciples, namely, to cure the sick, raise the dead, cleanse leapers, cast out demons, and so on. Yet as those who witness to the risen Christ engage with the various cultures to which they are sent, they need not — indeed, they should not — predetermine the form Christ will take as he comes alive in this new place. As necessarily particular, the language of witness must engage and converse with the concrete other, something Paul illustrates by, for instance, choosing whether he tells his story with or without Ananias in it. And this can give birth in each instance to particular new things that the world has yet to see.

As mentioned, the gospel brings a politics of speech, and the speech requires a form of life — and so a community who lives it. But further, the life gives room for us to come to learn to speak in new ways. For instance, Servais Pinckaers gives a fascinating account of how the term "person" was transformed by the Christian vision. Thomas appropriated the term, knowing that while it "cannot be found in the text of the Old or New Testament as referring to God . . . [w]e have to look for new words about God which express the old faith because we have to argue with heretics."[36] As Pinckaers concludes, "Here the powerful influence of Christian thought on language is apparent. The term 'person' is given a real impetus to transcend its original and then its social meaning, to rise to a universal level, and finally to be applied to the God of Revelation in his most intimate mystery, to the Persons of the Trinity."[37]

---

36. *Summa Theologiae*, I, 29, 3 ad 1, as quoted by Pinckaers, *The Pinckaers Reader*, p. 145.

37. *The Pinckaers Reader*, pp. 151-52.

Witness Exemplified: A Recent Example

More contemporarily, Emmanuel Katongole has written of the recent spread of Christianity through Africa. As he accents, the spread is of little merit if the newfound "faith" does little to challenge the accepted politics of modern Africa, namely, "that the nation-state is the only possible structure for modern social existence in Africa."[38] In contrast to such conventional assumptions, Katongole highlights stories of witness wherein the gospel meets specific conditions in Africa, such as child kidnappings by the Lord's Resistance Army (LRA) in Uganda or the tribal tensions between Hutu and Tutsi in Rwanda and Burundi. Rightly witnessed to, the gospel so transforms the social vision of those who receive it that the result appears, like Paul to Festus, to be a form of craziness. For instance, Maggy Barankitse of Burundi openly admits that "love has made me crazy."[39]

In 1993 Maggy witnessed the brutal execution of seventy-two Hutus in the bishop's compound in Ruyigi where she worked — all part of the ethnic violence between Hutu and Tutsis that has racked Maggy's part of Africa. Miraculously, seven orphan children she had taken to raise, four Hutus and three Tutsis, survived the slaughter. Rather than despair after so much horror, Maggy felt "an incredible resistance inside me, like strength" that filled her with one goal: "to raise the children beyond the hatred and bitterness that I came to see in their eyes."[40]

Since 1993 Maggy has founded a house for orphans called Maison Shalom. Beginning with twenty-five children, Maison Shalom has become home to more than 10,000 children. Underneath this extraordinary story is a conviction that the ethnic identities that have ruled the imaginations of many in Burundi and neighboring Rwanda are deeply false and are directly called into question by the new story that has come. As Katongole describes it,

> According to Maggy, love is our true identity. Love is the dignity that God gives each person in creation. Each person is created out of love

38. Emmanuel Katongole, *The Sacrifice of Africa: A Political Theology for Africa* (Grand Rapids: Eerdmans, 2011), p. 59.

39. Katongole, *The Sacrifice of Africa*, p. 193.

40. Katongole, *The Sacrifice of Africa*, p. 171.

as God's child, and is meant to live in the house of God as a member of God's family. Thus love is not only our identity; it is our unique vocation. "Love is the most beautiful calling of human beings. We are created out of love and to love." Maggy's hope was for Maison Shalom to become not simply an example of the identity and calling of God's love, but also the seed for a new culture — and indeed a new culture founded on the story of love. As she says, "I would like for Burundi to give birth to a new generation who will carry the light of love and forgiveness to all the surrounding hills."[41]

Maggy's story illustrates not only how the gospel brings new beginnings but also how this comes about as those who are called, like Paul and the other apostles, throw themselves with abandon into the task that is Christian witness. Behind the witness lies a "madness" whose root is a politics of hope that looks to the formation of communities in which the truth about human beings — that they are all children of God, made for love — can come to genuine realization. The church, which grows by witness, is also by its very existence a witness, an alternative politics to the politics of the old age.[42]

The Politics of Martyrdom

The politics of witness is necessarily a politics of speech. The witness that is the church requires Christians to be able to tell a story that we believe is not just our story but the story of the world. The story cannot be told without including such crucial terms as "sin," "confession," "redemption," "hope," and "church." But the terms are not to exclude but rather to invite: through the telling we hope those who do not share our story will be able to recognize how all that is exists as a witness to God. Likewise, we cannot and do not expect witness to be the end of arguments we need to have, but rather the beginning.

41. Katongole, *The Sacrifice of Africa*, p. 176.
42. In *With the Grain of the Universe* Hauerwas tries to show that Barth so understands the significance of the church; cf. pp. 199-200.

If we are to have arguments, we will need people to argue with, ones who do not begin from where we begin. Witness assumes this will be the case. Indeed, as one of us has commented elsewhere, it was precisely the relinquishing of the necessity that Christians witness that turned Christianity into a story that no longer needed telling — exemplified by the presumptions that held sway for the likes of Reinhold Niebuhr and William James. "Niebuhr assumed that the truth of Christianity consisted in the confirmation of universal and timeless myths about the human condition that made Christianity available to anyone without witness. So conceived, Christianity became a 'truth' for the sustaining of social orders in the West. In an odd way, James and Niebuhr offer accounts of religion and Christianity, respectively, that make the existence of the church accidental to Christianity."[43] Indeed, for Niebuhr, James, and most of their contemporaries, "Christianity makes sense only as a disguised humanism."[44] So, for instance, Christ's resurrection is no longer the beginning point for Christian witness, but rather a sign or metaphor for a spiritual or moral meaning for life that is better understood when placed in another language than that of the church.

These presumptions make Christianity too much at home in the world, but ironically also too little. If the story does not need to be told, it cannot compel, which also implies that it need not be embraced. Indeed, it need no longer trust those who hear it for the first time to embrace it and also to carry it on to others. It has settled things, meanings, without any need for the ongoing history of people who carry the news and those who hear it, either accepting or rejecting it.

In contrast to such a view, Christians as a people must be forever committed to the point of exchange, one person to another, implied by witness. Like St. Paul, Christians think they have been given something that needs to be given again. They want to go places and meet people and tell them the story that has gathered them in — and that they also suppose can and will gather in these new hearers. Moreover, they are prepared to receive the various ways those to whom they witness may have already embraced the gospel they preach — like Paul in Athens as he speaks of

43. Hauerwas, *With the Grain of the Universe*, p. 39.
44. Hauerwas, *With the Grain of the Universe*, p. 206.

their "unknown god." That language of Christian faith is in this sense not closed; rather, it remains open to receive gratefully what others have discovered and spoken, as, for example, it received (and also transformed) the language of "person" or the classical language of the virtues.[45]

Christians need, in other words, a profound trust both in the story that they tell about the Lord of the universe and in those to whom they tell it, who are all his children. Moreover, they must trust that the God who sends them to the ends of the earth is bringing forth something new in his redemptive action, in which they participate. This includes a trust that those to whom they witness will learn the gospel in a new and different light, drawing it out in ways hitherto unimagined. Indeed, as they witness, Christians joyfully anticipate that the language they bring will bear fruit, even explode into new, even more faithful expressions of God among us. This is how Christians are at home in the world to which they speak in witness.

Yet, in another way (which also cannot be well articulated if Christianity is taken up into another language that is supposed to express its "deeper meanings"), Christian witness is also *not* at home in the world to which it is given. As the stories in Acts demonstrate, true Christian witnesses know that the Christ to whom they bear witness is not always received gladly. This mirrors what John reports of the Christ: "He was in the world, and the world came into being through him; yet the world did not know him. He came to what was his own, and his own people did not accept him" (John 1:10-11).

This reminder of the possible rejection of the gospel by the world leads us again to the connection, indeed, the etymological equivalence, between Christian witness and martyrdom. Yet for the reasons just suggested regarding the trust Christians need as they witness, the connection must be carefully approached. As Craig Hovey writes,

> The first thing to say is that martyrdom is not the only mode of witness the church has. Christians bear a positive message to the world. That message speaks of salvation and good news before it speaks about con-

45. For a full treatment of this point, see our *Christians among the Virtues* (Notre Dame: University of Notre Dame Press, 1997).

demnation. The church is not first against the world but for the world. When it encounters hostility in a world that refuses to hear the gospel, the church must have a clear conscience before God that it has not courted that hostility.[46]

Christian martyrdom is in this sense not at all a necessity. It is not written into the foundations of the created world. It is, rather, one of the contingent parts of the ongoing story of God and the world. Hovey calls it an "empirical reality," which Christians must be schooled to treat as such. Christians should know that the "deaths of martyrs are not somehow an evangelistic strategy. With this awareness Christians are released from the thought that persecution is necessary for the church's witness. They are promised that persecution may be an empirical reality but that the salvation of the world does not rely on and depend on the opposition of the world to the kingdom of God."[47]

Nevertheless, as empirical reality, martyrdom also hits at the center of the story of the Christian gospel. For the Christ preached is Christ crucified. Christ came and the world killed him. But, as Hovey comments, his death is not the end of the story to which Christians bear witness. In fact, in the "ironic logic of the resurrection,"

[t]he way the world kills is not finally allowed to be antithetical to the way that God saves. Jesus's words from the cross in Luke "Father forgive them; for they know not what they do," can be read as precisely displaying this irony. They do not know what they are doing because their killing is becoming the very grounds for the possibility of their forgiveness. When the Father grants the Son's request for the forgiveness of his enemies, the Father's answer will be the cross and the resurrection. The ironic logic of this means that the connection between Jesus's death and the forgiveness of the Roman army is the gift of the Father to the Son, which will be good news for the whole world and constitute the content of all Christian proclamation. Martyrs are in-

46. Craig Hovey, *To Share in the Body: A Theology of Martyrdom for Today's Church* (Grand Rapids: Brazos, 2008), p. 37.
47. Hovey, *To Share in the Body*, p. 37.

cluded in the death and resurrection of Christ because their deaths witness to the Father's gift to the Son by contributing to the growth of the church in baptism.[48]

In this way martyrdom uniquely witnesses to cross and resurrection since it shows this ironic logic rather than simply telling it. As such, it instantiates the politics of hope that confronts and finally vanquishes (in its own peculiar, indeed, ironic way) the politics of violence to which the nations who know not Christ are so often tempted.[49] The growth of the church in connection to martyrdom, which Tertullian famously termed the "seed of the church," is itself a sign of the way in which God gathers the world unto himself. If it is to show forth this ironic logic, witness to it, the church in its ongoing life must live in such a way that martyrdom remains a consistent possibility.

As Hovey notes, this is written into the language of Christian baptism. When on the road to Jerusalem James and John ask Jesus to put them at his right and left hand in his coming Kingdom, he responds: "You do not know what you are asking. Are you able to drink the cup that I drink, or to be baptized with the baptism with which I am baptized?" (Mark 10:38). Although it does not require it, baptism prepares Christians for the death of the martyr.

Again, it is not up to the Christian to die, but for the world to kill. The early martyrs did not seek death but rather refused to do what the Romans required, namely, sacrifice to pagan gods — and for this the Romans killed them. What baptism does require, however, is that the church live in such a way as to make the crucified and resurrected Jesus fully present to the world. And here, as Hovey notes, the infrequency of Christian martyrdom

---

48. Hovey, *To Share in the Body*, p. 36.

49. For an account of martyrdom quite similar to Hovey's see Joshua J. Whitfield, *Pilgrim Holiness: Martyrdom as Descriptive Witness* (Eugene, OR: Cascade, 2009). Drawing on Wittgenstein, Whitfield, like Hovey, stresses the importance of speech for sustaining the memory of the martyrs. He notes, "given that martyrdom is intelligible according to the particular narrative of Israel, Jesus, and the Church; and also given the martyr's speech in particular discloses that narrative in an exemplary and reconciling fashion, it is possible to suggest that both martyr's speech and also the Church's memory of martyrs provide not only exemplifications and training of habits of truthfulness but also in the habits of unity" (p. 118).

may sometimes be read as an indictment of the church. "Does the world ignore the church out of goodwill? Or has the church often given the world too little to reject, too little witness, too few challenges, too small a God and a harmless Jesus?"[50]

As sacrament, baptism gathers the individual body into the corporate body of the church, a community whose politics is rooted in another way than that which predominates in the world. If this other way is lived clearly and plainly it will stand as a witness; and as such it can and sometimes will provoke a response among the nations that attempt to annihilate it as a rival. Of course, often enough "baptism" shows none of this. As Hovey remarks, "for many baptism only enshrines one's individual life apart from God and entrenches one's autonomous freedom from the church. It becomes a quaint ceremony for an innocuous blessing, a hopeful yet bland sign for receiving good things from life, a plea for calm and good luck, a positive omen, an exercise in superstition."[51]

Such sentimentality especially tempts Christians in Western individualized cultures; it is a "faith" that needs no church. Without church "witness" can present no new way of life, no new language or politics, and so no practical wisdom that, in its transforming power, opens to the renewal (or restoration) of all that is. In this role "church" must genuinely inhabit the world as church, that is, as Christ's body in the world. As William Cavanaugh argues, it has been tempted otherwise, especially in the past century in Latin America and primarily under the influence of Jacques Maritain. Despite his theological seriousness and depth, Maritain supposed that the church should define itself as the "soul of society" rather than as political body. This "social Catholicism" led to "the church's abandonment of social space to the state. The church construed itself not as a real body but as a 'mystical body,' hovering over the divisions of the 'temporal plane,' uniting all in soul but not in body."[52] This laid the church open to an especially virulent form of nationalism practiced under the regime of Augusto Pinochet in Chile. Here the state set about "not only to attack the church but to render it invisible. It does so by making bod-

50. Hovey, *To Share in the Body*, p. 39.
51. Hovey, *To Share in the Body*, p. 40.
52. William Cavanaugh, *Torture and Eucharist: Theology, Politics, and the Body of Christ* (Malden, MA: Blackwell, 2006), p. 16.

ies disappear and by torturing without having any visible effects on the bodies of its victims. The torture project learned how to attack the church without creating martyrs, who are the seed of future resistance, and who make the church visible as the body of Christ."[53]

As Cavanaugh holds, for the church to recover from this spiritualization, it must recover Eucharist, not as "object" but as "action."[54] Action, as Thomas Aquinas saw (and as both Pinckaers and Kerr have reminded us), roots any and every form of practical reason. So the action of Eucharist — which as sacrament is God's action in which we participate — anchors the practical reason (or the political prudence) of the church. Conceived as such, the church that is the "mystical body of Christ does not hover above national boundaries but dissolves them, making possible Christian resistance to the nation-state's violent designs."[55]

Here Christians' speech and action can unite in full witness to the God who created all that is and continues to reach out redemptively to re-create it. Rightly conceived and practiced, Christian witness is neither theoretical nor formulaic but engages the world as it is, as one person telling another. Eagerly awaiting, even expecting, its acceptance, witness also knows what to do in the face of its rejection, as discerned within the grammar of Christ's cross and resurrection, which remains always its fundamental idiom.

53. Cavanaugh, *Torture and Eucharist*, pp. 15-16.
54. Cavanaugh, *Torture and Eucharist*, p. 213.
55. Cavanaugh, *Torture and Eucharist*, p. 221.

PART TWO

Church and Politics

Church Matters: On Faith and Politics

The Theological Politics of the "And"

I am a Christian. I am even a Christian theologian. I observe in my memoir, *Hannah's Child*, that you do not need to be a theologian to be a Christian but I probably did. Being a Christian has not and does not come naturally or easily for me. I take that to be a good thing because I am sure that to be a Christian requires training that lasts a lifetime. I am more than ready to acknowledge that some may find that being a Christian comes more "naturally," but that can present its own difficulties. Just as an athlete with natural gifts may fail to develop the fundamental skills necessary to play his or her sport after the talent fades, so people naturally disposed to faith may fail to develop the skills necessary to sustain them for a lifetime.

By training I mean something very basic, such as acquiring habits of speech necessary for prayer. The acquisition of such habits is crucial for the formation of our bodies if we are to acquire the virtues necessary to live life as a Christian. For I take it to be crucial that Christians must live in such a manner that their lives are unintelligible if the God we worship in Jesus Christ does not exist. The training entailed in being a Christian can be called, if you are so disposed, culture. That is particularly the case

My title is a play on Herbert McCabe, O.P., *God Matters* (Springfield, IL: Templegate, 1991).

if, as Raymond Williams reminds us in *Keywords*, "culture" is a term first used as a process noun to describe the tending or cultivation of a crop or animal.[1] One of the challenges Christians confront is how the politics we helped create has made it difficult to sustain the material practices constitutive of an ecclesial culture to produce Christians.

The character of much of modern theology exemplifies this development. In the attempt to make Christianity intelligible within the epistemological conceits of modernity, theologians have been intent on showing that what we believe as Christians is not that different from what those who are not Christians believe. Thus MacIntyre's wry observation that the project of modern theology to distinguish the kernel of the Christian faith from the outmoded husk has resulted in offering atheists less and less in which to disbelieve.[2]

It should not be surprising, as David Yeago argues, that many secular people now assume that descriptions of reality that Christians employ are a sort of varnish that can be scraped away to reveal a more basic account of what has always been the case. From a secular point of view it is assumed that we agree, or should agree, on fundamental naturalistic and secular descriptions of reality, whatever religious elaborations may lie over them. What I find so interesting is that many Christians accept these naturalistic assumptions about the way things are because they believe that by doing so it is possible to transcend our diverse particularities that otherwise result in unwelcome conflict. From such a perspective it is only a short step to the key socio-political move crucial to the formation of modern societies, that is, the relegation of religion to the sphere of private inwardness and individual motivation.[3]

Societies that have relegated strong convictions to the private, a development I think appropriately identified as "secularization," may assume a tolerant or intolerant attitude toward the church, but the crucial characteristic of such societies is that the church is understood to be no

1. Raymond Williams, *Keywords: A Vocabulary of Culture and Society* (New York: Oxford University Press, 1976), pp. 77-78.

2. Alasdair MacIntyre, *The Religious Significance of Atheism* (New York: Columbia University Press, 1966), p. 24.

3. David Yeago, "Messiah's People: The Culture of the Church in the Midst of the Nations," *Pro Ecclesia* 6, no. 1 (1997): 147-48.

more than a "voluntary association" of like-minded individuals.[4] Even those who identify as "religious" assume that their religious convictions should be submitted to a public order governed by a secular rationality. I hope to challenge that assumption by calling into question the conceptual resources that now seem to be givens for how the church is understood. In particular I hope to convince Christians that the church is a material reality that must resist the domestication of our faith in the interest of societal peace.

There is a great deal going against such a project. For example, in his book *Civil Religion: A Dialogue in the History of Political Philosophy*, Ronald Beiner argues that in modernity the attempt to domesticate strong religious convictions in the interest of state control has assumed two primary and antithetical alternatives: civil religion or liberalism. Civil religion is the attempt to empower religion not for the good of religion but for the creation of the citizen. Indeed, the very creation of "religion" as a concept more fundamental than a determinative tradition has manifested itself in that, at least in Western societies, Christianity has become "civil."[5] Jean-Jacques Rousseau, according to Beiner, is the decisive figure who gave expression to this transformation, because Rousseau saw clearly that the modern state could not risk having a church capable of challenging its political authority.[6] In the process, the political concepts used to legitimize the modern state, at least if Carl Schmitt is right, have become secularized theological concepts.[7]

In contrast to civil religion, the liberal alternative rejects all attempts

4. I have no intention of entering into the never-ending debates about secularization and the corresponding discussions concerning the demise of "religion." Suffice it to say that I am in general sympathetic with David Martin's contention that secularization is best understood in terms of social differentiation correlative of the division of labor, with the result that discrete sectors of social life are assumed autonomous. See David Martin, *The Future of Christianity: Reflections on Violence and Democracy, Religion and Secularization* (Surrey, UK: Ashgate, 2011), p. 124.

5. Bill Cavanaugh provides an invaluable account of how the creation of "religion" was a correlative of the modern state. See his *The Myth of Religious Violence* (New York: Oxford University Press, 2009), pp. 60-71.

6. Ronald Beiner, *Civil Religion: A Dialogue in the History of Political Philosophy* (Cambridge: Cambridge University Press, 2011), pp. 1-7.

7. Carl Schmitt, *Political Theology: Four Chapters on the Concept of Sovereignty* (Chicago: University of Chicago Press, 2005), pp. 5, 35.

to use religion to produce citizens in service to the state. Liberalism, in its many versions, according to Beiner, seeks to domesticate or neutralize the impact of religious commitment on political life.[8] Liberalism may well result in the production of a banal and flattened account of human existence, but such a form of life seems necessary if we are to be at peace with one another. In other words, liberalism as a way of life depends on the creation of people who think there is nothing for which it is worth dying. Such a way of life was exemplified by President Bush, who suggested that the duty of Americans after September 11, 2001, was to go shopping. Such a view of the world evoked Friedrich Nietzsche's bitter condemnation, ironically making Nietzsche an ally of a Christianity determined by martyrdom.[9]

An extraordinary claim, to be sure, but, as Paul Kahn has observed, the Western state exists "under the very real threat of Christian martyrdom; a threat to expose the state and its claim to power as nothing at all."[10] The martyr does so, according to Kahn, because when everything is said and done sacrifice is always stronger than murder. The martyr wields a power that defeats the murderer because the martyr can be remembered by a community more enduring than the state. That is why the liberal state has such a stake in the domestication of Christianity by making it but another lifestyle choice.

In contrast, the modern nation-state, Kahn argues, has been an extremely effective sacrificial agent, able to mobilize its populations to make sacrifices to sustain its existence as an end in itself. The nation-state has therefore stepped into the place of religious belief, offering the individual the possibility of transcending our finitude. War becomes the act of sacrifice by which the state sustains the assumption that, though we die, it can and will continue to exist without end.[11]

I have earned the description of being a "fideistic, sectarian tribalist" because of my attempt to imagine an ecclesial alternative capable of re-

8. Beiner, *Civil Religion*, pp. 301-5.
9. Beiner, *Civil Religion*, pp. 374-94.
10. Paul Kahn, *Putting Liberalism in Its Place* (Princeton: Princeton University Press, 2005), p. 82. I am indebted to Sean Larson for suggesting the importance of Kahn's understanding of liberalism for the argument I am making in this essay.
11. Kahn, *Putting Liberalism in Its Place*, pp. 276-77.

sisting the politics Beiner (and Kahn) describe.[12] For, as Yeago observes, most churches in the West, with the possible exception of the Roman Catholic Church, have acquiesced in this understanding of their social character and have therefore collaborated in the eclipse of their ecclesial reality.[13] As a result, the church seems caught in a "ceaseless crisis of legitimation" in which the church must find a justification for its existence in terms of the projects and aspirations of that larger order.[14]

In his extraordinary book *Atheist Delusions: The Christian Revolution and Its Fashionable Enemies*, David Bentley Hart observes that the relegation of Christian beliefs to the private sphere is legitimated by a story of human freedom in which humankind is liberated from the crushing weight of tradition and doctrine. Hart, whose prose begs for extensive quotation, says the story goes like this:

> Once upon a time Western humanity was the cosseted and incurious ward of Mother Church; during this, the age of faith, culture stagnated, science languished, wars of religion were routinely waged, witches were burned by inquisitors, and Western humanity labored in brutish subjugation to dogma, superstition, and the unholy alliance of church and state. Withering blasts of fanaticism and fideism had long since scorched away the last remnants of classical learning; inquiry

---

12. Kahn argues that there is a liberalism of the will that can and does demand sacrifice. Liberalism of interest and reason, however, cannot acknowledge the sacrifices required by the state. The result is what Kahn calls the "paradox of democratic self-government"; that is, "the more the nation believes itself to be a product of the will of the popular sovereign, the less democratic it becomes — if by democratic, we mean subject to control through broadly participatory electoral mechanisms." Kahn suggests that this is the modern form of Rousseau's distinction between the general will and the will of all. *Putting Liberalism in Its Place*, p. 161.

13. For an extremely informative comparison of the Catholic and Protestant responses to secularization see Martin, *The Future of Christianity*, pp. 25-44. Emile Perreau-Saussine's *Catholicism and Democracy: An Essay in the History of Political Thought* (Princeton: Princeton University Press, 2011) is a fascinating account of the rise of the political importance of the papacy after the French Revolution; the importance of the papacy was at once the manifestation as well as the result of the Catholic agreement with the liberal presumption that there is "something irreducibly secular about the modern state" (p. 2).

14. Yeago, "Messiah's People," pp. 148-49.

was stifled; the literary remains of classical antiquity had long ago been consigned to the fires of faith, and even the great achievements of "Greek science" were forgotten until Islamic civilization restored them to the West. All was darkness. Then, in the wake of the "wars of religion" that had torn Christendom apart, came the full flowering of the Enlightenment and with it the reign of reason and progress, the riches of scientific achievement and political liberty, and a new and revolutionary sense of human dignity. The secular nation-state arose, reduced religion to an establishment of the state, and thereby rescued Western humanity from the blood-steeped intolerance of religion. Now, at last, Western humanity has left its nonage and attained its majority, in science, politics, and ethics. The story of the travails of Galileo almost invariably occupies an honored place in this narrative, as exemplary of the natural relation between "faith" and "reason" and as an exquisite epitome of scientific reason's mighty struggle during the early modern period to free itself from the tyranny of religion.[15]

This "simple and enchanting tale" is, Hart observes, captivating in its explanatory power. According to Hart, however, there is just one problem with this story. The problem is that every detail of the story, as well as the overarching plot, just happens to be false.[16] Hart's book provides the arguments and evidence to sustain that judgment. What I find so interesting, however, is that even if the narrative may be false in every detail it is nonetheless true that believer and unbeliever alike assume, though they may disagree about some of the details, that the main plot of the story is true.

That this story now has canonical status has deep significance for how Christians should understand the relation between faith and politics. Put even more strongly, in the interest of being good citizens, of being civil, Christians have lost the ability to say why what they believe is true. That loss is, I want to suggest, a correlative of the depolitization of the church as a community capable of challenging the imperial pretensions of the

15. David Bentley Hart, *Atheist Delusions: The Christian Revolution and Its Fashionable Enemies* (New Haven: Yale University Press, 2009), pp. 33-34.
16. Hart, *Atheist Delusions*, p. 34.

modern state. That the church matters is why I resist using the language of "belief" to indicate what allegedly makes Christians Christian.[17] Of course Christians "believe in God," but far more important for determining the character of Christian existence is that it is constituted by a politics that cannot avoid challenging what is normally identified as "the political." For what is normally identified as "the political" produces dualisms that invite questions such as "What is the relation between faith and politics?" If I am right, that "and" prematurely ends any serious theological reflection from a Christian perspective.

As I have already indicated, to make this argument necessarily puts me at odds with the attempt to make Christian convictions compatible with the epistemological and moral presumptions of liberal social orders. That project presumed a story very much along the lines suggested by Hart. Theologians trimmed the sails of Christian convictions to show that even if the metaphysical commitments that seem intrinsic to Christian practice cannot be intellectually sustained, it remains the case that Christianity can claim some credit for the creation of the culture and politics of modernity.

In particular, Christian theologians sought to justify Christian participation in the politics of democratic societies. The field of Christian ethics, the discipline with which I am identified, had as one of its primary agendas to convince Christians that their "beliefs" had political implications. The determinative representative who exemplified this mode of Christian ethical reflection was Reinhold Niebuhr. Thus his claim that "the real problem of a Christian social ethic is to derive from the Gospel a clear view of the realities with which we must deal in our common or social life, and also to preserve a sense of responsibility for achieving the highest measure of order, freedom and justice despite the hazards of

---

17. In his magisterial book *The Unintended Reformation: How a Religious Revolution Secularized Society* (Cambridge, MA: Harvard University Press, 2012), Brad Gregory observes that the Reformation placed an unprecedented emphasis on doctrine for identifying what made Christians Christians. Such an emphasis led Protestant and Catholic alike to emphasize the importance of an "interior assent to the propositional content of doctrinal truth claims, whatever they were." Gregory observes that this development "risked making Christianity seem more a matter of what one believed than how one lived — of making the faith a crypto-Cartesian matter of one's soul and mind, *rather than* a matter of what one does with one's body" (p. 155).

man's collective life."[18] Niebuhr reminded Christians that we do not live in a world in which sin can be eliminated, but we nonetheless must seek to establish the tentative harmonies and provisional equities possible in any historical situation.

Niebuhr, who prided himself in being a sober realist challenging what he took to be the unfounded optimism of liberal thinkers such as John Dewey, would have in a like manner called into question the optimism of the story Hart associates with the celebration, if not the legitimization, of modernity. But Niebuhr's support of liberal democratic political arrangements drew on a narrative very much like the one Hart identifies as the story of modernity.[19] The result is ironic, a category Niebuhr loved, because Niebuhr's arguments for political engagement by Christians presupposed a narrative that legitimates political arrangement that requires the privatization of Christian convictions — one of the consequences being the loss of any attempt to say what it might mean for the gospel of Jesus Christ to be true.

For instance, one of the curiosities associated with what have been popularly called "the new atheists" is their assumption that the most decisive challenges to the truthfulness of Christian convictions come from developments in the sciences or, perhaps more accurately put, the "method" of science. Such a view fails to appreciate that the most decisive challenge to the truthfulness of Christian convictions is political.[20] The politics of modernity has so successfully made Christianity but another lifestyle option that it is a mystery why the new atheists think it is important to show what Christians believe to be false. Such a project hardly

18. *Reinhold Niebuhr on Politics*, ed. Harry Davis and Robert Good (New York: Scribner's, 1960), p. 153.

19. For a fuller defense of this account of Niebuhr see my *Wilderness Wanderings: Probing Twentieth-Century Theology and Philosophy* (Boulder: Westview, 1997), pp. 32-62, and *With the Grain of the Universe: The Church's Witness and Natural Theology* (Grand Rapids: Brazos, 2001), pp. 87-140.

20. David Martin nicely shows that the assumption that science makes theological claims unintelligible is simply not sustainable. See his *The Future of Christianity*, pp. 119-31. Brad Gregory observes that "empirical investigation of the natural world has not falsified any theological claims." Much more troubling for the status of the truthfulness of Christian convictions, according to Gregory, were the unresolved disputes between Protestants and Catholics concerning the meaning of God's actions. *The Unintended Reformation*, p. 47.

seems necessary, given that Christians, in the name of being good democratic citizens, live lives of unacknowledged but desperate unbelief just to the extent that they believe what they believe as a Christian cannot be a matter of truth. As a result, Christians no longer believe that the church is an alternative politics to the politics of the world, which means they have lost any way to account for why Christians in the past thought they had a faith worth dying for.

The Witness of Karl Barth

I need an example of what the connection between the truthfulness of Christian speech and politics might look like. An example is necessary because I am not sure we know what Christianity so understood would look like. I think, however, we have the beginnings in the work of Karl Barth. Barth, more than any other theologian in modernity, recognized that the recovery of the language of the faith entailed a politics at odds with the world as we know it. For Barth there is no kernel of the Christian faith because the faith begins and ends with the extraordinary claim that what we mean when we say "God" is to be determined by Mary's willingness to be impregnated by the Holy Spirit.

That is not where Barth began. Barth began by presuming that the work of Protestant liberal theologians was a given. It was, however, a political event that called into question Barth's liberalism. On a day in early August of 1914 Barth read a proclamation in support of the war policy of Wilhelm II signed by ninety-three German intellectuals. To Barth's horror, almost all of his venerated theological teachers were among the names of those who had signed in support of the war. Barth confessed that he suddenly realized that he could no longer follow their theology or ethics. At that moment the theology of the nineteenth century, the theology of Protestant liberalism, came to an end for Barth.[21]

Barth characterized the theology he thought must be left behind, a theology identified with figures such as Schleiermacher and Troeltsch, as the attempt to respond to the modern age by underwriting the assump-

---

21. Karl Barth, *The Humanity of God* (Richmond: John Knox, 1963), p. 14.

tion that Christianity is but an expression of the alleged innate human capacity for the infinite. From such a perspective Christianity is understood to be but one particular expression of religion. Such a view of the Christian faith presumes that the primary task of Christian theology is to assure the general acceptance of the Christian faith for the sustaining of the achievements of Western civilization. Barth observed that theology so conceived was more interested in man's relationship with God than with God's dealings with man.[22]

For Barth, however, a theology understood as the realization in one form or another of human self-awareness could have no ground or content other than ourselves. "Faith as the Christian commerce with God could first and last be only the Christian commerce with himself."[23] The figure haunting such an account of Christianity is Ludwig Feuerbach, whom Barth thought had powerfully reconfigured the Christian faith as a statement of profound human needs and desires.

Drawing on Søren Kierkegaard, Fyodor Dostoyevsky, and Franz Overbeck, as well as his discovery of what he characterized as "the strange new world of the Bible," against the theology of his teachers, Barth proclaimed: "God is God."[24] Barth did not think such a claim to be redundant. Rather, he thought it to be the best expression of who God is; it is a response to the particularity of a God who has initiated an encounter with humankind. Barth says, "the stone wall we first ran up against was that the theme of the Bible is the deity of *God*, more exactly God's *deity* — God's independence and particular character, not only in relation to the natural but also to the spiritual cosmos; God's absolutely unique existence, might, and initiative, above all, in His relation to man."[25]

So Barth challenged what he characterized as the accommodated the-

22. Barth, *The Humanity of God*, p. 24. Barth noted, however, that theology so understood could be in continuity with Melanchthon's emphasis on the benefits of Christ. So there is no reason why an attempt should not be made to develop a Christian anthropocentrism in which theology is done, so to speak, from the bottom up.

23. Barth, *The Humanity of God*, p. 26.

24. Timothy Gorringe suggests that Barth may well have seen *A Midsummer Night's Dream*, whose "Well roared, Lion!" he liked to use to characterize his reaction against Protestant liberalism. See Gorringe, *Karl Barth: Against Hegemony* (Oxford: Oxford University Press, 1999), p. 25.

25. Barth, *The Humanity of God*, p. 41.

ology of Protestant liberalism, using expressions such as God is "wholly other" and God breaks in upon us "perpendicularly from above." There is an "infinite qualitative distinction" between God and us, rendering any presumption that we can know God on our terms to be just that, namely, a presumption based on sinful pride. Thus Barth's sobering claim that God is God and we are not means that it can never be the case that we have the means to know God unless God first makes himself known to us.

Barth would later acknowledge that his initial reaction against Protestant liberal theology was exaggerated, but any theology committed to clearing the ground for a fresh expression of the Christian faith could not help but sound extreme. Barth acknowledged that his first salvos against Protestant liberalism seemed to be saying that God is everything and man nothing. Such a God, the God who is wholly other, isolated, and set over against man, threatens to become the God of the philosophers rather than the God who called Abraham. The majesty of the God of the philosophers might have the contradictory results of confirming the hopelessness of all human activity while offering a new justification of the autonomy of man. Barth wanted neither of these results.

In retrospect, however, Barth confessed that he was wrong exactly where he was right, but at the time he did not know how to carry through with sufficient care the discovery of God's deity.[26] For Barth the decisive breakthrough came with the recognition that "who God is and what He is in His deity He proves and reveals not in a vacuum as a divine being-for-Himself, but precisely and authentically in the fact that He exists, speaks, and acts as the *partner* of man, though of course as the absolute superior partner."[27] In short, Barth discovered that it is precisely God's deity that includes and constitutes God's humanity.

We are not dealing with an abstract God, that is, a God whose deity exists separated from man, because in Jesus Christ there can be no isolation of man from God or God from man. In Barth's language: "God's deity in Jesus Christ consists in the fact that God Himself in Him is the *subject* who speaks and acts with sovereignty. . . . In Jesus Christ man's freedom is wholly enclosed in the freedom of God. Without the condescension of

---

26. Barth, *The Humanity of God*, p. 44.
27. Barth, *The Humanity of God*, p. 46.

God there would be no exaltation of man. . . . We have no universal deity capable of being reached conceptually, but this concrete deity — real and recognizable in the *descent* grounded in that sequence and peculiar to the existence of Jesus Christ."[28]

I am aware that this all-too-brief account of Barth's decisive theological turn may seem but a report on esoteric methodological issues in Christian theology. But I ask you to remember that Barth's discovery of the otherness of God, an otherness intrinsic to God's humanity, was occasioned by his recognition of the failure of the politics and ethics of modern theology in the face of the First World War. I think it not accidental, moreover, that Barth was among the first to recognize the character of the politics represented by Hitler. Barth was a person of unusual insight, or, as Timothy Gorringe describes him, he was a person of extraordinary vitality who was a profoundly political animal.[29] But his perception of the threat the Nazis represented cannot be separated from his theological turn occasioned by his reaction against his teachers who supported the war.

Tim Gorringe rightly argues in his book *Karl Barth: Against Hegemony* that Barth never assumed that his theology might have political implications because his theology was a politics. That way of putting the matter — that is, "his theology was a politics" — is crucial. The very structure of Barth's *Dogmatics*, Gorringe suggests, with its integration of theology and ethics displayed in his refusal to separate law from gospel, was Barth's way of refusing any distinction between theory and practice. Barth's Christocentrism meant that his "theology was never a predicate of his politics, but [it is] also true that politics is never simply a predicate of his theology."[30]

Gorringe's argument that Barth was a political theologian is confirmed by an event in 1934, the same year Barth wrote the Barmen Declaration, when Barth responded to a challenge by some American and English critics that his theology was too abstract and unrelated to actual lives. Barth begins his defense by observing that he is after all "a mod-

28. Barth, *The Humanity of God*, p. 48.
29. Gorringe, *Karl Barth*, p. 11.
30. Gorringe, *Karl Barth*, p. 9.

ern man" who stands in the midst of this age. Like his questioners, he too must live a life not merely in theory but in practice in what he characterizes as the "stormy present." Accordingly, he tells his antagonists that "exactly because I was called to live in a modern world, did I reach the path of which you have heard me speak."[31]

In particular, Barth calls attention to his years as a pastor in which he faced the task of preaching the gospel in the face of secularism. During this time he was confronted with the modern world, but he was also confronted with the modern church. It was a church — a church of great sincerity and zeal, with fervid devotion to deeds of charity — too closely related to the modern world. It was a church that no longer knew God's choice to love the world by what Christians had been given to do in the light of that love, that is, to be witnesses to the treasure that is the gospel. The problem, according to Barth, is that the church of the pious man, this church of the good man, this church of the moral man, became the church of man.[32] The result was the fusion of Christianity and nationalism.[33]

Consequently, the modern church is a near relative to the godless modern world. That error, Barth suggests, began two hundred years before the present with pietism's objections to orthodoxy. In the Reformation the church heard of God and of Christ, but love was not active.[34] The fatal error was the Christian response: they did not say, let God be

---

31. Karl Barth, *God in Action* (Eugene, OR: Wipf and Stock, 2005), p. 133. This little gem of a book contains lectures Barth gave in response to the Nazis in 1934.

32. The role of pietism in the development of Protestant liberal theology as well as the legitimating discourse for the subordination of the church to the state is a story in itself. It is not accidental that Barth was the great enemy of pietism. David Martin suggests that pietism was the ultimate working out of the implications of the Protestant Reformation for the development of the centralized sovereignty necessary to legitimate the formation of the nation-state. Martin observes: "German Pietism inculcated disciplines that helped ensure the smooth running of the state." *The Future of Christianity*, p. 199.

33. Barth, *God in Action*, pp. 134-35.

34. In his book *The Unintended Reformation*, Brad Gregory convincingly argues "that the Western world today is an extraordinarily complex, tangled project of rejections, retentions, and transformations of medieval Western Christianity, in which the Reformation era constitutes the critical watershed." The secularization that was the result of the Reformation was, according to Gregory, unintended but no less a reality (p. 2).

even more God and Christ be even more the Christ, but instead they said, let us improve matters ourselves. Reverence for the pious man became reverence for the moral man, and finally when it was found that man is of so large an importance, it became less important to speak of God, of Christ, of the Holy Spirit. Instead, men began to speak of human reason.[35]

Barth then directly addresses his questioners, whom he identifies as "friends," to tell them that he is well aware of what is happening and that is exactly why he insists that he must speak of God. He must speak of God because he must begin with the confession, "I am from Germany." Because he is from Germany he knows that he stands in a place that has reached the end of a road, a road that he acknowledges may be just beginning in social orders like America and England. Yet Barth claims that he is sure that what has been experienced in Germany, that is, the remarkable apostasy of the church to nationalism, will also be the fate of those who think Barth's theology to be a retreat from political engagement. Thus Barth's challenge to his critics: "if you make a start with 'God *and* . . .' you are opening the doors to every demon."[36]

Barth early recognized that such a demon had been let loose in the person of Hitler. Barth was able to do so because Hitler's attempt to make Christianity a state religion by creating the German Church meant that the free preaching of the gospel was prohibited. Theological speech and politics were inseparable. It is, therefore, no accident that Barth in the Barmen Declaration challenged the "German Christians" on Christological grounds.[37] He did so because he assumed that Jesus' claim "I am the way, and the truth, and life; no one comes to the Father, but by me" (John 14:6) is the defining politics of Christianity. Barth writes:

> Jesus Christ, as he is attested for us in Holy Scripture, is the one word of God which we have to hear and which we have to trust and obey in life

35. Barth, *God in Action*, p. 137.
36. Barth, *God in Action*, p. 138.
37. The Barmen Declaration was the statement of protest by the Confessing Church, that is, the church in opposition to Hitler's formation of the German Christian Church. The synod met in Barmen on January 4, 1934. Though the Barmen Declaration was a joint effort of several theologians, Barth was the primary author.

and in death. We reject the false doctrine, as though the Church could and would have to acknowledge as a source of its proclamation, apart from and beside this one word of God, still other events and powers, figures and truths, as God's revelation.[38]

The witness that is Karl Barth — that is, how such a life fits into the ongoing story we must tell as Christians of our faithful and unfaithful living out the gospel — means there is no way we can avoid making clear to ourselves and the world that we believe a new world began in the belly of Mary.

Where Are We Now? Where Do We Need to Go?

You may be rightly wondering, if not worried, where all this has gotten us. I should like to be able to say more about where we are now and where we need to go, but I am unsure who the "we" or the "us" may be. I have assumed I should, or perhaps more truthfully, I can only speak from a first-person perspective, but hopefully it is one shaped by my Christian identity. Yet just as Barth confessed that he was German, so I must acknowledge that I am American. Indeed, it may be I am more American than Christian and thus I may be tempted to confuse the Christian "we" and the American "we." That confusion tempts Americans to assume that we represent what any right-thinking person should say because our "we" is the universal "we."

American presumption is always a problem, but the problem is deeper than my American identity. For I think none of us can assume an agreed-upon "we" or "us" to be a manifestation of cultural and political challenges confronting those who claim to live in a world that is "plural." Given the difficulty of locating the "we," some may worry that directing attention to Barth in order to show the political character of Christian convictions is morally and politically the exemplification of a profoundly reactionary position. In Nazi Germany a Barmen Decla-

---

38. I am quoting from Arthur Cochrane, *The Church's Confession under Hitler* (Philadelphia: Westminster, 1962), pp. 172-78.

ration may have seemed "prophetic," but "after Hitler" a Barmen-like account of the politics of Christian convictions suggests theocracy.[39]

I confess I often enjoy making liberal friends, particularly American liberal friends, nervous by acknowledging that I am of course a theocrat. "Jesus is Lord" is not my personal opinion; I take it to be a determinative political claim. So I am ready to rule. The difficulty is that following a crucified Lord entails embodying a politics that cannot resort to coercion and violence; it is a politics of persuasion all the way down. It is a tiring business that is slow and time-consuming, but then we, that is, Christians, believe that by redeeming time Christ has given us all the time we need to pursue peace. Christ, through the Holy Spirit, bestows upon his disciples the long-suffering patience necessary to resist any politics whose impatience makes coercion and violence the only and inevitable response to conflict.

For fifteen hundred years Christians thought Jesus' lordship meant they should rule the world. That rule assumed diverse forms, some beneficial and some quite destructive. "Constantinianism" and "Christendom" are descriptions of the various ways in which Christians sought to determine the cultural and political life of the worlds in which they found themselves. Some Christians look with nostalgia on that past, seeking ways to recapture Christian dominance of the world. That is obviously not my perspective.

For as David Hart observes, Christianity's greatest historical triumph was also its most calamitous defeat. The conversion of the Roman Empire was supposed to mean that the faith had overthrown the powers of "this age"; instead, the faith itself had become subordinate to those very powers. Like Hart, I have no reason to deny the many achievements of Christendom. I think he is right to suggest that the church was a revolution, a slow and persistent revolution, a cosmic sedition, in which the human person was "invested with an intrinsic and inviolable dignity" by being recognized as God's own.[40] But this revolution, exactly because it was so

39. During a visit to the Holocaust Museum in Washington, D.C., my wife and I encountered schoolchildren wearing shirts emblazoned with the slogan "Celebrate Diversity." There is much good, no doubt, in training the young to enjoy difference, but I worry for those who think the celebration of diversity is an adequate response to a movement like National Socialism.

40. Hart, *Atheist Delusions*, p. 167.

radical, was absorbed and subdued by society until nominal baptism became the expression of a church that was reduced to an instrument of temporal power and the gospel was made a captive to the mechanism of the state.[41]

In *The Stillborn God: Religion, Politics, and the Modern West,* Mark Lilla has written in defense of what he calls "the great separation" of politics and religion represented by Thomas Hobbes. Lilla observes that, although Christianity is inescapably political, it has proved incapable of integrating this fact into Christian theology.[42] The problem, according to Lilla, is that to be a Christian means being in the world, including the political world, but somehow not being of it. Such a way of being, Lilla argues, cannot help but produce a false consciousness. Christendom is the institutionalization of this consciousness just to the extent that the church thought reconciliation could be expressed politically.[43] Politics so constituted cannot help but suffer from permanent instability.

Lilla, I think, is right that the eschatological character of the Christian faith will challenge the politics of the worlds in which it finds itself. But that is why, even at times when the church fails to be true to its calling to be a political alternative, God raises up a Karl Barth. For as Barth insisted, this really is all about God, the particular God of Jesus Christ. The humanity of that God, Christians believe, has made it possible for a people to exist who do in fact, as Nietzsche suggested, exemplify a slave morality. It is a morality Hart describes as a "strange, impractical, altogether unworldly tenderness" expressed in the ability to see as our sisters or brothers the child who is autistic or has Down syndrome or is disabled,

---

41. Hart, *Atheist Delusions,* p. 194. It is true, nonetheless, as Brad Gregory argues in *The Unintended Reformation,* that the church was never coextensive with or absorbed by any secular political entity. A thousand years after Constantine, from the papacy to the parishes into which Christendom was parceled, the church remained distinct from secular political entities such as medieval kingdoms, principalities, duchies, cities, and city-states (pp. 136-37). One of the great virtues of Gregory's book is his treatment of the often ignored Anabaptists. He rightly understands the Anabaptists to represent a political alternative to the magisterial Reformers just to the extent that the latter led to the increasing control of the church by the state.

42. Mark Lilla, *The Stillborn God: Religion, Politics, and the Modern West* (New York: Knopf, 2007), p. 85.

43. Lilla, *The Stillborn God,* p. 169.

a child who is a perpetual perplexity for the world, a child who can cause pain and only fleetingly charm or delight; or the derelict or broken men and women who have wasted their lives; or the homeless, the diseased, the mentally ill, criminals, and reprobates.[44]

Such a morality is the matter that is the church. It is the matter that made even a church in Christendom uneasy. From the church's standpoint today, Christendom may be a lamentable world now lost, but it is not clear what will replace it or shape the resulting culture or politics. Hart observes that when Christianity passes from a culture, the resulting remainder may be worse than if Christianity had never existed. Christians took the gods away, and no one will ever believe them again. Christians demystified the world, robbing good pagans of their reverence and hard-won wisdom derived from the study of human and nonhuman nature. So once again Nietzsche was right that the Christians shaped a world that meant that those who would come after Christianity could not avoid nihilism.[45]

Why this is the case is perhaps best exemplified by how time is understood. Christians, drawing as they must on God's calling of Israel to be the promised people, cannot help but believe that time has a plot. That is to say, Christians believe in history — a strange phrase to be sure, but one to remind us of how extraordinary it is for Christians to believe we come from a past that will find its fulfillment in the future. Accordingly, we believe that time has a narrative logic, which means that time is not just one damn thing after another. The story of creation is meant to remind us that all that exists lends witness to the glory of God, giving history a significance otherwise unavailable. Creation, redemption, and reconciliation are names that, Christians believe, constitute the basic plotline that makes history more than a tale told by an idiot.[46]

Yet the very assumption that history has a direction is the necessary condition that underwrites the story of modernity earlier characterized by Hart — the story that has underwritten the new atheists' presumption that, if history is finally rid of Christianity, we will discover how, through

---

44. Hart, *Atheist Delusions*, pp. 213-14.
45. Hart, *Atheist Delusions*, pp. 229-30.
46. Hart, *Atheist Delusions*, pp. 201-2.

unconstrained reason, our politics can be made more just and humane. Thus Hart speculates that the violence done in the name of humanity, a violence that is now unconstrained, might never have been unleashed if Christianity had not introduced its "peculiar variant of apocalyptic yearning into Western culture."[47] Hart rightly observes that such a judgment is purely speculative, given the reality that past great empires prior to Christianity claimed divine warrants for murder. Yet Hart thinks the secularization of Christian eschatological grammar is the "chief cause of the modern state's curious talent for mass murder."[48] An exaggerated claim, perhaps, but it is at least a reminder that it is by no means clear why the killing called war is distinguishable from mass murder.[49]

This last observation, I hope, draws us back to Karl Barth's theological work. I suggested that Barth exemplifies the politics of speech that is at the heart of Christian convictions. At the heart of Christian convictions is the belief in "the humanity of God," a humanity made unavoidable by our faith in Jesus Christ as the second person of the Trinity. Christ's humanity means that no account of the church is possible which does not require material expression that is rightly understood as a politics. Church matters matter not only for the church; but we believe what is a necessity for the church is a possibility for all that is not the church.

I suspect humans always live in times of transition; what is time if

---

47. Hart, *Atheist Delusions*, pp. 222-23.

48. Hart, *Atheist Delusions*, pp. 223-24.

49. In a recent blog post entitled "Bend Your Knee," www.hoodedutilitarian.com, Noah Berlatsky defends my arguments for pacifism against Eric Cohen's critique of my book *War and the American Difference* that appeared in the conservative magazine *First Things*. Cohen described my views as "a form of eschatological madness" — a description that Berlatsky quite rightly suggests I would happily accept. Berlatsky suggests that Cohen missed my argument that war produces its own logic and morality. In fact, according to Berlatsky, Cohen's defense of war as a heroic story exemplifies the view of war I was criticizing; when war becomes a "heroic story" it becomes idolatry. He observes that, though I would like to get rid of war, what I really want to get rid of is a church of war. What Cohen missed is that my argument is aimed at Christians. Berlatsky then makes what was for me the surprising claim that he finds this to be a relief for someone like him because he is an atheist, so he can cheerfully continue to support Caesar. Yet he observes that there is a bit of discomfort in the thought, because if Christians began to take up nonviolence, and he hates to have to say it, "it would be hard to escape the suspicion that that might actually be the work of God." http://hoodedutilitarian.com/2012/04/bend-your-knee/.

not transition? But I believe we are living in a time when Christendom is actually coming to an end. That is an extraordinary transition whose significance for Christian and non-Christian has yet to be understood. But at the very least it means that the church is finally free to be a politics. If I may summarize what I take to be one appropriate response to this observation, it is quite simply this: let Christians make the most of it.

The End of Protestantism

Until I was asked to provide my vision of the twenty-first-century church, I did not realize that I do not think we — and in particular, theologians — should try to anticipate what the church should look like as we face this new century. Twenty centuries have passed since the birth of Christ. I suspect the form the church has taken as the centuries have passed could not have been anticipated by those in each preceding century. For example, how could anyone have imagined monasticism as one of the most effective forms of Christian evangelism? Our future is in God's hands. We had best not try to anticipate what God is doing and is going to do to us. Indeed, it is not even clear what a century might mean in God's time. We had best keep on keeping on hoping in the hope God can make use of us in ways we cannot imagine.

The church seldom wills herself to be faithful. Faithfulness is more likely the result of necessity. Here our guide must be Israel and the people Israel became, that is, the Jews. Israel sought to be a great nation, Israel sought like other nations to have a king, but Israel was exiled. Through exile Israel developed the skills of survival necessary when you find you are not in control. Christians, as we face whatever our future may be, hopefully will relearn by rediscovering our Jewish identity how to live by our wits.

Of course, you can hardly anticipate the future when you are not sure what is happening to you in the present. But if we do not know what is happening to us in the present, we also are not sure how to tell the story of our past. Church history is a determinative theological enterprise requiring some account of what is deemed important for the challenges facing us in our time. I think, for example, we may be coming to a time when the story we call the Reformation will not determine our understanding of where we are as Protestant Christians.

Bluntly put, we may be living during a time when we are watching Protestantism coming to an end. What that means for the future I am not sure. The very name "Protestant" denotes a protest movement, a reform movement, in the church catholic. When Protestantism became an end in itself, when Protestants became denominations, we became unintelligible to ourselves. Our inability to resist the market, our inability as Protestants not to become consumers of our religious preferences, is but an indication that we are in trouble. Of course, Catholicism is also beset by the challenge of choice, which helps explain why Catholicism in America may now be a form of Protestantism.

The Protestant world is beset by the Groucho Marx problem. Groucho Marx said he would not want to be a member of a country club that would have him as a member. In like manner I suspect most of us distrust a church that we have chosen. We do so because we do not trust our own ability to choose because we think our lives are also the result of our arbitrary choices. We therefore have great difficulty passing on our faith in God to our children because we think they ought to make up their own minds about such important matters.[1] As a result, too often our children think they get to make up the kind of Christianity they will practice, which usually means after a time they quit practicing altogether. It is interesting to note that often parents who believe they should let their children make up their own minds about being a Christian (or a Jew) do not think their children can or should make up their minds about their loyalty to an entity called America.

That we find ourselves in this unhappy situation helps us account for the moral confusion that surrounds the church and the challenges we face. There is no better indication of our confusion than the current attention religious denominations are giving to questions concerning ho-

---

1. Sentimentality, not atheism, is the deepest enemy of the Christian faith. Unfortunately, sentimentality is the sentiment that possesses Protestant Christianity.

mosexuality. C. S. Lewis's Screwtape could not have wished for a better result to make the church look silly. In a time of war, when bishops ought to be exercising their authority to help Christians discern how to think about war, bishops find they have no authority at all. Bishops have no authority because they now understand their office primarily in terms of being a CEO of a dysfunctional company. As a result, the Protestant denominations of America have simply not had anything useful to say about the current doctrine of preemptive war that guides America's foreign policy. All we have left to talk about is sex because we have accepted the concordat of liberal political theory that the church gets to occupy the space called "the private."

I once wrote an essay called "Why Gays (as a Group) Are Morally Superior to Christians (as a Group)" in which I argued that gays had done an extraordinary thing — they had got themselves banned from the military as a group.[2] Why, I asked, could not Christians as a group get themselves banned from the military? The essay was not really, of course, about gays but rather was a way to help Christians discern why their arguments about gays reflect more the class character of the church than the theological convictions that should inform such discussion. Ask yourself what arguments about gays might look like if Christians were seen as so subversive that they could not be trusted to be in the military. The ethics of sex would not be considered primarily in terms of what is or is not fulfilling for an individual, but rather in terms of what kinds of discipline are necessary to sustain a community distrusted by the wider society. Would gays (who have enough trouble already) want to be members of such a group? Moreover, if they did want to be Christians, they would have to understand that their "sexuality" could not be the most important thing the church has to consider. Rather, Christians must lead lives of faithfulness that make them warriors against war.

Of course, the failure of the church to challenge the current war in Iraq is also the result of the inability of Christians to distinguish our reaction to September 11, 2001, from the general American response. If there is any mood that characterizes current American culture, it is the mood

2. In Stanley Hauerwas, *Dispatches from the Front: Theological Engagements with the Secular* (Durham, NC: Duke University Press, 1994), pp. 153-55.

of fear. The most powerful nation in the world runs on fear. We are scared literally to death because we have used our wealth to live lives that are lived to deny death. Being wealthy makes those who possess wealth stupid, and America is very wealthy. The people of the world have to know who we are, but we do not have to know anything about who they are. At least we do not have to know anything about the rest of the world except what we need to know to sell Coca-Cola.

For example, Americans cannot understand why "they" (that is, the September 11, 2001, terrorists) came here. We cannot understand why a few people could want so desperately to harm Americans in our own country. It never seems to occur to us that they came here because Americans are there. Moreover, we never ask, "Why are we there?" There may be some very good answers to why we are "there," but we never hear what those answers may be because we never ask the questions necessary to elicit the answers. All is blurred by the need of American foreign policy "to keep America strong."

So Americans, Christians and non-Christians, now find our lives dominated by the need for security. We not only want to feel safe; we want to *be* safe. We rightly want to lead normal lives, that is, lives that allow us to get on with the everyday. We want to fall in love, we want to be of use to others through work, we want to go to universities, we want to live in communities that can sustain trust. These are goods we should want. But those goods cannot be guaranteed by trying to erect walls that give the impression that there is nothing to fear. We live in a dangerous world, often made more dangerous by the goods we rightly desire. Our deepest immorality results from our attempt to avoid the dangers constitutive of a worthy way of life. We have forgotten that the courageous have fears the coward can never know because to be courageous makes the world more dangerous.

Of all people, Christians should know that this is a dangerous world. We are, after all, a church of the martyrs. That our entry doors are painted red is not an accident. Those doors make clear that the Christian "we" cannot always be the American "we." "We" Christians are different. Sometimes the Christian "we" may find much in common with the American "we." But that commonality must be found, not assumed. At the very least Christians know that we are bound to other Christians around the world, which makes it impossible for us to think we can easily go to war. The Mennonite poster, "A Modest Proposal for Peace: Let the Christians of the World Agree That They Will Not Kill One Another," is surely what it means to be made one through the body and blood of Lord Jesus.

But it is exactly the issue of unity that bedevils Protestantism. If we are coming to the end of Protestantism, I suspect one of the reasons God is killing us is due to our inability to avoid nationalistic identifications of the church. We are American Lutherans, Presbyterians, Episcopalians, Methodists, not Methodists who happen to live in America. I am often introduced as the theologian who was named by *Time* as America's best theologian. It is a terrible burden to have been so designated, but at least I can point out that I was named not America's best theologian but the best theologian in America. Where the qualifier stands is not unimportant.

It may be objected that Catholics and Mennonites often are just as willing to embrace nationalistic identification as those in Protestant denominations. Of course that is true, but at least Catholics and Mennonites have resources Protestants do not have to suggest why such identification is a problem. That they do, moreover, is the reason why Mennonites discover that they may well have more in common with Catholics than with mainstream Protestant denominations that trace their beginnings to Luther and Calvin.

The account I have given of why we may now be coming to the end of Protestantism is just one version of the story I have been telling for some time. That story suggests that for better or worse we are coming to the end of the Constantinian settlement. Allegedly the so-called American doctrine of the separation of church and state means that America has never had an established church. Yet such a reading of Constantinianism is too unimaginative. You do not need legal establishment when you have social and cultural power. America has been and continues to be the great experiment in Protestant cultural formation. Will Willimon and I argued, however, in *Resident Aliens* that the social and cultural power of Protestantism is fading.[3] Accordingly, we tried to make suggestions as to

---

3. Will Willimon and Stanley Hauerwas, *Resident Aliens: Life in the Christian Colony* (Nashville: Abingdon, 1989).

how the church should reclaim the political significance of the practices that make the church the church.

Of course, the presidency of George Bush seems to give the lie to the claim that the power of Protestant Christianity, and in particular what is described as the Christian right, is fading in America. However, I am not convinced that President Bush or the Christian right is an indication of the continuing power of Christianity in America. What needs to be said is that no doubt George Bush is a sincere Christian, but that is but a reminder of how little sincerity has to do with being a Christian. The difficulty is that the Christianity that seems to be important to President Bush and the Christianity of the religious right is such a pathetic form of Christianity. It is the individualistic kind of Christianity that a capitalist economy is so adept at producing. It is important, however, to remember that the kind of Christianity represented by the religious right is but the mirror image of liberal Protestantism. Both are forms of Christianity that cannot survive the loss of the civil religion necessary to sustain the general presumption that everyone ought to believe in something.

Because Willimon and I tried to imagine a different future for the church in America in *Resident Aliens*, we were called *sectarian, fideistic, tribalist*. Some of those who would so label us did so because we challenged the assumption that the Christian way of securing justice in societies like America consisted primarily in being on the left wing of the Democratic party. We had nothing against people being on the left wing of the Democratic party, though we think it is increasingly unclear if there is any Left left in America. But we were trying to remind Christians that our politics was first and foremost to be the church of Jesus Christ. I am not sure if such a way of conceiving of the task of the church constitutes "a vision of the twenty-first-century church," but I am sure if the church is to be faithful to the task of first and foremost being the church of Jesus Christ, then we must recover what it means for the church to be an alternative politics in the world in which we find ourselves.

I am aware that talk of the church as an alternative politics may sound overblown. The church is a far too accommodated institution to be any kind of alternative. Moreover, it is not clear why this emphasis on the church as an alternate polity is the kind of emphasis that is at the heart of Methodism. After all, Methodism is a movement that by accident became a church in America. At best we have emphasized sanctification, not ecclesiology, as what makes Methodism distinctive. Our emphasis on sanctification, moreover, became confused with a pietistic construal of the faith shaped by revivals. So holiness was thought to be about the individual rather than the church. Methodists confused salvation with having a personal relationship with God, which meant the church simply became the place that confirmed your prior relation with God. The scholarship of Frank Baker, Albert Outler, Robert Cushman, Thomas Langford, Richard Heitzenrater, and now Randy Maddox on Wesley certainly challenged this understanding of Methodism; but unfortunately their recovery of the Catholic Wesley had little effect on church practice.

It is interesting to ask why the good work done on John Wesley has had so little influence. Certainly it may be, as a Methodist bishop once told me, that American Methodism owes nothing to Wesley. Our founders are Cokesbury and Asbury. As troubling as such a view may be, I think even more disturbing is the profound anti-intellectualism that has characterized Methodism over most of the twentieth century. No doubt there are many explanations for Methodist disdain of serious theological work — for example, the identification of Methodist theology with liberal Protestantism, the emphasis on experience, concern for social action, theology primarily understood as being on behalf of the oppressed, the concern with church growth. But I think, for whatever reasons, Methodists have not been distinguished for our theological contributions to our own life or to the church catholic.

I think, however, Methodism could make a real contribution to our common life as Protestant Christians if we took seriously the ecclesial implications of Wesley's stress on sanctification. I think Maddox is quite right to say that Wesley understood that without God's grace we cannot be saved; but without our (grace-empowered but uncoerced) participation, God's grace will not save.[4] Wesley, of course, was not unique in this emphasis — thus Augustine's observation that the God who created us without us will not save us without us. Participation is, of course, signaled

---

4. Randy Maddox, *Responsible Grace: John Wesley's Practical Theology* (Nashville: Kingswood Books, 1994).

by baptism, by which we are made members of a community in which we are made accountable by one another. In short, Methodists are free church Catholics.[5]

I am aware of course that some may think that, given the character of Methodist churches, this is not a realistic proposal. However, my views have been shaped by participation in a Methodist church. Broadway United Methodist Church taught me that the kind of alternative politics I think the church must be is as real as the people that claimed me when I lived in South Bend, Indiana. Indeed, when I received the invitation to join the faculty at Duke, I told the congregation they could tell me to go or stay. I hope I would have stayed if they had told me to do so. Instead, they told me that I could go as long as I taught what I had learned there. I have tried to do what they told me to do and it has gotten me into a lot of trouble.

I need to be clear. I do not think every church should be a small-membership church. I want churches to be like Broadway in their own way. For the politics of the church is a local politics that requires constant discernment developed through argument and time. In his wonderful account of Broadway, *Vital Ministry in the Small-Membership Church*, Mike Mather uses E. B. White's description of his wife's bulb planting in their garden — that is, she was "calmly plotting the resurrection" — to describe Broadway.[6] He notes that the small-membership church has time to nurture the opportunities for resurrection that arise from pain and suffering. Mather observes that taking the time to know one another's name and the story that gives that name life is an indication of a people who believe that God has given them all the time in the world to honor and worship God.

Mather suggests that the life given by God's Spirit comes from the lives of the people of the parish. Such life "means we can take the time to trust that God has put inside each one of us gifts for the building of community. We trust that to be true both inside of our walls and outside

---

5. One of the great virtues of Richard Heitzenrater's *Wesley and the People Called Methodist* (Nashville: Abingdon, 1955) is how we get to see the importance of the church for Wesley. See p. 19.

6. Mike Mather, *Vital Ministry in the Small-Membership Church: Shaping Stories, Shaping Community* (Nashville: Discipleship Resources, 2002), p. 20.

them."[7] Such a people can take the time to ask those who come to the food pantry not how poor they are or how deeply they are in need, but what assets they can bring to the church. Exactly because Broadway does not have many resources, they need all the help they can get. Money too often makes it possible for us not to need one another. But the people at Broadway will always need one another because they certainly do not have any money.

I find it quite interesting that Ephraim Radner in his recent book *Hope among the Fragments: The Broken Church and Its Engagement of Scripture* (a book that quite effectively argues that even Anglicans should not give up on the church), in a manner quite similar to Mike Mather's, calls attention to the importance of time. Radner notes that Anglicanism in America has probably always been unintelligible just to the extent that the church in America lacked the support of the establishment it had in England. Now that Anglicanism in America is coming unraveled, the temptation is to believe that we do not have the time to make the adjustments necessary for the church to survive. In Radner's words,

> We do not have time in our hands — time to make the changes we need to make in order to convert cultures, historical diseases, and so on — but God does. We do not have the power any longer to embrace a culture as a whole with our religion and so, in a deliberate squeeze, to transform it — but God does. We do not have the focused Spirit to quench the passions of human hatred that poison even the heart of religion — but God does. What we have are the forms that tie themselves to God's time and to God's power and to God's transformation. We have such forms, and whoever we are, and to whatever church we belong, we can submit to them.[8]

The forms that tie us to God's time are as common as the worship, how we govern ourselves, and our respect for our past teachers. I do not think Broadway could have ever become Broadway, nor could it remain

---

7. Mather, *Vital Ministry in the Small-Membership Church*, p. 24.

8. Ephraim Radner, *Hope among the Fragments: The Broken Church and Its Engagement of Scripture* (Grand Rapids: Brazos, 2004), p. 50.

Broadway over the years, without the time the church took to move to every-Sunday Eucharist. Ministers will come and go. They will have differing pastoral styles. The challenges before the neighborhood will change. The politics of the city will change. New members will come with new agendas. Yet Sunday after Sunday the word will be preached and the Eucharist will be served, the church year will be kept, and Lent will climax with Holy Week. Broadway is able to remain Broadway because the connection between worship, service, and politics is never lost.

Because Broadway has been a small-membership church, I am sure it is hard to imagine that Broadway could have been able to be Broadway if it had been a larger church. I have no doubt that there are many virtues to being small. Indeed, I am convinced that size is one of the crucial issues that determines whether a polity is capable of sustaining the politics necessary for the discovery of goods in common. Of course, Plato and Aristotle also thought that size mattered. However, I do not think being small necessarily insures that the church will be faithful.

Some may think that a church of resident aliens would necessarily be small. I do not assume that to be the case. But I am sure if God is in the process of making his church leaner and meaner, it becomes all the more important for the churches to be connected with other churches. A church is constituted, as Mike Mather suggests, by many small stories. We learn to be the gospel for one another by having our lives narrated by God's life. Yet we are subtle sinners, constantly tempted to make our story more important than the story God would tell of us. One of the gifts God has given us to test whether we have distorted the gospel is our connections with churches around the world. That connection is called "catholic."

If I have any hope, if I have any vision that I would wish for the church of this century, it is that we might discover how desperately we need one another. This need is often described as the ecumenical movement, but the unity we must discover is deeper than simply acknowledging that the reasons for our divisions in the past no longer pertain. As Cardinal Kasper has said,

> The ecumenical aim is not a simple return of the others into the fold of the Catholic Church, nor the conversion of individuals to the Catholic

Church (even if this must obviously be mutually acknowledged when it is based on reasons of conscience). In the ecumenical movement the question is the conversion of all to Jesus Christ; in him we move nearer to one another. Only by a renewal of the spiritual ecumenism, by common prayer, and common listening to the Word of God in the Bible can we hope to overcome the present ecumenical impasses and difficulties.[9]

Such a movement is all the more important for Christians who live in the United States. For we are constantly tempted to confuse the universality of the church with the universal pretensions of liberal regimes. The small stories we learn to tell one another at churches like Broadway offer some hope and resistance to the seductive story that America represents the "end of history." But we must also learn to hear and retell the small stories of our brothers and sisters in other countries that suffer from our pretentious empire — an empire all the more dangerous just to the extent that it lacks the resources to acknowledge that it is an empire.

I make no apology for celebrating a church like Broadway United Methodist Church. God through this church has quite literally saved some of its members' lives. The work done in the church's neighborhood and in South Bend, Indiana, by Broadway is good work. But also let us not forget that we are not only members of the church of Jesus Christ. We are also Americans.[10] If we are to survive that fate, we are going to need all the help we can get from Christians around the world. God help us.

---

9. Walter Cardinal Kasper, "Present-Day Problems in Ecumenical Theology," *Reflection* 6 (Spring 2003): 64-65. For a fascinating and compelling exploration of the holiness movement, see John Wright, "Catholicity Before Identity: The Catholicity of the Church of the Nazarene and Its Membership Ritual," in *It's All about Grace: Wesleyan Essays in Honor of Herbert L. Prince* (San Diego: Pont Loma Press, 2004), pp. 46-55.

10. In *After Virtue: A Study in Moral Theory,* 2nd ed. (Notre Dame: University of Notre Dame Press, 1984), Alasdair MacIntyre observes, "The story of my life is always embedded in the story of those communities from which I derive my identity. I am born with a past; and to try to cut myself off from that past in an individualist mode, is to deform my present relationships. The possession of an historical identity and the possession of a social identity coincide. Notice that rebellion against my identity is always one possible mode of expressing it" (p. 221). By acknowledging that we are Americans, Christians rightly confess that we owe America much. That debt we hopefully rightly return with loving criticism made possible by our participation in the church.

Which Church? What Unity? or,
An Attempt to Say What I May Think about
the Future of Christian Unity

A Question with an Inadequate Response

In a chapter entitled "Ecumenisms in Conflict: Where Does Hauerwas Stand?" George Lindbeck asks why, given my often declared commitment to the significance of the unity of the church, I have not been engaged in the ecumenical movement.[1] Lindbeck observes that not only have I been largely absent from events and forums dedicated to overcoming separation between churches but I have also neglected to address such endeavors in what I have written. Lindbeck suggests that there may be good reasons for my disengagement from ecumenical work, but he would like to know what those reasons may be. Given all that I have learned from George Lindbeck, given my regard for him and his work, I would like to give a satisfactory answer to his question, but I am not sure I even know my own mind well enough to know how to respond to his question.

Lindbeck's question is perfectly legitimate, but I am a bit uneasy with accepting the question at face value. For it seems to presume that how I answer the question might make a difference for how others might understand their involvement or lack of involvement with the ecumenical movement. In short, any attempt to answer the question can invite me to

---

1. George Lindbeck, "Ecumenisms in Conflict: Where Does Hauerwas Stand?" in *God, Truth, and Witness: Engaging Stanley Hauerwas*, ed. L. Gregory Jones, Reinhard Hütter, and C. Rosalee Velloso Ewell (Grand Rapids: Brazos, 2005), pp. 212-28.

indulge in a fantasy that what I think about ecumenism actually makes a difference. I do not believe that anyone who has given their life to the ecumenical movement will think they need my support.[2] Given my ambiguous ecclesial status, it is not even clear which church I would represent.

Of course, my ambiguous ecclesial status is one of the reasons I have not been a good citizen of the ecumenical movement. I have not needed to be engaged in efforts to unify the church because I have thought of myself, no doubt in a manner that threatens self-deception, as more or less a living ecumenical movement. Raised Methodist, teaching and worshiping first among the Lutherans at Augustana College, then with the Catholics at Notre Dame, and finally ending up with the Methodists at the Divinity School at Duke have given me a distinct, if not confused, ecclesial identity. Add to that mixture my sympathies for the Anabaptists and the fact that for the last ten years I have been a communicant at the Episcopal Church of the Holy Family. I would not blame anyone for thinking this is a person who should not be trusted to represent a particular tradition in ecumenical discussions.

I should like to think, however, that the promiscuous character of my ecclesial practice and theology reflects my Methodist commitments. A strange claim, to be sure, but one I think makes some sense.[3] Methodism is a movement that by accident became a church in America. As a result, it is not clear that Methodists have ever been able to develop a coherent ecclesiology. For example, our bishops are not an order of ministry but rather are understood to be a function. Methodists, of course, did not worry whether we had a coherent account of the church because

2. My longtime colleague, Geoffrey Wainwright, is an exemplary participant in the ecumenical movement. I stand in awe of his willingness to do hard and patient work to reach agreements about such matters as ministry and Eucharist. His theological work on these matters deserves close attention. See for example his books *The Ecumenical Movement: Crisis and Opportunity for the Church* (Grand Rapids: Eerdmans, 1983) and *Worship with One Accord: Where Liturgy and Ecumenism Embrace* (New York: Oxford University Press, 1997). Needless to say, Geoffrey brings to the work of ecumenical dialogue the kind of theological intelligence and knowledge I simply do not possess.

3. For a more extended account of the role of Methodism see my "The End of Protestantism and the Methodist Contribution," *Wesleyan Theological Journal* 41, no. 1 (Spring 2006): 7-17.

Methodists in America had such a genius for organization that we did not need to ask how the emerging church order did or did not reflect an ecclesiology that was theologically defensible. A genius for organization, however, is not necessarily a "good thing" because too often you become trapped by what worked in the past. Habits are hard to break.

Important for me, however, as I've tried to understand what it meant to be a Methodist was the attempt by Wesley scholars and theologians like Albert Outler and Robert Cushman to locate Methodism centrally in the great Catholic traditions. From Outler and Cushman I learned to read Wesley as a theologian whose account of sanctification entailed an ecclesiology that had deep ecumenical implications. Even before I had read Yoder I thought Methodism might be understood as a free church in the Catholic tradition, one that hopefully might be a model for other traditions to recognize that churches so constituted already share a unity that only Christ can give. So I thought I was being ecumenical by trying to be a theologian who helped the Methodist church to be faithful to Wesley's fundamental theological vision.

Of course, the problem with that project was and is the reality of Methodism. The way I had learned to read John and Charles Wesley had little purchase on the actual practices of the Methodist church in America. Most Methodists have no idea what it might mean for the Methodist church to be identified as a church committed to recovering holiness as one of the essential marks that makes the church the church. The kinds of disciplines I imagined as constituting the practices of a church committed to holiness were simply not on the Methodist radar screen.[4] My

4. My favorite footnote in *With the Grain of the Universe: The Church's Witness and Natural Theology* (Grand Rapids: Brazos, 2001) is my report of Barth's reaction to the Harnack-Peterson exchange over church authority for theology. Barth sides with Peterson, but Barth acknowledges that the churches, even regional denominations, fail to indicate which creeds or doctrines are normative. Barth observes that as a result the theologian is left in a situation like King Nebuchadnezzar's wise men, who were not only supposed to interpret the king's dream but also to tell him what he had dreamed. As a Methodist theologian, or at least a theologian who is Methodist, I often feel like one of Nebuchadnezzar's wise men. We are in Michael Hollerich's debt for translating and making available Erik Peterson's important work, which continues to have crucial relevance for issues of church unity. See Erik Peterson, *Theological Tractates*, ed., trans., and with an introduction by Michael Hollerich (Stanford: Stanford University Press, 2011).

presumption that Methodism might be a church uniquely suited to help discover the unity of the churches may have been naïve, but that is what I thought.

I should also acknowledge that I was never particularly interested in the movements concerned with the institutional unity of mainstream Protestant denominations. I am not sure why I was uninterested in those attempts to overcome theological and ecclesial differences of the past, but I must admit I just did not see any reason to think, for example, that the joining of mainstream American denominations would be interesting from a theological point of view. I suspected that the theological differences that were once thought so important that they could not be compromised in the interest of unity, only to be considered later to be no obstacle to the merger of churches, meant these were churches that had given up on the importance of theology for discerning what we believe to be true.

Of course, it could work the other way. Sometimes attempts to reach agreements meant an intensification of differences. Those differences may not have much to do with the actual life of the churches so identified, but the differences had to be identified for this or that particular denomination to get its market share in the decreasing market. For most Christians I suspect the differences they noticed between the Protestant denominations had less to do with "doctrine" and more to do with the way the particular church was governed. The problem with that understanding of the differences between the churches is that there was little appreciation of how governance itself is a theological matter.

Those actually engaged in the ecumenical discussions seeking unity between particular churches often found that they represented positions that they understood to be definitive of their tradition, but that understanding was not widely shared by those who identified as members of that denomination. The representatives discovered that they were more likely to get agreements between different traditions than they were to reach agreement within their own tradition. The problem was not union between churches that had been long separated, but union within the various churches themselves. I assume that is a problem that has not gone away.

Timing is also very important. Vatican II was in process during my years in seminary and graduate work. I did not get to take courses from Lindbeck because he was in Rome as an observer representing the Lutheran Church in America.[5] But I remember reading with great excitement Lindbeck's book *The Future of Roman Catholic Theology*, which was published in 1970, and thinking that his presentation of the theological developments of Vatican II represented the kind of work I wanted to be about.[6] Insofar as I thought about ecumenical relations because of Lindbeck, I was much more interested in questions of Protestant/Catholic relations than I was with the relation between Protestant denominations.

Another reason for my lack of interest in ecumenical engagement is that I am a lousy churchman. Readers of *Hannah's Child* I believe would find adequate documentation there to confirm that judgment.[7] I am an enthusiastic participant in *a* church, but I have never been particularly concerned with denominational identity. At least I have seldom sought to participate in church life beyond the local parish. I am a congregationalist with Catholic sensibilities. Which probably explains how I ended up in an Episcopal church.

That may seem odd, given my account above of the role Methodism played in my understanding of my ecumenical commitments. But note that I began my reflection on the importance of Methodism with the avowal that I encountered Outler and Cushman because I was trying to understand what it meant to be Methodist. I had not come, so to speak, from the belly of the beast identified as institutional Methodism, and I was not planning to be ordained. So I have never been an "establishment Methodist." Conference Methodism for me was a distant reality in which I had little interest.

I have provided these "explanations" for my lack of ecumenical engagement in an effort to respond to Lindbeck's question. I do not think

---

5. For Lindbeck's reflections on his time at Vatican II see *Postliberal Theology and the Church Catholic: Conversations with George Lindbeck, David Burrell, and Stanley Hauerwas*, ed. John Wright (Grand Rapids: Baker, 2012), pp. 61-68. I think it quite interesting that Lindbeck singles out Albert Outler, whom he had as a teacher at Yale, as one of the most significant observers at Vatican II.

6. George Lindbeck, *The Future of Roman Catholic Theology: Vatican II — Catalyst for Change* (Philadelphia: Fortress, 1970).

7. Stanley Hauerwas, *Hannah's Child: A Theologian's Memoir* (Grand Rapids: Eerdmans, 2012).

they are particularly interesting reasons to explain why I have not been involved in the ecumenical movement. Nor do they represent an adequate response to the more profound challenge raised by Lindbeck. That challenge I take to be whether, given my emphasis on the importance of Christian unity so that the world can have a visible sign of reconciliation, I know for what I am asking. For example, Lindbeck calls attention to my attempt in *With the Grain of the Universe: The Church's Witness and Natural Theology* to make John Howard Yoder and John Paul II allies in the formation of a church capable of being a witness to peace in a world of war.[8] He then observes that Yoder and John Paul II were people with deep commitments to ecumenism. Which makes my lack of attention to the actual work necessary for Christian unity seem odd.[9]

Lindbeck charitably suggests that I am not without some response to his question concerning my seeming lack of interest in the ecumenical movement. For example, he thinks it quite possible that I assume that the visibility of the church's unity is independent of ecumenism. Such a view, Lindbeck rightly believes, would be consistent with my general presumption that practice precedes theory. So the visible unity of Christ may be present in the broken fragments of the church even when that unity is not institutionally assumed to be present. It may be, according to Lindbeck, that I assume that whenever the Holy Spirit uses the diversity of the church to unite faithful lives we see what it means to be "ecumenical."[10] I confess I am quite sympathetic to that understanding of how unity between Christians happens.

Yet Lindbeck is not about to let me off the hook so easily. He observes that even though ecumenism is logically dispensable in my work, it is a practical precondition for the way I do theology. If the Roman Catholic opening occasioned by Vatican II, for example, had not taken place, I would have never gotten to know John Howard Yoder at Notre Dame. Lindbeck puts it this way: "While it is true that ecumenism is impossible apart from witnesses who visibly enact the division-transcending unity that is in Christ, Hauerwas's lifework — his efforts to spread the recog-

---

8. Hauerwas, *With the Grain of the Universe*, pp. 218-41.
9. Lindbeck, "Ecumenisms in Conflict," pp. 217-18.
10. Lindbeck, "Ecumenisms in Conflict," p. 218.

nition of such enactments and encourage their occurrence — is in part dependent on ecumenical developments."[11] That surely seems right, forcing me to recognize that I am a theologian who has avoided acknowledging the conditions of possibility necessary for positions I have taken.

Yet even as I acknowledge Lindbeck's point, I am not sure what follows. I do not know how to go on. It is not just that I do not know how to go on, but if Lindbeck is right that the high tide of the ecumenical movement is over, it is not clear that we even know how to think about Christian unity. At a conference held at the Nazarene Seminary in Kansas City concerning whether or not the Reformation is over, Lindbeck made the following observation:

> What the good God is doing to the church, it seems to me, is destroying us bit by bit. And I think that God wants us to be united. And destroying each denomination's identity is precisely the way in which we will be eventually united. But nevertheless, if you are going to be really ecumenical, you are going to have to love your own tradition and love it to its depths. I don't know what that means in Nazarene terms, but for those of you who are Nazarene, I've discovered one wonderful thing about [it] in the last day — namely, that you are trying to keep together internationally. Outside of the Roman Catholics, the Nazarenes are the only ones who are trying to keep together internationally. I hope you succeed even if it means that Americans become a minority and have to let newer and newer mission extensions of the Nazarenes be the dominant group. If you succeed in that you will be doing the type of Christian sacrifice that brings us closer to Christ.[12]

11. Lindbeck, "Ecumenisms in Conflict," p. 219.

12. Lindbeck, *Postliberal Theology and the Church Catholic*, p. 118. This is not a new theme with Lindbeck. See, for example, his 1968 lecture, "Ecumenism and the Future of Belief," in his book *The Church in a Postliberal Age*, ed. James Buckley (Grand Rapids: Eerdmans, 2002), pp. 91-105. Lindbeck observes in this lecture that the ecumenical movement is in part the product of pressures that produce price-fixing and monopolies in the business world. That process may help strip various traditions of excess ecclesial baggage, but it can also lead to the church being even more accommodated to the secular world. As a result, the churches lose their distinctive identities that are crucial for an ecumenical sectarianism (pp. 100-101). Lindbeck's attempt to develop

What Then Might Unity Look Like? The Yoder Alternative

I think Lindbeck may be wrong to say that only Roman Catholics and the Nazarenes are trying to hold their churches together internationally.[13] But that is a small matter. Far more important from my perspective is his claim that God is destroying the church bit by bit so that we might discover our unity. I want to explore that claim by directing attention to John Howard Yoder's understanding of Christian unity and the ecumenical imperative. I do so not only because, as Lindbeck suggests, I could and should learn from Yoder's ecumenical work, but also because I hope to show that Yoder provides a quite distinctive understanding of the ecumenical task. In particular, Yoder helps us see that too often the divisions in the church reflect the accommodation of the church to worldly divisions.

In spite of Michael Cartwright making available Yoder's reflections on Christian unity in *The Royal Priesthood: Essays Ecclesiological and Ecumenical*, Yoder's extensive engagement with the ecumenical movement is not well known.[14] Yoder was deeply committed to the ecumenical movement, often attending and participating in the work of the World Council of Churches.[15] He was so committed because, as Cartwright observes in his informative introductory essay to *The Royal Priesthood*, Yoder understood the obligation to work for Christian unity as a correlative to his understanding of the faithfulness of the church displayed by the apostolic practice of discipleship. Yoder's focus on discipleship as a crucial practice for discerning the unity of the church brought through the work of the

---

an ecclesiology shaped by the continuity with Judaism reflects, I suspect, this understanding of the future of the church.

13. After reading this essay, in a personal communication Lindbeck agreed that he was over-generalizing when he said only Roman Catholics and Nazarenes are trying to hold their churches together internationally.

14. John Howard Yoder, *The Royal Priesthood: Essays Ecclesiological and Ecumenical*, ed. Michael Cartwright (Grand Rapids: Eerdmans, 1994).

15. For a good account of Yoder's ecumenical involvement see Gayle Gerber Koontz, "Unity with Integrity: John H. Yoder's Ecumenical Theology and Practice," in *Radical Ecumenicity: Pursuing Unity and Continuity after John Howard Yoder*, ed. John C. Nugent (Abilene, TX: Abilene Christian University Press, 2010), pp. 57-84.

Holy Spirit is not surprising for someone representing the Anabaptist movement.[16]

Yoder's commitment to the ecumenical movement, therefore, was shaped by his ecclesial identity as a Mennonite, but Cartwright argues that it would be a mistake to think Yoder saw his ecumenical work as representing a denominational perspective.[17] To be sure, Yoder thought the witness to peace to be constitutive of Christian unity, but, as Cartwright observes, Yoder's peace witness took "shape within a consistently articulated belief that the unity of the church is a gift of God's Holy Spirit, which *enables* Christians to embody God's *shalom* in the world."[18] Yet that perspective made Yoder quite critical of how Christian unity was understood by many in the ecumenical movement.[19]

For example, Yoder observed that "mainstream ecumenism" assumes that the unity sought between churches is analogous to the unity that is assumed to be present in the denomination they represent. The unity sought, therefore, is the unity of government that reproduces, particularly in churches after the Reformation, national boundaries. As a result, churches lack the means to recognize one of the most significant barriers to the unity of the church. Therefore, from Yoder's perspective, the unification of Methodists and Presbyterians is not of theological significance, though it might be a bureaucratic achievement. Such a union would do little to challenge the divisions of the churches determined by nationalism, race, rich and poor, liberal and conservative.[20]

Yoder had no use for what he called "the American pluralistic cafete-

16. Michael Cartwright, "Radical Reform, Radical Catholicity: John Howard Yoder's Vision of the Faithful Church," in *The Royal Priesthood*, pp. 1-49.

17. In a chapter in *The Royal Priesthood* entitled "The Free Church Ecumenical Style," Yoder puts it this way: "The position of the believer's church or the free church is not simply a doctrinal stance that certain denominations may represent in the ecumenical free-for-all of American pluralism: the genius of the free church calls rather for a unique form of ecumenical expression as well" (p. 232).

18. Cartwright, "Radical Reform, Radical Catholicity," p. 3.

19. Mark Nation has provided the best account we have of Yoder's concerns about many of the aspects of the ecumenical movement; see his *John Howard Yoder: Mennonite Patience, Evangelical Witness, Catholic Convictions* (Grand Rapids: Eerdmans, 2006), pp. 77-108.

20. Yoder, "The Free Church Ecumenical Style," in *The Royal Priesthood*, pp. 233-34.

ria" as a way to imagine Christian unity. Celebrations of "pluralism," he argued, can be a way to avoid holding one another accountable by asking if we believe what we say to be true. The gospel is about matters of life and death. Too often ecumenical tolerance leads to the presumption that our differences can be settled by the difference being described as "true for me." But the "for me" turns out to indicate a lack of seriousness that betrays the gospel.

Too often celebrations of diversity are attempts to avoid "the hard duties of reconciliation, postponing long-range investment in tasks that take time and that demand occasional readiness for suffering."[21] Yoder is not denying the importance of diversity within a church; but, drawing on Paul's understanding of the church as a body, he argues that in contrast to pluralism that posits diversity with no purpose, the appeal to the body to characterize the diverse gifts of difference assumes that diversity serves a common purpose.

Yoder certainly thought "doctrine matters," but he also thought one of the unfortunate results of the Reformation was the isolation of doctrine from the ecclesial practices that constitute the Christian relation to the world.[22] For example, he assumes that it goes without saying that a church whose worship and church order are determined by a state is ecumenically handicapped. But even more deleterious are churches that are not institutionally bound to a state but that nonetheless give "unhesitating consent to nationalism in its demonic mil-

21. Yoder, "The Imperative of Christian Unity," in *The Royal Priesthood*, p. 293.

22. In *The Unintended Reformation: How a Religious Revolution Secularized Society* (Cambridge, MA: Harvard University Press, 2012), Brad Gregory observes that the Reformation did not simply refocus the church on certain doctrines, for example, *Sola Scriptura;* in addition, doctrine was now all-important as a means to establish authority. Gregory is appropriately critical of the pre-Reformation church, but he is surely right to suggest that prior to the Reformation Christianity was embedded in social life, political relations, and the wider culture with its principal purpose being the sanctification of the baptized through the practice of the Christian faith. Accordingly, Gregory maintains that Christianity paradoxically combined sharp limits on orthodoxy with a wide tolerance of diverse local beliefs and practices. To be sure, the very presumption that there is something called orthodoxy implied heterodoxy, but Gregory argues that orthodoxy is but a corollary of the fact that the church makes truth claims. Doctrine served Christian unity; but doctrine was also, as it was to become in the Reformation, that which in and of itself constituted Christian unity (pp. 82-84).

itary form."[23] The continuing temptation of churches to "consent" to nationalism Yoder understood to be the continuing habit derived from Constantinianism. That habit, the Constantinian habit, was intensified by the Magisterial Reformation just to the extent that the Reformers found it necessary to seek safety by appeal to the local prince.

For Yoder, to seek the unity of the church, a unity grounded in the memory of Christ, requires the "disavowal of Constantine."[24] To disavow Constantine means that the church must confess its fallibility, which requires that claims of the church's indefectibility must be given up. In Yoder's words, Christians must be able to say, "We were wrong. The picture you have been given of Jesus by the Empire, by the Crusades, by struggles over holy sites, and by wars in the name of the 'Christian West' is not only something to forget but something to forgive. We are not merely outgrowing it, as if it had been acceptable at the time: we disavow it and repent of it."[25]

Crucial for Yoder's understanding of the challenge of unity is how the story of our faithfulness and unfaithfulness is told. History matters, and in particular the history of apostasy matters if the church is to confess the sin of disunity.[26] Yoder observes that, without exception, most

23. Yoder, "The Nature of the Unity We Seek," in *The Royal Priesthood*, pp. 226-27.

24. Yoder, "The Disavowal of Constantine," in *The Royal Priesthood*, pp. 242-61.

25. Yoder, "The Disavowal of Constantine," in *The Royal Priesthood*, pp. 250-51. In his book on Christian unity, *A Brutal Reality: The Spiritual Politics of the Christian Church* (Waco, TX: Baylor University Press, 2012), Ephraim Radner develops an account of Christian unity that I suspect many will find not only challenging but also quite similar to Yoder's account. Radner not only argues, as Yoder does, that crucial for ecumenical work is a recognition and confession of the sin of the church, but he also worries that consensual accounts of unity merely reproduce the politics of liberalism that make as well as occlude the divisions that are finally murderous. Radner's book is in every sense far too "thick" to be briefly discussed. I mention it only to recommend that it be read by anyone concerned with the subject of this essay.

26. In particular, the history that matters is the history of the Reformation. The decline of Protestant churches no doubt will make possible a retelling of the Reformation that may well reduce the significance of that time. The very description "Protestant" indicates a movement of reform of the Roman Catholic Church. But "Protestant" came to be associated with churches that, in the hope of unity, no longer cared about reform of the Catholic Church. Protestantism became an end in itself, which means it was not clear how it should understand itself. Brad Gregory has begun to raise questions about how this history requires a retelling if we are to understand the world in

of the serious divisions in the church resulted in one party in the conflict calling the other apostate. Yet because modern manners do not allow the use of such descriptions in modern ecumenical discussions, no serious investigation of apostasy is explored. What is required is the same kind of "realism" concerning the failure of the church to be the church that we find in the story of Israel in the Old Testament. In short, what is required is a theological telling of the story of the church.[27]

It is not surprising, therefore, that Yoder's understanding of ecumenicity assumes a process of conflict based on Matthew 18. That it does so reflects the Anabaptist understanding of the necessary confrontation by brothers and sisters concerning sins that need to be confessed and forgiven if the church is to be a reconciling people.[28] That conflict is part and parcel of Christian unity means that the unity of a church is not a unity based on agreements, but rather one that assumes that disagreements should not lead to division but rather should be a testimony to the existence of a reconciling people. For the believers' church, the unity sought is a unity that is first and foremost a unity between people. We do

---

which we now live. For example, Gregory suggests that the story we need to tell cannot be one only about the Protestant/Catholic divide; it must also be about how that division shaped the world as we know it. For instance, Gregory observes that it is not the empirical investigations associated with the sciences that have falsified theological claims. "Rather, incompatible Catholic and Protestant views about the meaning of God's actions created an intellectually sterile impasse because of the objections they inevitably provoked from theological opponents, and the intractable doctrinal controversies they constantly reinforced." Gregory, *The Unintended Reformation*, p. 47.

27. Yoder, "The Free Church Ecumenical Style," in *The Royal Priesthood*, pp. 236-40. Yoder observes, for example, that it is important to say that the early ecumenical councils were not ecumenical, though that does not mean that their results are to be ignored. It is also the case that there has been no time when Christians did not have serious disagreements and differences. So unity is not some "state" once achieved and now lost, but rather unity is always an eschatological gift. John Howard Yoder, "The Ecumenical Movement and the Faithful Church," in Nugent, ed., *Radical Ecumenicity*, pp. 208-9.

28. Nation points out, for example, that Yoder thought the 1982 Faith and Order Commission statement entitled *Baptism, Eucharist, and Ministry* gave insufficient attention to repentance as necessary if ecumenical unity is to be achieved. Nation observes that Yoder particularly had in mind the need for repentance for the killing of Anabaptists for their views on baptism. Nation notes not only that Yoder wanted these wrongs acknowledged but also that there were and are significant theological issues at stake regarding believer's baptism. Nation, *John Howard Yoder*, pp. 100-101.

not so much encounter another tradition as we encounter one another as brothers and sisters. Crucial for the recognition of a unity that is the unity of persons is worship. Of course, nothing is more divisive than worship, yet that is exactly why nothing is more important than the discovery that where two or three are gathered in the name of Christ the Spirit is present.[29]

For Yoder, the unifying of Christians through worship is a theological imperative required by Jesus' prayer in the Gospel of John that just as he is one with the Father so may his followers be one (John 17:20-24). The imperative of unity is a trinitarian imperative because "the function of the unity of the future believers is . . . to make credible the fundamental Christian claim . . . and to reflect the nature of the unity between the Son and Father, to render that credible witness substantial."[30] Where Christians are not united, according to Yoder, quite simply the gospel is not true in that place.

An extraordinary claim, but one I think true about the kind of truth the gospel is. What I find particularly compelling about this claim is that truth is determined by "place." This is not a vulgar relativism, but rather an implication that the gospel by its very nature requires the witness of a community. Yoder puts it this way: "At least for Christians, the continuing pertinence of the historical memory of Jesus, via the New Testament, as a lever for continuing critique, is part of the message itself. The capacity for, or in fact the demand for, self-critique is part of what must be shared with people of other faiths and ideologies."[31]

For Yoder, truth and the enactment of unity as the catholic characteristic of the church are first and foremost to take place in a locality. He observes that it is simply the case that for most Christians the locus of visibility of our oneness is where they live and go to church. Accordingly, the locus of visible unity should be local.[32] From Yoder's perspective, catho-

29. Yoder, "The Free Church Ecumenical Style," in *The Royal Priesthood*, pp. 240-41.

30. Yoder, "The Imperative of Christian Unity," in *The Royal Priesthood*, p. 291. For an account of the importance of the Trinity for Yoder see David Parler, *Things Hold Together: John Howard Yoder's Trinitarian Theology of Culture* (Harrisonburg, VA: Herald, 2012).

31. Yoder, "The Disavowal of Constantine," in *The Royal Priesthood*, p. 251.

32. Mark Nation identifies three steps Yoder thinks necessary for locating catho-

licity is not a reality that can be simply "located" but is itself a process of a people committed to being in communion with one another through the work of the Holy Spirit.[33]

I think it quite interesting that in this context Yoder uses the description "catholic" to characterize the kind of communion that ought to exist between Christians, rather than the language of unity. I am not suggesting that what it means for the church to be catholic is not unrelated to what it means for us to be united, but I take it that "catholic" may be the more basic term, suggesting as it does that there is a union that does not deny difference in a manner the language of unity does not. Christians are obligated to love one another, which, I think, means that such love determines what it means to be united.

For it certainly seems to be the case that locality means difference. Difference can threaten unity, but unity cannot be catholic without difference. Yoder is well aware that locality can tempt Christians to identify the church with a given society or assume some way of being church in one context to be necessary for all churches. The only safeguard against these temptations is the demand that the church be in mission. For it is through mission that the church finds that there are different ways to worship Jesus. The difference, moreover, is not right or wrong. It is just different. But these differences must be tested so that Christians moving from one Eucharistic assembly to another Eucharistic assembly can have confidence that they are worshiping the same God.[34]

I should like to think that Yoder's emphasis on locality as the locus for the visibility of Christian unity may well be a way to help us go on at a time when the ecumenical movement at the highest level seems unsure.

---

licity: (1) the renunciation of privilege or power to enforce our understanding of the Word we believe to be catholic, (2) the acknowledgment of the fallibility of our witness and ministry by making clear the ongoing need for reformation, and (3) the formulation of ecclesiology in such a manner that it is capable of being expressed elsewhere. *John Howard Yoder*, pp. 95-96.

33. Yoder, "The Imperative of Christian Unity," in *The Royal Priesthood*, pp. 297-99.

34. For a fascinating defense of Yoder's understanding of the Eucharist as an alternative to Roman Catholic and Zwinglian accounts see Branson Parler, "Spinning the Liturgical Turn: Why John Howard Yoder Is Not an Ethicist," in Nugent, ed., *Radical Ecumenicity*, pp. 181-85.

I am sure some will worry that a focus on the local threatens the catholic character of the church. But if Yoder is right, as I believe him to be, the catholicity of the church is necessarily local. Of course, what constitutes "locality" and how the local is identified is itself an ongoing challenge. But at the very least "local" means that claims of unity begin with the concrete life of actual congregations.

Does that mean Yoder was a "congregationalist"? Am I, as one influenced by Yoder, a congregationalist? As I confessed above, I so understand myself and am ready to be so identified. That does not mean, however, that I can be thought to be in agreement with the denomination that bears that name. For I see no reason why a congregational understanding of the church necessarily means that there is no role for bishops. Bishops, after all, are those charged with the responsibility of helping diverse Eucharistic assemblies keep from being isolated from one another across time and space. Such a task is appropriately described as "apostolic."

In responses to this essay, Joe Mangina has suggested to me that in effect, influenced by Yoder, what I am about is trying to change the ecumenical subject. In short, I cannot answer Lindbeck on his own terms because I am challenging, for example, the ecumenical movement's attempt to distinguish between matters of faith and order and faith and works. I have often directed attention to the poster that reads: "A Modest Proposal for Peace: Let the Christians of the World Agree They Will Not Kill One Another." That "Proposal," a proposal that makes sense only if Christ has been raised from the dead, I assume is the condition for any serious attempt to achieve Christian unity. If that is to change the subject, then so be it.

Yoder obviously drew on his understanding of what his Anabaptist forerunners thought was at stake during the time of the Reformation to inform his understanding of the ecumenical imperative, but I think it would be a mistake to describe his ecumenical vision as only representing the "Mennonite denomination." Indeed, it is not clear to me if the Mennonites can be classified as a denomination. For it is my judgment that as soon as a church understands itself as a denomination the ecumenical passion is lost.

Moreover, Yoder's understanding of the ecumenical imperative not only is based on his understanding of the Anabaptist vision but also is shaped, as was the Anabaptist vision itself, on Scripture and, in particular, on Paul's attempt to keep unity even with those who seek division. For Yoder, the emphasis on unity for Paul did not mean that faithful living was to be overlooked, but that the discipline needed required the work of discernment. That such a view is not limited to the Anabaptist I hope to show by suggesting that the tradition called Anglicanism can be understood in terms very close to Yoder's understanding of Christian unity.

Reality and Form in Catholicity

Some may think I could not have chosen a worse example for exemplifying Christian unity than those churches currently identified in quite diverse contexts as the Anglican Communion. Moreover, Anglicanism is a state church, which from Yoder's perspective makes it a doubtful ecumenical paradigm. The Anglican Communion is obviously in turmoil. But it is not clear to me why that is a problem. Bruce Kaye has argued that the Church of England has always been in turmoil.[35] This is not the place to rehearse Kaye's extremely important argument that Anglicanism is best understood as a form of Gallicanism — that is, Anglicanism is the expression of a form of catholic Christianity in a locality called England.[36] But what I take to be so important about Kaye's argument is how he helps us understand that the history of the Church of England does not begin with Henry VIII.[37]

35. Bruce Kaye, *Conflict and the Practice of the Christian Faith* (Eugene, OR: Cascade, 2009).

36. Kaye, *Conflict and the Practice of the Christian Faith*, pp. 33-35.

37. One of the strengths of Anglicanism, as well as of those churches generally classified as Anabaptist, is that they have no decisive "founder" such as Luther or Calvin. Accordingly, they are not tempted to think that everything that needs to be said about the church must be found or justified by Luther or Calvin. Nor are they committed to the view that the faithful church only begins with the Reformation. Yoder's critique of Constantinianism complicates this stance, but he was always insistent that God never abandoned the church, even during its most accommodated times. Brad Gregory argues that how the story of the Reformation has been told has not paid sufficient attention to the Anabaptists because it is assumed that their social impact was minimal. Gregory suggests, however, that the Anabaptists were closer to the Catholics than to the magisterial Reformers on many of the issues raised by the Reform-

Anglicanism is the name for the ongoing attempt to enact the interdependent character of churches in a manner that, in Kaye's words, accomplishes "Catholicity without Leviathan."[38] That reality, the Catholic reality, according to Kaye, makes the relationships and the attitudes of the local church key for the expression of our need for one another. Kaye argues that it is not the existence of a single great church to which others relate and on which they depend that determines catholicity. "Rather it is the universality of the Gospel which expresses itself in different circumstances and creates an ecclesial life in those local circumstances which needs the influence of catholic interdependence for its prospering and faithfulness."[39]

I noted above that Yoder makes the extraordinary claim that where Christians are divided — and by divided Yoder means at the very least that they have commitments that could lead them to kill one another — the gospel cannot be true. I think that claim can be sustained by suggesting, and I realize for some this may seem to come from left field, how Kaye's account of Anglicanism can be understood as an ecclesial expression of Alasdair MacIntyre's account of tradition-constituted rationality.[40] If I can sustain that claim, I hope to show the vital connection between the Christian commitment to be in communion and why we believe what we believe to be true.

For MacIntyre, there is no rationality qua rationality, but various claims about the way things are tradition-dependent. But the diversity of traditions does not mean that there can be no meaningful disagreements between traditions because the agents of traditions make claims to truth.[41]

---

ers. *The Unintended Reformation*, pp. 92-96. Yoder notes that the "free church" is also a tradition, so it is important that guidance be received from the past, but the way that guidance is received is less firmly structured than in certain Protestant denominations because it does not understand fidelity to be determined by any one figure such as Luther or Calvin. Yoder, "Reformed versus Anabaptist Social Strategies: An Inadequate Typology," *Theological Students Fellowship Bulletin* (May-June 1985): 5.

38. Kaye, *Conflict and the Practice of the Christian Faith*, pp. 41-61.

39. Bruce Kaye, "Reality and Form in Catholicity," *Journal of Anglican Studies* 10, no. 1 (May 2012): 10.

40. Kaye made this suggestion about MacIntyre's account of tradition in a personal communication.

41. Alasdair MacIntyre, "Moral Relativism, Truth, and Justification," in *Moral*

Accordingly, only if members of a tradition are committed to showing that what they assert and how what they assert is appropriated can we "adequately understand how, in case of each rival moral standpoint, given the historical, social, psychological, and intellectual circumstances in which that standpoint has been theoretically elaborated and embodied in practice, it is intelligible that this is how things should seem to be to the adherents of those standpoints."[42] Therefore, members of a tradition must be able to explain why other traditions see things differently from the way they see the world.

For MacIntyre, traditions are seldom self-contained because they are always undergoing change made necessary by the tensions present in any substantive tradition. Change, moreover, means that the first stage of a tradition in which the beliefs, utterances, texts, and persons are assumed to be authoritative gives way to the discoveries of inadequacies that require reformulations.[43] The reformulation characteristic of mature traditions makes it possible for a tradition to be subject to or to subject another tradition to an "epistemological crisis" — that is, the recognition by a tradition that, by its own standards, it cannot provide an adequate response to a challenge that exposes a problem it cannot help but recognize as a problem.[44]

From MacIntyre's perspective, for a tradition to undergo an episte-

---

Truth and Moral Tradition: Essays in Honour of Peter Geach and Elizabeth Anscombe, ed. Luke Gormally (Dublin: Four Court Press, 1994), p. 8.

42. MacIntyre, "Moral Relativism, Truth, and Justification," p. 21. I am indebted to Jeffrey Nicholas for calling attention to this important article by MacIntyre as well as for his general account of MacIntyre's views in his book *Reason, Tradition, and the Good: MacIntyre's Tradition-Constituted Reason and Frankfurt School Critical Theory* (Notre Dame: University of Notre Dame Press, 2012), pp. 191-92.

43. Alasdair MacIntyre, *Whose Justice? Which Rationality?* (Notre Dame: University of Notre Dame Press, 1988), pp. 354-55. MacIntyre's account of the stages a tradition goes through is very important for helping us understand the limits and possibilities of the ecumenical movement. He assumes that the beginning of a tradition consists in authority being bestowed on certain texts and people. Such a bestowal in the light of later developments may appear arbitrary, but it is exactly through continuing questioning that the beginnings can be made coherent in the light of an ongoing narrative. Accordingly, it may be possible that the story we now call the Reformation can be made of service to the ecumenical task just to the extent that it is open to re-narration.

44. MacIntyre, *Whose Justice? Which Rationality?* p. 361.

mological crisis is a great achievement, requiring as it must conceptual innovation. These innovations must, however, be seen as having some continuity with the past through narrative display. So for a tradition to be judged to have passed successfully through an epistemological crisis, the adherents of that tradition must be able to rewrite the history of that tradition in a more insightful manner than previously was possible.[45] It remains a possibility on MacIntyre's grounds that some traditions do not have the crisis they should have or are unable to resolve a crisis successfully.

Kaye can be understood to be providing an account of the Anglican tradition as one that, by recognizing itself as such, acknowledges that no one tradition, no one congregation, can claim to adequately comprehend the whole Christian truth. Catholicity now can be seen as the commitment by the church, the Anglican Church in this instance, to be ready to challenge as well as be challenged by other Christian traditions. For it turns out that what is at stake is truth.

In support of this understanding of catholicity Kaye quotes Rowan Williams's 2011 Christmas letter to the Primates of the Anglican Communion in which he makes the point that catholicity is a dynamic of church life that is necessarily expressed locally. Williams writes:

> Throughout my time of my service as Archbishop I have tried to keep before my eyes and those of the Communion the warnings given by St Paul about the risk of saying "I have no need of you" to any other who seeks to serve Jesus Christ as a member of His Body. I make no apology for repeating this point. Advent is a good time to recall that we all live in imperfect churches, that we all must draw together in hope for the fuller presence of Our Lord, and that we all therefore must be willing to receive from each other whatever gifts God has to give through them.[46]

Kaye observes that such a view of catholicity challenges any account of the autonomy of any particular church in Anglicanism. Again, catho-

---

45. MacIntyre, *Whose Justice? Which Rationality?* p. 363.
46. Quoted in Kaye, "Reality and Form in Catholicity," p. 10.

licity names the need of the churches to need one another for their ability to live faithfully. Interdependence so understood means that argument is an enduring feature of ecclesial life. This view of catholicity resonates with Yoder's argument that agreement is not an indication of Christian unity, but rather the crucial issue is "faithfulness in our confession of Jesus Christ in personal and ecclesial life in the gospel virtue of love."[47] So understood, catholicity names the quality of life of the church that makes possible the cultivation of the virtues of humility and love.[48]

Kaye argues, therefore, that the unity that makes a church community a Christian community is the unity of love. The test of the various institutional arrangements within as well as between churches is whether those arrangements foster the virtues that help us recognize that our faithfulness depends on our willingness to be helped by other ecclesial communities. Kaye acknowledges that for some "the peaceable kingdom of a Christian community may often look like a shambolic confusion of arguments."[49] Yet it is love that makes such arguments possible, and such love constitutes the unity that makes a church community Christian.

I confess I am uneasy using this appeal to love as indicative of the unity we seek as Christians. Love threatens sentimentality that avoids questions of truth. Love also can become a general attitude of acceptance that is a correlative of a weak Christology. Yet a cruciform-shaped love, a love capable of patience, surely must be at the heart of the ecumenical imperative. For such a love has no reason to suppress difference in the name of unity. And it is surely the case that, whatever form our unity will take, it must be one that sees what we have learned through our differences as gifts.

What matters, therefore, is the reality of the interdependence that gives visibility to our catholicity. The form — that is, the institutional ar-

---

47. Kaye, "Reality and Form in Catholicity," p. 11.

48. Sam Wells observes that if the "Episcopal faith has a central conviction, it is that doctrine and ethics, belief and practice, find their meeting place and testing ground in common prayer. If there were one symbol of the convergence of Scripture, tradition, and reason, it would be the Book of Common Prayer." *What Episcopalians Believe: An Introduction* (New York: Morehouse, 2011), p. 50. I call attention to Wells's claim because I think it makes clear how holiness has always been central to the Church of England.

49. Kaye, "Reality and Form in Catholicity," p. 12.

rangement — that expresses our interdependence is valuable but secondary.[50] What is crucial is the effectiveness of how the gospel is lived out so that the gift and grace of God are apparent by the very fact that such a people exist. As Kaye puts it, "the truth of that catholicity can be seen when it produces the virtues of love and humility."[51]

Anabaptists and Anglicans are seldom thought to share a common ecclesiology, but Kaye and Yoder have very similar understandings of the catholic character of the church.[52] I have often described my ecclesial identity to be that of a "high church Mennonite" — to be sure, a description originally designed to confuse my critics. But in light of the account of the catholic character of the church Yoder and Kaye provide, I hope my self-designation can be understood as a viable future for the church. For if God is killing us, as Lindbeck suggests, I suspect our death is due to the habits of Christendom. The future may well be a church that has the disciplines of mutual accountability necessary for the unity constituted by the body and blood of Jesus.

Let me end by being as candid as I can be. I think the churches, Protestant and Catholic, have for some time been in an "epistemological crisis." That crisis reflects the tension in the gospel in which the lordship of Christ seems to require Christians to acquire social and political power, but at the same time the very means to achieve that end are in conflict with the One in whose name Christians act. In other words, Constantinianism and/or Christendom can be understood as a working out of the logic of the resurrection and ascension of Jesus.

Whatever one may or may not think about the establishment of the

50. I served on the search committee for a new rector for the Church of the Holy Family. In the process I discovered that the Episcopal Church is a congregational polity with bishops. I quite like that form of government. After all, we are all congregationalist now no matter to what church we belong.

51. Kaye, "Reality and Form in Catholicity," p. 12.

52. It would be quite interesting to compare Yoder's and Kaye's understanding of the unity of the church to that of Yves Congar, O.P. For example, Congar notes that the fundamental unity of the church is not to be found in fundamental dogmas or even in the baptismal confession of faith, but rather in the sacramental character of the church herself. I suspect what Congar means by "sacramental" is not all that different from Yoder's and Kaye's understanding of the creation of the people of God through the work of the Holy Spirit. See Congar's *Diversity and Communion* (Mystic, CT: Twenty-Third Publications, 1984), p. 21.

church through social and political power, and I am among those who have been quite critical of such an arrangement, that reality is drawing to an end. That it is so not only means a rethinking of what we mean by church, but in fact to do theology from "below" means everything Christians say we believe will need to be rethought. In particular, I suspect theology needs to be much more concrete and specific. When you are in a survival mode you do not need an "atonement theory" if you take seriously that through the church, and in particular the Eucharist, we are made participants in Christ's very life. In such a circumstance churches may well discover that what was thought to be church dividing turns out to be less significant than they thought.

John Howard Yoder and Karl Barth represent the beginning, to use MacIntyrian terms, of a narration of Christian existence and theology in which the familiar is made unfamiliar. This task is not one that is limited to Protestantism; Roman Catholicism faces the same challenge. It is my conviction that the challenge of Christian unity will depend on how Christians discover how they need one another if they are adequately to learn to live in a world that Christians created but no longer control. If I have an ecumenical vocation it is to try to help the church think through this challenge.

If I have made any contribution toward our becoming a more faithful and united church, it has been through being a teacher of theology committed to thinking through the loss of Christendom. One of the features of my work to which Lindbeck calls attention is my ability "to interest an astonishing range of students and readers from Eastern Orthodox to Pentecostals on both sides of the Atlantic and including secularists such as Jeff Stout of Princeton University."[53] I am grateful to Lindbeck for calling attention to the diversity of students who have entrusted me with their training. I should like to think I have introduced them to the task of theology in a manner that makes them part of a common effort to discover what God is doing to make us adequate witnesses to God's desire to have a people in the world who refuse to let worldly divisions determine their relation to one another.

53. Lindbeck, "Ecumenisms in Conflict," p. 215.

War and Peace

Europe and War

In his *Confessions* Augustine asks, "What, then, is time?" He responds by observing, "I know well enough what it is, provided that nobody asks me; but if I am asked what it is and try to explain, I am baffled."[1] Odd though it may seem, I suspect the same is true if we ask, "What, then, is war?" There is little reason to think we do not know what war looks like. After all, unlike time, we assume we can "see" war. Yet if we are asked why we do not describe a conflict between mafia families, a conflict in which organized groups of people kill and are killed, as "war," we may well discover that war, like time, is not easily explained.

John Keegan has even written a book entitled *A History of Warfare*.[2] If you can write a history of a subject then it would seem you must know what makes a war a war. Yet Keegan wisely disavows any attempt to distinguish in a decisive fashion war from other forms of killing. He does so because he thinks war is an "essentially contested concept." The best he can do, the best anyone can do, is to stipulate what he understands war to name. Though many assume that they know a war when they see one, they may well miss the fact that what they have come to "see" is in service to a particular ideology.[3]

1. Augustine, *Confessions*, trans. R. S. Pine-Coffin (Harmondsworth: Penguin, 1970), p. 264.
2. John Keegan, *A History of Warfare* (New York: Vintage, 1994).
3. Although the subject I am addressing is "war and peace," I have assumed that

For example, Michael Howard worries that how war is understood by "liberal intellectuals," that is, as a pathological aberration from the norm of peace, does not do justice to the reality that war names. The problem, according to Howard, is that if war is assumed to be pathological and abnormal, then all conflict must be similarly regarded. But from Howard's perspective war is a particular kind of conflict between very specific kinds of social groups, namely, sovereign states. Howard draws on Karl von Clausewitz's and Jean-Jacques Rousseau's argument that if one had no sovereign states one would not have wars. "As states acquire a monopoly of violence, war becomes the only remaining form of conflict that may legitimately be settled by physical force."[4]

Howard's claim that war is properly so called only after the creation of sovereign states is a strikingly modern presumption. To so understand war reflects a construal of war that goes hand in hand with the creation of that entity we now call modern Europe. How one determines when "modern Europe" begins is a matter of dispute, but at the very least "modern" indicates the loss of Christendom. That loss had deep implications for how war and the justification of war and peace were and are to be understood. When Christendom was presupposed, those at war with one another had a sense that they were part of a wider civilization. Accordingly, a conflict between two princes could be mediated by a king or a bishop because both sides assumed they shared the same standards. That was not true when war was against the "infidels."[5]

After the Reformation, bishops no longer were political actors. They no longer had the power to restrain the use of war by kings and princes as an expression of political interest. That did not mean, however, that some did not try to establish grounds for understanding as well as limit-

---

my primary responsibility was to write about war, and I have done so. However, the very presumption that war is to be treated before peace can give the impression that "peace" is but the absence of war. Such a presumption, however, is surely a mistake if peace both ontologically and morally is a more determinative reality than violence. That does not mean that "peace" is no less a "contested concept" than war. These are matters I unfortunately must leave aside in this context.

4. Michael Howard, *The Causes of War* (Cambridge, MA: Harvard University Press, 1983), p. 11.

5. John Howard Yoder, *Christian Attitudes to War, Peace, and Revolution*, ed. Theodore Koontz and Andy Alexis-Baker (Grand Rapids: Brazos, 2009), pp. 120-21.

ing war between the emerging political realities. Hugo Grotius is rightly given credit for first expressing the significance of this new reality, that is, how a legal order between sovereign states might be possible as a way to limit war. His *De Jure Belli ac Paci* (1619) presumed that there exists a common human nature that makes possible cooperative agreements between states. Grotius, therefore, represents the attempt to develop an ethics of war after the loss of Christendom.

To ask what makes a war a war therefore turns out to be extremely important for how the ethics of war is to be understood. The ethics of war does not begin with the question of whether a particular war can or cannot be justified on just war grounds. For example, it is instructive to ask: "If a war is not just, what is it?" The question is instructive because many assume that even if a war cannot be justified on just war grounds it nonetheless may be necessary and therefore an obligation for the citizens of a particular state. This position is often identified as a form of "realism" that presumes the development of the nation-state system of Europe.

To so understand war as the expression of the reality of Europe may seem arbitrary, but Howard's position is widely shared by some of the most thoughtful writers on war and peace. For example, W. B. Gallie argues in his extremely important book *Philosophers of Peace and War: Kant, Clausewitz, Marx, Engels, and Tolstoy* that the very idea of international politics — that is, the systematic study of the use of the threat of war and expansion of commercial and cultural contacts — awaited developments in the eighteenth century that recognized that to establish a civil constitution was dependent on a law-governed relation between states.[6]

Philip Bobbitt complicates Howard's and Gallie's account by suggesting that the development of what we now call war must begin with a history of the evolution of the modern state from the princely states of the fifteenth century to the kingly states of the seventeenth century, climaxing in the development of the nation-states from the state-nations of the eighteenth century.[7] The most important difference between these states for understanding war as a correlative of European developments is the transition

6. W. B. Gallie, *Philosophers of Peace and War: Kant, Clausewitz, Marx, Engels, and Tolstoy* (Cambridge: Cambridge University Press, 1978), p. 1.

7. Philip Bobbitt, *The Shield of Achilles: War, Peace, and the Course of History* (New York: Knopf, 2002), pp. 69-213.

from the state-nation to the nation-state. The former, according to Bobbitt, is a state that mobilizes a national, ethnocultural group to act on behalf of the state, whereas a nation-state creates a state to benefit the nation it governs.[8] Bobbitt argues that the state-nation was Napoleon's great creation through the military innovation of universal conscription.[9] Even though Napoleon lost, he had insured the triumph of the state-nation as those who had beaten him had to mirror his achievement.

Bobbitt's account of the development of the states that constituted Europe is the background necessary to justify his contention that the very character of the states so conceived was "a by-product of rulers' efforts to acquire the means of war."[10] Such a state is the consequence of the necessities required to sustain the military expenditures necessary to insure the support of the administrative professionals who commanded the battle fleets to control the seas. But it is also the case that the democratic revolution of these states brought about a bureaucratization of force structures that changed the character of war itself.[11] As a result, the wars of the state-nations were wars of the state that were made into wars of the peoples, whereas the wars of the nation-states were wars that championed causes that had popular support by being fought for popular ideals.[12]

Though Bobbitt thickens Howard's and Gallie's understanding of the relation of war and the state, he is in fundamental agreement with their contention that war is constitutive of the development of international constitutional orders. From such a perspective war is not good or bad. Rather, war simply "is." In a series of lectures at the College de France in 1975 through 1976 entitled *Society Must Be Defended*, Michel Foucault argued in a similar fashion that Clausewitz's famous proposition, "War is the continuation of politics by other means," should be inverted. Fou-

---

8. Bobbitt, *The Shield of Achilles*, p. 146.

9. Bobbitt, *The Shield of Achilles*, p. 151.

10. Bobbitt, *The Shield of Achilles*, p. 174. Bobbitt is quoting Charles Tilly.

11. Bobbitt, *The Shield of Achilles*, p. 174.

12. Bobbitt, *The Shield of Achilles*, p. 204. Bobbitt observes that the nation-state gains its legitimacy from the claim that it is doing something unique in history, that is, maintaining, nurturing, and improving the conditions of its citizens (p. 177). That is why the nation-state, unlike the state-nation, depends on the success of maintaining modern life. Thus a severe economic depression undermines the legitimacy of those who would govern such states in a way in which the state-nation is not delegitimated.

cault observed, "the role of political power is perpetually to use a sort of silent war to reinscribe that relationship of force, and to reinscribe it in institutions, economic inequalities, language, and even the bodies of individuals. This is the initial meaning of our inversion of Clausewitz's aphorism — politics is the continuation of war by other means. Politics, in other words, sanctions and reproduces the disequilibrium of forces manifested in war."[13]

According to Foucault, the inversion of Clausewitz's proposition helps us see that a crucial transition in the practices and institutions of war, which were initially concentrated in the hands of a central power, became associated both in *de facto* and *de jure* terms with emerging state power. "The State acquired a monopoly on war," which had the effect of making war seem to exist only on the outer limits of the great state units. War became the technical and professional prerogative of a carefully defined and controlled military apparatus. The army now became an institution. This means, Foucault argued, that we cannot assume that society, the law, and the state are like armistices that put an end to wars. Beneath the law, war continues to rage. "War is the motor behind institutions and order. In the smallest of its cogs, peace is waging a secret war. To put it another way, we have to interpret the war that is going on beneath peace; peace itself is a coded war. We are all inevitably someone's adversary."[14] Contrary to Thomas Hobbes, sovereignty is not the result of the war of all against all; rather, what we should learn from Hobbes is that it is not that war gives birth to states but rather that sovereignty is always shaped from below by those who are afraid.[15]

Kant on War

It is extremely important that the account of war correlative to the institution of an international order exemplified by the development of the

13. Michel Foucault, *Society Must Be Defended*, ed. Mauro Bertani and Alessandro Fontana, trans. David Macey (New York: Picador, 2003), pp. 15-16.

14. Foucault, *Society Must Be Defended*, pp. 50-51.

15. Foucault, *Society Must Be Defended*, p. 96. Foucault seems to echo themes from the words of Carl Schmitt.

nation-states of Europe not be seen as antithetical to the rule of law. For, as Foucault implies, the developments in international law worked to legitimate war as an essential function of the state. Paul Kahn observes that law and war are "common expressions of the modern political culture of the sovereign nation-state. The state writes itself into existence by drafting a constitution. It expresses the historical permanence of that law by defending it at all costs. It demonstrates its own ultimate significance in the life of the individual citizen through the act of sacrifice that war entails. . . . All citizens become appropriate subjects of sacrifice and all history becomes coterminous with the continuation of the state."[16]

The connection between law and war, W. B. Gallie argues, was given its strongest theoretical justification by Immanuel Kant in his pamphlet *Perpetual Peace*, written in 1795. In that pamphlet Kant was intent on providing an account of the emerging order he thought might create a more lasting peace.[17] Though often identified as a pacifist, Kant, like Howard and Bobbitt, thought war could not be abolished, though he sought to make war less likely. By doing so he made articulate the presuppositions that continue to shape modern assumptions about war and peace. If we are to understand where we are today, it is therefore necessary to understand Kant, or at least Gallie's account of Kant, because few have seen as clearly as Kant how the attempt to establish political order by reason ironically results in making war inevitable and, thereby, morally necessary.[18]

Kant begins *Perpetual Peace* by putting forward the conditions he thinks nations must adhere to in order to maintain peace between themselves. Nations must pledge not to enter into secret treaties; they must refuse to acquire other states through inheritance, purchase, or gift; they cannot have standing armies, though they can create citizen militias for

16. Paul Kahn, *Putting Liberalism in Its Place* (Princeton: Princeton University Press, 2005), p. 279.

17. Kant's *Perpetual Peace* can be found in *Kant's Political Writings*, ed. H. Reiss, trans. H. Nisbit (Cambridge: Cambridge University Press, 1970). I will, however, be referencing Gallie's account of this important work.

18. I draw on Gallie's account of *Perpetual Peace* because, as Gallie notes, Kant's pamphlet, which Kant wrote in a "popular" style in the hopes that it might be widely read, has led to a mass of contradictory interpretations, many of which can be justified by the text. I use Gallie not only because I think his reading to be right but also because how he reads Kant also makes clear Kant's relevancy for the subject of this chapter.

defense; they cannot go into debt to sustain the military; they must not interfere with the internal constitution of another state; nor can they use assassins or try to subvert other governments. Those who can sign a treaty so conceived must be constituted by representative government, because Kant knew such a treaty would only be the beginning of the process of peace.

Gallie rightly argues that Kant thought his understanding of the conditions necessary to sustain a more lasting peace between nations to be an expression of his central philosophical ideas. He sought to show how reason could lead to the formation of the relation between nations that could result in unity and peace. In particular, Kant's project in *Perpetual Peace* was "to construct a framework of ideas within which the generally acknowledged rights and duties of states *vis-à-vis* their *own* citizens can be shown to require, logically, acknowledgement of certain equally important rights and duties towards each other (and each other's citizens) if their traditionally recognized tasks are ever to be effectively discharged."[19] In effect, Kant gave a philosophical defense of Grotius's presumption that a common humanity exists sufficient to sustain a law-like relation between nation-states.

Like Rousseau, whom Kant admired, Kant wrote of international relations assuming the arrangements of eighteenth-century Europe. Kant thought that European states represented an advanced stage of development because they shared the inheritance of a common civilization. Kant therefore believed that, even though wars continued to break out, the greatest threat to civilization — that is, the overthrow of established political units within their own borders — was made less likely by the equilibrium between states in the nation-state system (p. 18). It was thus assumed that if a European power threatened its neighbor, an alliance of powers would oppose it. "War, therefore, was not simply a necessary evil within the European system, it was also the indispensable safeguard of the survival and independence of the different European states" (p. 18).

Kant, of course, did not think that war was a "good thing." Rather, he thought war to be one of the greatest evils humans endure. Yet he also

---

19. Gallie, *Philosophers of Peace and War*, pp. 13-14. Page references to Gallie's book will be given in the text in parentheses.

thought that an international order must have as its task to keep the peace between like-minded states. Accordingly, Kant thought an essential precondition of an international order is the non-interference in the internal affairs of other states. He assumed that the task of creating such an order would take many years. Though he thought like-minded states could sign a non-aggression treaty, he nonetheless assumed that every citizen "should be prepared to defend his country from foreign invasion" (p. 21).

Kant knew that various philosophers and political leaders had sought to escape war by two means: (1) by imagining a vast empire that could control all subject people, or (2) by creating a strong federation of sovereign states united by their mutual defense. The latter was Rousseau's position, yet Kant rejected it as well as the presumption of peace through empire. He rejected empire as a solution to the problem of inter-state relations because an empire would only substitute one form of tyranny for another. On the other hand, federations are not strong enough to enforce peace, which meant that Kant thought any attempt to enforce peace between sovereign states to be delusion (p. 24).

Thus Kant's belief that, until there is asymmetry between establishing and maintaining just constitutions and maintaining a relationship between states, the use of force in self-defense could not be ruled out. Gallie summarizes Kant's position, noting that for Kant "an act of defensive war may be justified as preserving a (relatively) just state in existence; but it cannot be justified in respect of that kind of relation between states which Reason positively requires that all states should strive to bring into being" (p. 24). Kant recommended, therefore, that states form confederations so that the "peace" between them could be extended to like-minded powers.

Gallie notes that Kant's "cosmopolitan ideal" is neither a world-state nor an anarchistic Utopia, but rather the hope of a world in which the rights of individuals can transcend the boundaries of their own nations. Peace would be secured, not by a supernational authority, but by the mutual recognition of states constituted by citizens who recognize the rights and duties incumbent on rational beings to respect other nationals who are also so constituted (p. 27). Kant therefore expresses in *Perpetual Peace* his commitment to the rational consciousness of the free individual, who too often is tragically blind and wayward. Thus he took the task of "perpetual peace-*making* as, like all the other major tasks of mankind, essentially a matter of man's remaking of himself" (p. 35).

Kant's position has been endlessly critiqued and qualified, but his fundamental perspective continues to shape how war has been understood by those committed to maintaining the nation-state system. Kant was the ultimate liberal, if liberal names the attempt to create a politics of reason enshrined in law. Yet the question remains whether the liberal state so conceived can comprehend the reality of war. Gallie suggests that the reality of war received its most determinative expression in the work of Tolstoy and Clausewitz.

Tolstoy's great work *War and Peace*, a work that, like *Perpetual Peace*, was a response to the Napoleonic Wars, is Tolstoy's attempt to show how little wars can be understood (p. 101). That is why in *War and Peace* the most coherent units of action are relatively small groups of men who share the demands of war. They do not nor can they experience the battle as a whole. Yet Tolstoy is at pains in his great novel to show that neither do those who are in command of the armies have control or knowledge of the total action of the armies in battle. According to Gallie, however, what most bothered Tolstoy was not the killing itself, but rather the progressive dominance of life by "the anonymous, irresistible, seemingly irreversible-bureaucratic state machines" (p. 126).

Though Tolstoy and Clausewitz seem to represent antithetical positions, in a quite remarkable way how they understood war is quite similar. In particular, Clausewitz's understanding of Absolute War — that is, war fought for the complete destruction of the enemy no matter what the cost, war that cannot be comprehended by "reason" — is not that different from Tolstoy's (pp. 50-52). Clausewitz and Tolstoy, in quite different but complementary ways, support Paul Kahn's claim that the sacrifice that war requires cannot "find a moral foundation in a theory of the democratic legitimacy of law."[20]

According to Kahn, the fundamental feature of war is killing and being killed. War is not about the life and death of individuals who participate in war, but rather war is about the existence of "the sovereign as an imagined

---

20. Paul Kahn, *Sacred Violence: Torture, Terror, and Sovereignty* (Ann Arbor: University of Michigan Press, 2008), p. 103.

reality of transcendent value."[21] In short, Kahn suggests that war is the way states sanctify their existence — an ironic result, given the widespread presumption that the creation of the modern nation-state system was necessary to stop Catholics and Protestants after the Reformation from killing one another. It is that presumption to which I must now turn.

"The Myth of Religious Violence"

In *The Myth of Religious Violence* William Cavanaugh challenges the widespread presumption that religions promote violence. The presumption that religious violence is uncontrollable reflects Kantian-like justifications of the nation-state system of Europe. From such a perspective religion is identified with trans-historical and trans-cultural aspects of human life that are allegedly not subject to rational control. Accordingly, religion must be restricted to the "private" region of our lives and prohibited from having a public role. In contrast to religious communities, the secular nation-state represents universal and timeless truth, making possible the resolution of differences short of war.[22]

Cavanaugh explores the historical record used to justify the presumption that religious violence cannot be controlled because religions are not subject to reason. Thus it is alleged that in the aftermath of the Protestant Reformation, in which Christendom was divided between Catholics and Protestants, the "wars of religion" devastated Europe. Because Catholics and Protestants were unable to settle their doctrinal differences, they embarked on a century of chaos and bloodletting that ravaged Europe. Peace between the warring religious communities was made possible only by the rise of the secular nation-state. The Peace of Westphalia in 1648 was the expression of this new reality. The state now had a monopoly on use of violence, requiring Protestants and Catholics to submit to the religiously neutral sovereign state.[23]

The power of this story, a story in which the state becomes the prin-

21. Kahn, *Sacred Violence*, p. 150.
22. William Cavanaugh, *The Myth of Religious Violence: Secular Ideology and the Roots of Modern Conflict* (New York: Oxford University Press, 2009), p. 3.
23. Cavanaugh, *The Myth of Religious Violence*, p. 123.

cipal agent, is evident in the role the story plays in the thought of Baruch Spinoza, Thomas Hobbes, John Locke, Jean-Jacques Rousseau, Edward Gibbon, and Voltaire. The story is repeated endlessly, moreover, by contemporary political theorists such as Quentin Skinner, Jeffrey Stout, Judith Shklar, John Rawls, and J. G. A. Pocock. Thus Pocock's characterization of the Enlightenment "first, as the emergence of a system of states, founded in civil and commercial society and culture, which might enable Europe to escape from the wars of religion without falling under the hegemony of a single monarchy; second, as a series of programmes for reducing the power of either churches or congregations to disturb the peace of civil society by challenging its authority."[24]

The only problem with this story, according to Cavanaugh, is that it is not true. Cavanaugh observes that if it were true one would expect to find that Catholics killed Protestants and not fellow Catholics. Likewise, one would think that Protestants killed Catholics but not necessarily other Protestants. Moreover, if the story were true, then the wars named the wars of religion must have had as their primary cause the cause of religion rather than political, economic, or social purpose.

Yet Cavanaugh argues that it is simply impossible to isolate something called religion from politics and economics. That Catholics killed Catholics and Protestants killed Protestants in the so-called religious wars is sufficient to suggest that more was at stake than being Catholic or Protestant. At the very least what was at stake were the beginnings of the development of the modern state system, which had begun, we now can see, prior to the Reformation. For what is clear is that the political actors who represented the beginnings of such states used antagonism between Catholics and Protestants to legitimate the growth of the state.[25]

The historical record simply does not support the story of the "religious wars." Cavanaugh points out that Charles V spent much of the decade following Luther's excommunication fighting the pope, even sacking Rome in 1527. Charles was also more frequently at war with France than with the Protestants in Germany. In the Schmalkaldic War of 1546-1547 the Protestant princes supported the Catholic emperor in the wars against

---

24. Quoted by Cavanaugh in *The Myth of Religious Violence*, p. 139.
25. Cavanaugh, *The Myth of Religious Violence*, p. 142.

France. In 1552 the Catholic king Henry II of France attacked the emperor's army while the Catholic princes of the empire took a position of neutrality. In 1583 the Protestant Jan Casimir of the Palatinate joined the Catholic duke of Larraine to fight against Henry III. In 1631 Cardinal Richelieu of France made a treaty with Sweden to subsidize the Swedish war effort. Indeed, in the latter half of what we now call the Thirty Years' War the battle was largely between Catholic France and Catholic Habsburgs.[26]

These examples, and Cavanaugh provides many more, make clear that any attempt to isolate "religion" from social, economic, and political realities cannot be sustained. Indeed, it is crucial for Cavanaugh that the very creation of the category "religion" is a correlative of the attempt to legitimate state control of the church. For as Cavanaugh observes, the creation of the category "religion" has a history. In the pre-modern West it would have never occurred to Christians that their faith might be a species of a more universal category called religion. To be sure, religion in the Middle Ages was associated with bodily disciplines of "the religious," but that use of the term meant that what it meant to be "religious" was a concrete expression of a set of practices.[27]

It may seem a small point to argue, as Cavanaugh does, that the very category of "religion" is a construct. But he suggests rightly that when "religion" became a description of an alleged reality more comprehensive than a specific faith, it served as an ideological justification of the nation-state. In other words, the creation of "religion" went hand in hand with the growth of the nation-state, which was justified as necessary to save Europe and later the whole world from religious violence. From Cavanaugh's perspective, the state so understood, moreover, is not a secularized state, but rather one that is sacralized. For in the name of controlling religious violence the nation-state "replaced the church in its role as the primary cultural institution that deals with death. Christianity's decline in the West necessitated another way of dealing with the arbitrariness of death. Nations provide a new kind of salvation; my death is not in vain if it is for the nation, which lives on into a limitless future."[28]

26. Cavanaugh, *The Myth of Religious Violence*, pp. 142-50.
27. Cavanaugh, *The Myth of Religious Violence*, p. 81.
28. Cavanaugh, *The Myth of Religious Violence*, p. 114. Cavanaugh is here characterizing Benedict Anderson's views.

The myth of religious violence is, therefore, anything but innocent. Cavanaugh characterizes the myth as part of the folklore of Western societies that has no basis in reality other than the reality it creates by its constant repetition. The repetitive character of the story, however, is necessary just to the extent that the story legitimates the power of the nation-state in the West to wage war. It is a story of salvation in which the nation-state claims a monopoly on legitimate violence to save us from the violence of religion. The story is used to foster the idea, particularly in the United States, that secular social orders are inherently peaceful. The power of the story is evident just to the extent that a nation that spends more on its military than all the other nations of the world combined prides itself on being a peace-loving country.[29]

The Ethics of War and Peace

I began by observing that to know what makes war a war is not obvious. I have tried to elaborate that claim by suggesting how the development of the modern state system of Europe produced an account of war that made war unavoidable but hopefully seldom necessary. The irony, however, of war so understood was that subsequent wars were "total" in a manner that made it impossible for those who were not in the military to be protected from the war. Equally ironic was the use of the "Enlightened" ideology of the European powers to justify their imperial ambitions in wars against people who were not advanced enough to be "nations."

The reality of war, particularly the war described as the First World War, seemed so senseless and the loss of life so massive and purposeless that many were led to conclude that war could not be justified. The "pacifism" that followed in the wake of that war was a "liberal" position that assumed that war simply was "irrational." A pacifism so conceived reflected some of the rationalist presumptions Kant had developed in *Perpetual Peace*. Indeed, many read Kant as an advocate of pacifism. Though to so read Kant was a mistake, such a reading did suggest how difficult it was to try to think ethically about war.

29. Cavanaugh, *The Myth of Religious Violence*, p. 127.

In 1960, a church historian at Yale Divinity School, Roland Bainton, wrote *Christian Attitudes toward War and Peace: A Historical Survey and Critical Re-Evaluation,* in which he provided a typology that determined for many what they took to be the ethical alternatives for how war should be understood.[30] Bainton identified three stances Christians have taken toward war: pacifism, just war, and crusade. It is important to remember that Bainton understood these to be "types"; that is, they are characterizations that in reality might be more complex. For example, a crusade — that is, a war fought for a cause that is so important that the means used to achieve victory cannot be limited — was often thought to be just in the Middle Ages.[31]

By contrast, a just war is a war fought to accomplish a limited end. This requires that the means used must be appropriate to the end. Though Bainton named just war as historically one of the major Christian options, in truth the use of just war criteria for justifying or critiquing war was largely absent from Christian and non-Christian reflection on war after the Reformation. It was only with the work of Paul Ramsey that just war again became a viable way to think about the ethics of war. In particular, Ramsey in 1961 published *War and the Christian Conscience: How Shall Modern War Be Conducted Justly?*[32] In the book Ramsey drew on Augustine to suggest that just war is best understood as a response to an unjust attack on the innocent rather than an act of self-defense. Therefore those who would defend the innocent should seek only to use as much violence as necessary to deter the attack on the innocent. For a war to be just, therefore, a declaration of war is required by the legitimate authority to make clear to the enemy the limited nature of the war and the conditions for surrendering.

---

30. Roland Bainton, *Christian Attitudes toward War and Peace: A Historical Survey and Critical Re-Evaluation* (Nashville: Abingdon, 1960).

31. This way of putting the matter can be misleading because the Crusades for the Holy Land were often fought as "just," requiring knights to distinguish between combatants and non-combatants. Though this was often thought to be a matter of honor required of knights, it nonetheless suggested that a war whose end was "religious" was still assumed to be just. All of which is a reminder that the just war criteria were developed over many centuries and could appear quite different at different times.

32. Paul Ramsey, *War and the Christian Conscience: How Shall Modern War Be Conducted Justly?* (Durham, NC: Duke University Press, 1961).

Moreover, the war once begun must, if it is to be just, be fought in such a manner that the intention for going to war not be different from the reason declared for the war. A legitimate authority is therefore required to insure that the war is a public matter. The war must be fought, moreover, in a manner that clearly distinguishes the killing in war from murder. That is why the principle of discrimination was so important for Ramsey, because it requires that non-combatants be distinguished from combatants.

Ramsey was deeply influenced by the "realism" of Reinhold Niebuhr. Niebuhr justified the Christian participation in war by arguing that the relative justice between nations was possible only if war was not disavowed. Crucial for maintaining justice (and peace) within as well as between nations was the establishment, as near as possible, of more or less equal balances of power. Accordingly, Niebuhr was a sworn enemy of all attempts by Christians to think that war might be avoided. The question for Niebuhr was never whether war could be justified, but how soon a war might need to be fought or how long it could be avoided to make less likely a larger or more destructive war.[33] Though he would have been critical of Kant's "rationalism," Niebuhr assumed a world not unlike the one Kant tried to justify in *Perpetual Peace*.

Ramsey was deeply appreciative of Niebuhr's perspective, but he worried that there was inadequate control on Niebuhr's justification of war as crucial for securing justice in a nation-state system that lacked any legitimate authority. Ramsey therefore attempted to show how just war could be understood as an expression of the kind of realism represented by Niebuhr. Such a view of just war has been questioned by Daniel Bell for failing to see that just war is not, as Ramsey sometimes seemed to suggest, a checklist to see if a war passes the just war criteria; rather, just war is a way in which the church discerned whether Christian participation in war can be understood as a form of discipleship.[34]

Though Bainton made reference to the Anabaptist understanding of Christological pacifism in his book, he seems to have thought some

33. Reinhold Niebuhr, *Moral Man and Immoral Society* (New York: Scribner's Sons, 1932).

34. Daniel Bell, *Just War as Christian Discipleship: Recentering the Tradition in the Church Rather Than the State* (Grand Rapids: Brazos, 2009).

form of liberal Protestant understanding of nonviolence to be the most persuasive. It was the kind of liberal pacifism John Howard Yoder associated with secular humanism, based on the presumption that humankind names a sufficient community to make possible an appeal across differences that can secure agreements short of war.[35] As an alternative to secular pacifism, Yoder, drawing on his Anabaptist tradition, developed an account of Christological pacifism that is political exactly because it is non-coercive. Pacifism, according to Yoder, is required by the cross of Christ, for it is in the cross that God refuses to save coercively. Jesus therefore does not fit the Kantian mold, because he is not commending his ethic for just anyone, but for those who would be his disciples.[36]

Yoder represents a form of pacifism that assumes that a Christian understanding of war draws on an eschatological perspective unavailable to those who do not share the Christian worship of Christ. Accordingly, he is not convinced that questions about effectiveness, which can be quite important, should determine how the Christian is to think about war. He puts it this way: "Jesus was not successful. Jesus did not promise his followers that if they did things right, they would conquer with time. The non-coerciveness of agape includes renouncing the promise of power; it includes renouncing the mechanical model of how to move history. Yet that acknowledgement does not mean simple despair or unconcern. It rather means a promise of victory, the paradigm of which is the Resurrection."[37]

Yoder's arguments for Christian nonviolence are clearly dependent on theological claims and, in particular, on an understanding of the priority of the church to the world. Accordingly, he represents an alternative to the Christendom assumptions that shaped how Christians understood war in war-riven Europe. For Yoder, the primary agent is not the emerging nation-states or the international system, but the church. That

---

35. Yoder, *Christian Attitudes to War, Peace, and Revolution*. Though Yoder used Bainton's typology, he argued that the "blank check" needed to be added to Bainton's three. For, as Yoder argued, in fact most Christians, particularly after the Reformation, were schooled not to call into question those who ruled them. Accordingly, they simply killed whoever their ruler asked them to kill. In short, they simply gave a "blank check" to war.

36. Yoder, *Christian Attitudes to War, Peace, and Revolution*, p. 316.

37. Yoder, *Christian Attitudes to War, Peace, and Revolution*, p. 359.

does not mean that he would fail to recognize the world that has developed, a world that the Howards and the Bobbitts describe, but he refuses to believe that that world must be assumed as necessary. At the very least, Yoder represents a challenge to the role war too often plays in providing the sacrifices thought necessary to justify the ethos of the modern state.

I referred above to Paul Kahn's contention that the political meaning of the modern state, the state created by European thought, is sustained by the practice of sacrifice, of killing and being killed. It is hard to see how that claim can be denied after the wars of the twentieth century.[38] Through sacrifice, and in particular the sacrifice of war, citizens are created just to the extent that they are subjects who can be called on to make the sacrifices war demands.[39] That is why the Christian alternative to war is best thought of not as an "ethic"; rather, the Christian alternative to war is Eucharist.[40] Christ is the end of all sacrifices not determined by his cross.

38. See, for example, Allen Frantzen, *Bloody Good: Chivalry, Sacrifice, and the Great War* (Chicago: University of Chicago Press, 2004), and Ivan Strenski, *Contesting Sacrifice: Religion, Nationalism, and Social Thought in France* (Chicago: University of Chicago Press, 2002).

39. Kahn, *Sacred Violence*, p. 35.

40. Stanley Hauerwas and Samuel Wells, "Breaking Bread: Peace and War," in *The Blackwell Companion to Christian Ethics*, ed. Stanley Hauerwas and Samuel Wells, 2nd ed. (Oxford: Wiley-Blackwell, 2011), pp. 415-26.

PART THREE

Life and Death

Bearing Reality

Listening to Elizabeth Costello

Elizabeth Costello, the central character of J. M. Coetzee's 2003 novel of the same name, has come from Australia to Altona College in Williamstown, Pennsylvania, to receive the Stowe Award.[1] The Stowe Award is made biennially to a major world writer. Elizabeth Costello is sixty-six years old. She has written nine novels, but her fourth, *The House on Eccles Street*, a novel that gave life to Marion Bloom, the wife of Leopold Bloom, of Joyce's *Ulysses*, had made her reputation. Her son, John, who teaches physics at a college in Massachusetts, has joined her for the bestowing of the award. He learns that one of the reasons his mother has been given the Stowe Award is because the judges judged it was the year an Australian should win.

Elizabeth is subject to the inevitable dinners and interviews one must go through on such occasions. One young interviewer, who has come from Boston for the event, asks, "What would you say is your main message?" Put off by the question, Elizabeth responds, "My message? Am I obliged to carry a message?" Later, in an interview for the radio station, she surprises herself by not using a canned response to a routine question about the difficulty of writing from the perspective of a male. She con-

---

1. J. M. Coetzee, *Elizabeth Costello* (New York: Penguin, 2003), pp. 1-2. Page references to the novel will appear in the text.

fesses that to so write is hard work but it is work worth doing, because it is important to make up a world in which a man moves, particularly if you are to write as an Australian.

The dinner is finished, the award is given, the acceptance speech, which is entitled "What Is Realism?" must now be given. Elizabeth begins by reflecting on the transience of fame, noting that someday the copies of her books in the British Library will be destroyed by acid and ants. She continues by calling her audience's attention to Franz Kafka's story of an ape dressed to give a speech before a learned society. Kafka's story is a monologue, making it impossible for the reader to know if the speaker is really an ape or a human thinking or presenting himself as an ape. Kafka has written in such a manner as to make it impossible for us to know if the story is about a man speaking to men or an ape speaking to apes or even a parrot speaking to parrots.

Elizabeth observes that there used to be a time when we would know. There was a time when we believed that when the text said, "On the table stood a glass of water," there was a table with a glass of water on it. But, as Kafka's story suggests, all that has ended. Words, Elizabeth observes, "no longer stand up to be counted." She continues: "There used to be a time, we believe, when we could say who we were. Now we are just performers speaking our parts. The bottom has dropped out. We could think of this as a tragic turn of events, were it not that it is hard to have respect for whatever was the bottom that dropped out — it looks to us like an illusion now, one of those illusions sustained only by the concentrated gaze of everyone in the room. Remove your gaze for but an instance and the mirror falls to the floor and shatters" (pp. 19-20).

She ends by expressing gratitude for the award, but observes, "Despite this splendid award, . . . despite the promise it makes that . . . I am beyond time's envious grasp, we all know, if we are being realistic, that it is only a matter of time before the books which you honour, and with whose genesis I have had something to do, will cease to be read and eventually cease to be remembered. And properly so. There must be some limit to the burden of remembering that we impose on our children and grandchildren. They have a world of their own, of which we should be less and less part. Thank you" (p. 20).

I begin with Coetzee's novel *Elizabeth Costello* because I think Coetzee, the great South African now Australian novelist, is a writer who thinks our humanity depends on our ability to live without the illusions used to protect ourselves from the terrors that seem constitutive of our humanity. Coetzee makes no apology for using his novels to give voice to as well as explore what he takes to be the moral challenges, challenges such as the cruelty we inflict on animals, we face. Of course, one can never be sure if Coetzee shares the positions taken by Elizabeth Costello. This created a problem for his respondents at Princeton when he gave the Tanner Lectures in 1998. The lectures, which are now the centerpieces of the novel *Elizabeth Costello,* consisted in Costello's speeches concerning our treatment of animals. Coetzee's respondents could not be sure if they were responding to Coetzee or Costello.[2]

Coetzee is a writer. In a scene late in the novel in which Elizabeth Costello appears before "her judges," who are all male, she defends herself, using Czeslaw Milosz's description, as a "secretary of the invisible." Her calling, and she may speak for Coetzee at this point, is to be a dictation secretary whose task is not to interrogate or judge what is given to her. "I merely write down the words and then test them, test their soundness, to make sure I have heard them right." She exercises what she calls "negative capability" in the hope she may contribute to the humanity of those who read her (pp. 199-200).

Coetzee denies that he is a philosopher, though, as the phrase "negative capability" suggests, he is philosophically knowledgeable and astute.[3] His late novels, such as *Elizabeth Costello,* have turned into an art

---

2. Coetzee's Tanner Lectures were published as *The Lives of Animals* (Princeton: Princeton University Press, 1999). The book was introduced by Amy Gutmann, with responses by Marjorie Garber, Peter Singer, Wendy Doniger, and Barbara Smuts. Gutmann and Singer assume that Costello is making a typical philosophical/ethical case against our use of animals. As we will see, however, there are strong reasons to question that reading of her speech exactly because that reading ignores Coetzee's depiction of Costello as the "wounded animal."

3. In a collection of his interviews and essays entitled *Doubling the Point: Essays and Interviews,* ed. David Attwell (Cambridge, MA: Harvard University Press, 1992), Coetzee describes himself as someone who is not a trained philosopher and claims to be rather slow and myopic in his thinking. So he simply does not have a mind for philosophy. It is, moreover, the case that he likes the feel of writing fiction, creating as it does a sense of responsibility toward something that has not yet emerged but lies somewhere at the end of the road (p. 246).

form philosophical lectures that are embedded and re-embedded in fictional narratives.[4] Coetzee seems to be testing the distinction between philosophy and literature by doing philosophy and literature through his writing of fiction.[5] In the process, he seeks to reveal the limits of accounts of rationality dominant in contemporary ethical theory in an effort to show that "the moral life is less about conclusive arguments of revelatory discoveries than it is the small actions of every day existence."[6]

Given Coetzee's philosophical interest, it is not surprising that his work, and in particular *Elizabeth Costello,* has attracted the attention of philosophers such as Cora Diamond, Stanley Cavell, and Stephen Mulhall. It is no accident, moreover, that these are philosophers deeply influenced by Wittgenstein who sense that Coetzee's attempt to confront "the fact of suffering in the world" is not unrelated to Wittgenstein's effort to help us recognize the limits of philosophy.[7]

Coetzee and Wittgenstein, to be sure in quite different ways, try to help us discover the possibilities and limits of what it means to be human in our times. We live after a century piled high with corpses produced by an inhumanity too often justified by an overconfident humanism.

4. For an insightful account of the way Coetzee's work involves such "embeddedness" see Ido Geiger, "Writing the Lives of Animals," in *J. M. Coetzee and Ethics: Philosophical Perspectives on Literature,* ed. Anton Leist and Peter Singer (New York: Columbia University Press, 2010), pp. 158-59.

5. This way to put the matter I owe to Jennifer Flynn in her essay *"The Lives of Animals* and the Form-Content Connection," in *J. M. Coetzee and Ethics,* p. 318.

6. Martin Woessner, "Coetzee's Critique of Reason," in *J. M. Coetzee and Ethics,* p. 241. Andy Lamey suggests that Mary Midgley's account of sympathy has had a decided influence on Coetzee, but Lamey also argues, I think rightly, that neither Midgley nor Coetzee thinks sympathy to be without reason. We may, for example, have a duty to feel one way rather than another. Lamey, "Sympathy and Scapegoating in J. M. Coetzee," in *J. M. Coetzee and Ethics,* pp. 173-81. Andy Lamey provides a very constructive comparison of Hobbes's and Kant's (to be sure quite different) contractarian accounts of moral rationality to suggest that what Kant and Hobbes have in common is the question of who is included in the social contract. For Coetzee to even produce that question is to have made a mistake. See Lamey, p. 176.

7. The phrase "the fact of suffering in the world" is Coetzee's. It appears in his *Doubling the Point,* where he says, "I, as a person, am overwhelmed, . . . my thinking is thrown into confusion and helplessness, by the fact of suffering in the world, and not only human suffering. These fictional constructions of mine are paltry, ludicrous defenses against that being-overwhelmed" (p. 248).

That humanism was often underwritten by Christian theologians in the hope that Christians might be counted among the progressive forces that would determine the future. We now live in a time, however, in which Christian and non-Christian alike are no longer sure what it means to be a human being. Is it finally all ruins?

T. S. Eliot is said to have remarked that humankind cannot bear much reality. Coetzee, however, seems to think that to be human entails the ability to bear reality even when the reality that must be borne is quite terrible. The question before us, at least the question Coetzee puts before us, is how much reality we can bear and remain human. Could it be, as Elizabeth Costello late in the novel reflects on evil, that if we are to save our humanity there are certain things that, because we are human, we may want to see, but from which we should turn our eyes?[8] These may well be questions, and I wonder if they are the same question, that cannot and, perhaps, should not be answered. Yet they are questions that will not go away. They are questions, moreover, that must be at the center of our work in Christian theology and ethics if that work is to be more than academic play.

I have begun by calling attention to Costello's lecture at Altona College because I cannot help but identify with her. I fear being self-indulgent, but I need to make clear why Costello gives voice to what I feel as I must now address you. Like Costello, I am old and trapped by a track record whose defense can stop thought from meeting the demands necessary to say as best one can what is true. The temptation is to resort to the well-worn responses to the stupid question asked by the uninformed reporter or to give once again the stump speech. That I have tried to counter the high humanism of our time with an equally high account of what it means to be Christian may seem to make the kind of challenge Coetzee's novel represents something Christians can avoid. I do not want that result.[9]

8. Coetzee, *Elizabeth Costello*, pp. 168-69. Costello even suggests that she is no longer sure that people are improved by what they read or write. She is not sure "that writers who venture into darker territories of the soul always return unscathed. She has begun to wonder whether writing what one desires, any more than reading what one desires, is in itself a good thing" (p. 160).

9. Peter Dula puts it well by suggesting that the appeal of my work comes from my "uncanny ability to give voice to the reader's secrets." According to Dula, I seem to know what no one could fail to know, but such attentiveness too often "gets sacrificed

Focusing on the question of how much reality we can bear and remain human, a question I should hope can defeat any attempt by me to "posture," also invites the exploration of the kind of work we must be about if we are to serve God and our neighbor through the modest office called Christian ethics. It is the kind of question that I think has been at the heart of Stanley Cavell's work, as Cavell has sought — as Stephen Mulhall suggests by commenting on Cavell's exploration of the paradox of photography — to make us see what is not there. For Cavell thinks philosophy, like much photography, is the attempt to achieve clarity about the obscurities that constitute our lives without the clarity so achieved banishing those same obscurities.[10] The challenge for those of us who would do the work of Christian theology is how to speak unapologetically as Christians without denying the obscurities.

The question can be put this way in terms of my own work: "How can I think that it is possible consistently to think with theologians like Karl Barth and John Howard Yoder and at the same time learn from philosophers like Ludwig Wittgenstein, Iris Murdoch, and Cora Diamond?" In what follows I hope to suggest why I think the kind of work Cora Diamond does by way of commentary on Coetzee's *Elizabeth Costello* is so important for helping us recognize what she calls "the difficulty of reality." For I hope to show how Diamond develops an account of the difficulty of reality that can help us better understand how Yoder depicts the difficulty that being a Christian entails.

"The Difficulty of Reality"

The "difficulty of reality" names for Diamond experiences we have in which something in reality is so resistant to our thinking that the inexplicability with which we must live is painful or difficult, or perhaps awesome and astonishing in its inexplicability.[11] Diamond recognizes that

in order to promote the ecclesiological project." Peter Dula, *Cavell, Companionship, and Christian Theology* (Oxford: Oxford University Press, 2011), pp. 201-2.

10. Stephen Mulhall, *The Wounded Animal: J. M. Coetzee and the Difficulty of Reality in Literature and Philosophy* (Princeton: Princeton University Press, 2009), p. 92.

11. Cora Diamond, "The Difficulty of Reality and the Difficulty of Philosophy," in

what she is trying to describe begs for exemplification. She uses, and I wonder if "use" is the right word, another event in Coetzee's *Elizabeth Costello* to display what she takes to be the inexplicability that is characteristic of our lives. Two years have passed since Elizabeth was at Altona College. She has come to Appleton College, the college where her son teaches, to deliver the annual Gates Lecture. The sponsors of the lecture would have liked for her to speak about herself and her work, but she has chosen to speak about animals. She is a vegetarian.

In her lecture, without going into details of the horror of the lives and deaths of animals, Costello calls attention to the cruelty of factory farming of animals. What particularly troubles Costello, however, is that this horror is treated by most of us as a given. In short, we do not have to think about what we do to animals because if we did think about what we do to animals we are not sure we could continue to live as we do. Our humanity seems to require or make possible that we acknowledge our cruelty to animals, but at the same time the same humanity cannot comprehend what it seems we need to acknowledge.

According to Diamond, however, it is crucial, if we are to understand the performance Costello's speech enacts, to recognize that she is not trying to make a philosophical case against cruelty to animals. Rather, Diamond argues that Coetzee wants us to see Costello as someone who is wounded and haunted by what we do to animals. Yet our inability to recognize what we do to animals is present in the inability of Costello's hearers to recognize how she suffers from their inability to recognize her suffering.[12]

Costello refuses to make a philosophical case against our cruelty toward animals because she sees our reliance on argumentation as a way we make unavailable to ourselves what it means for us to be living animals. She therefore does not seek to start a debate, but rather to make us aware of our own bodily life so that we might be able to imagine the bodily life of others.[13] Diamond argues that too often philosophical argument is an attempt at "deflection," a term she borrows from Cavell to describe the way we make our bodies mere facts that may or may not be relevant to the

---

Stanley Cavell, Cora Diamond, John McDowell, Ian Hacking, and Cary Wolfe, *Philosophy and Animal Life* (New York: Columbia University Press, 2008), pp. 45-46.

12. Diamond, "The Difficulty of Reality," p. 47.

13. Diamond, "The Difficulty of Reality," p. 53.

issue at hand. Just as, when we consider the death of an animal, we refuse to think we have the capacity to inhabit its body in our imagination, so we cannot identify with the wounded body of Elizabeth Costello.[14]

Diamond's reading of Costello's speech is confirmed later in the novel by an exchange at the dinner at the faculty club. After a heated discussion about Costello's speech, the president of the college attempts to come to Costello's aid by observing that her vegetarianism demands respect, rooted as it must be in a firm moral conviction. But Costello refuses the compliment, observing, "No, I don't think so. . . . It comes out of a desire to save my soul." The president responds, nonetheless, expressing respect for her taking a strong moral position, but Costello again refuses the compliment, pointing out that she is wearing leather shoes and carrying a leather purse (p. 89).

Stephen Mulhall, whose book *The Wounded Animal* is an extended analysis of as well as meditation on Coetzee's novel and the subsequent philosophical debates it has produced, defends Diamond's reading of Coetzee's novel. Like Diamond, he thinks Coetzee is intent that we see that Costello is the wounded animal. She is wounded, her very sanity is under threat, because she is experiencing as a horror what is not so experienced by others. It is this alienation between herself and her fellow human beings that is inexplicable.

Her tenuous hold on reality is made even more tenuous by her use of Holocaust imagery to suggest that the killing of the Jews is analogous to our cruelty toward animals. For the horror of the camps was that those who did the killing, as well as those who lived in the areas surrounding the camps, refused to think themselves into the place of the victims. We might like to think that the Germans and the Poles, some of whom did and some of whom did not know of the killing, would have been haunted by their victims. But Costello argues that the evidence suggests they were not rendered helpless by guilt or shame. She takes that to mean that "we can do anything and get away with it; that there is no punishment" (p. 80).

Costello's use of the Holocaust is challenged by a poet, Abraham Stern, who was to be one of the participants the next day in a symposium on Costello's work. Stern writes Costello a respectful letter, explaining

---

14. Diamond, "The Difficulty of Reality," p. 59.

that he cannot appear with her because the suggestion that the Jews were treated like cattle does not mean it follows that cattle are treated like Jews. Commenting on this passage, Mulhall thinks Stern fails to see that Coetzee is using Costello's appeal to the Holocaust, a use that gives us a way of seeing reality to which Costello is blind, to show that we cannot "simultaneously use the Holocaust as an image for what we do to animals and retain a grip on the reality of the Holocaust itself, on what it shows us about what we are (inexplicably, agonizingly) capable of doing to other human beings." In short, Mulhall observes, just to the extent that we strive to keep one sort of difficulty of reality in view we cannot humanly see other horrors.[15]

Diamond ends her article by suggesting that Costello's depiction of our imaginative incapacity to inhabit the bodily existence of others is not unconnected to Stanley Cavell's lifelong engagement with skepticism. For Cavell, the very fact of skepticism is revealed by the problem created by the possibility of knowing that another is in pain, to which "certainty is not enough." Even if we "know" the other is in pain, the knowledge we have cannot be a function of certainty. Therefore to acknowledge the pain of another means that I give voice to the fact that the other's suffering makes a claim on me, but by doing so I reveal my powerlessness to do more than acknowledge the other's pain.[16]

15. Mulhall, *The Wounded Animal*, p. 70. Mulhall calls attention to Rai Gaita's argument, in Gaita's *Good and Evil: An Absolute Conception* (London: Macmillan, 1991; 2nd ed. 2005), that human beings are "absolutely or unconditionally precious or valuable in the sense that, no matter how profoundly evil their actions and character may be, they may never be killed in the spirit of ridding the world of vermin." Mulhall observes that this view is morally serious only if we are prepared to regard some actions as absolutely evil. Which means that no human being can be thought to be beyond remorse. That is, people who have done great evil should not be compelled to think of themselves as utterly worthless. They will, however, find what they have done essentially mysterious. They will not be able to understand what they have done, which means, according to Mulhall, that the existence of evil is both undeniable and yet beyond our comprehension. That such is the case is an expression "of the incomprehensible truth that it [evil] nevertheless exists in the world and so is something with which we can and do make contact in our experience." Mulhall thinks Costello's sense of absolute evil involves this sense of the mysterious. *The Wounded Animal*, pp. 205-6.

16. I am indebted to Pieter Vermeulen for this characterization of Cavell's views in his "Being True to Fact: Coetzee's Prose of the World," in *J. M. Coetzee and Ethics*, pp. 278-79. In *Cavell, Companionship, and Christian Theology* Peter Dula provides a com-

Diamond's calling attention to Cavell makes clear that she is not simply trying to suggest that it is difficult to be ethical. Such a suggestion would only reproduce rationalistic ethical convention. Rather, by the difficulty of reality she is trying to help us see how our brutality resides in what makes us human. That the slave owner could see the humanity of the slave yet remain a slave owner is but one instance of the difficulty of reality.

Diamond thinks that Cavell's attention to skepticism, his refusal to think that skepticism is to be or can be defeated, is but an expression of his attention to ordinary language. In particular, Cavell helps us see how difficult it is to bring words, as Ludwig Wittgenstein sought to do, back from their metaphysical to their everyday use. For it is in the everyday that we discover the hiddenness, the separateness, the otherness of the other. Skepticism, therefore, just is the difficulty we have, often the deflections we enact, to avoid wounded bodies like Elizabeth Costello's body.[17]

In an essay entitled "Companionable Thinking," in *Philosophy and Animal Life*, Cavell, with some qualifications, accepts Diamond's suggestion that his understanding of skepticism — that is, the chronic difficulty we have in expressing ourselves that is manifest in our difficulty with or disappointment with language — bears a family resemblance to her understanding of "the difficulty of reality."[18] Cavell, however, confesses that, without knowing the proper response to learning and knowing the existence of concentration camps, mass starvation, or hydrogen bombs, it is his "persistent feeling that a sense of shame at being human (at being stigmatized for having a human body) is more maddeningly directed

---

pelling account of the significance of "acknowledgment" for Cavell. In particular he helps us see how acknowledgment is a knowledge without possession (pp. 136-42).

17. Diamond, "The Difficulty of Reality," p. 77. Diamond's account of Cavell on skepticism is confirmed by Dula's analysis of Cavell. Dula observes that, for Cavell, "the question of skepticism is a question about the human. In his response to skepticism, Cavell continually circles back to the question of human nature and repeatedly identifies skepticism with a 'denial of the human.' He will also say that 'only a God, or the son of God, could bear being human.'" Skepticism in short is the denial of finitude and the human by trying to convert the condition of being human into an intellectual difficulty. Dula, *Cavell, Companionship, and Christian Theology*, pp. 167-68.

18. Stanley Cavell, "Companionable Thinking," in *Philosophy and Animal Life*, p. 101. Mulhall provides an illuminating analysis of Cavell's reaction to Diamond in *The Wounded Animal*, pp. 69-87, 91-94.

to the human treatment of human animals than to its treatment of its non-human neighbors."[19] He recognizes that we may actually be able to take personal measures to avoid cruelty to non-humans, but in the human case we sense our helplessness. But what then? he asks. "Shall we unblushingly publish our guilt in remaining sane in a mad world?"[20]

I see no reason why anyone should think we must choose between Diamond's concern with our cruelty toward animals and Cavell's sense that the cruelty we perpetrate on one another should more likely drive us to madness. I am, however, sympathetic with Cavell because at the very least his calling attention to our everyday inhumanity reminds us of those cruelties, cruelties such as war, which we take for granted. We may, as Paul Kahn observes, compliment ourselves for no longer approving of torture, but our general disapproval of torture hides from us that "the destruction of bodies in modern warfare moves toward a generalized practice of torture."[21] Yet the torture that war is seems necessary as a sacrificial practice to establish and legitimate the sovereignty of the state over matters of life and death.[22] In short, war, like the eating of animals, is a cruel everyday reality we literally cannot live without, making it impossible to acknowledge reality.

Acknowledging Difficulty: A Yoderian Response[23]

To interject war as the exemplification of Diamond's "difficulty of reality" may seem an attempt to avoid what she takes to be "difficult." After all, we are ethicists well versed in strategies that deflect the reality of

19. Cavell, "Companionable Thinking," p. 125.
20. Cavell, "Companionable Thinking," p. 126.
21. Paul W. Kahn, *Sacred Violence: Torture, Terror, and Sovereignty* (Ann Arbor: University of Michigan Press, 2008), p. 43.
22. Kahn, *Sacred Violence*, pp. 144-45.
23. I use the language of acknowledgment because I have learned from Peter Dula how important such language is for Cavell. As Dula puts it, "For Cavell, there is no acknowledgment without self-revelation. There is no acknowledgment of another that is not an acknowledgment of *my* relation with the other.... The self is implicated and must be recognized. It is not always easy to tell the difference between acknowledgment and individualism." *Cavell, Companionship, and Christian Theology*, pp. 182-83.

war. I may well represent such a strategy just to the extent that I am self-identified as an advocate of Christian nonviolence. Yet one of the frustrations with being so identified is that too often the identification tempts the one so committed as well as one's critics to think nothing more needs to be thought after one is declared to be nonviolent. Yet to be nonviolent does not make the difficulty of reality disappear. Indeed, it may intensify the difficulty, given that the nonviolent may have to watch the innocent suffer for their convictions.

In order to explore how we might respond to Diamond's "difficulty of reality" as Christian theologians, I want to direct our attention to another speech. In 1988 John Howard Yoder gave the presidential address at the Society of Christian Ethics. The speech was entitled "To Serve Our God and to Rule the World."[24] The title does not seem promising for a response to Diamond, suggesting as it might that service to God makes possible a rule of the world that does not take into account "the difficulty of reality." Yet I hope to show that, as Alex Sider has argued, Yoder's understanding of holiness requires the acknowledgment of difficulty not unlike the difficulty Diamond finds present in Costello's speech.[25]

I think it not unimportant that the dying Paul Ramsey listened to Yoder's presidential speech with rapt attention. Death and the difficulty of reality are not unrelated, which makes all the more significant the mutual respect Ramsey and Yoder had for one another, a respect born I think of the faith they shared and the care with which they went about the work of Christian ethics. That care was well on display in Yoder's address, which remains I believe one of the most eloquent statements we have that describes the work of Christian ethics. For I believe that Yoder helps us see what it means to know how to go on without the difficulty of reality being ignored or denied.

Yoder begins with the Apocalypse:

---

24. John Howard Yoder, "To Serve Our God and to Rule the World," in *The Royal Priesthood: Essays Ecclesiological and Ecumenical*, ed. Michael Cartwright (Grand Rapids: Eerdmans, 1994), pp. 128-40. Hereafter page references to this essay will appear in the text.

25. J. Alexander Sider, *To See History Doxologically: History and Holiness in John Howard Yoder's Ecclesiology* (Grand Rapids: Eerdmans, 2011), pp. 1-2.

They sang a new hymn:
"You are worthy to take the scroll and to break its seals
Because you were sacrificed and with your blood you bought
For God
people of every tribe and tongue, people and nation,
and made them a priestly royal lineage
to serve our God and to rule the world."   (5:9-10)

These lines from the Apocalypse, according to Yoder, provide the context that makes the work of Christian ethics not only necessary but possible. For according to Yoder all ethics, Christian and non-Christian, is in service to some cosmic commitment and, therefore, always embedded in larger life process. For Christians that cosmic commitment is expressed in praise of God, making it possible to see history doxologically (p. 129).

To see history doxologically does not mean that we have a handle on history.[26] To think we have a handle on history would deny the difficulty that seeing history doxologically creates. For to see history doxologically not only demands but also enables modes of witness that "explode" the limits of our systems through which we seek to be in control of the world. Apocalypse is not the only mode of discourse in the Christian tradition, but it is the discourse in which God is praised as the ruler of the world. To so praise God, given the way the world is and our lack of control over that world, is surely one of the most challenging forms of Christian discourse.

To be among those who praise God as the ruler of this world, however, has often tempted Christians to think they are or must be in control if this is in fact God's world. Caesar's throne can be or must be usurped to insure that justice be done. The difficulty of being a creature wounded by sin is forgotten. Indeed, we forget or deny that we are creatures subject to the illusions we create to insure our significance. As a result, we lose the necessities that create imaginative alternatives that make it possible for us to live without denying the difficult task of acknowledging our humanity and that of our neighbors.

---

26. For extensive reflection on Yoder's understanding of what it means not to have a handle on history, see Chris K. Huebner, "Unhandling History: Anti-Theory, Ethics and the Practice of Witness" (Ph.D diss., Duke University, 2001).

Yoder is often criticized for idealizing the early church, but he assumed that church was unfaithful in its own way. After all, he read the New Testament. What he found remarkable, however, is that, given the insignificance of the early church, it nonetheless claimed that "Jesus Christ is *kyrios*." The church did so because it rightly thought that is the way the world really is. But if that is the way the world really is, the church had the time to build an alternative way of life in a world that did not believe there is an alternative way of life.

For such a people to see history doxologically is not a pious declaration about their subjectivities but rather the way a community is empowered to discern in and through time more humane ways to live. " 'To rule the world' in fellowship with the living Lamb will sometimes mean humbly building a grassroots culture, with Jeremiah. Sometimes (as with Joseph and Daniel) it will mean helping the pagan king solve one problem at a time. Sometimes (again as with Daniel and his friends) it will mean disobeying the King's imperative of idolatry, refusing to be bamboozled by the claims made for the Emperor's new robe or his fiery furnace" (p. 135).

None of these alternatives is without difficulty. None of them is free of ambiguity. That is why they require a mutual accountability in the hope that our desire to justify ourselves does not lead, as it so often does, to self-deception. By being held accountable, moreover, we can develop criteria to help us discriminate between what has been helpful and what has been unhelpful. Being capable of such discernment is aided by the necessity to appropriate, as Jesus did, that most difficult of histories, that is, the Jewish record of ambivalence about kingship and exile (p. 133). Demands for accountability, demands that are constitutive of what it means to see history doxologically, provide space for a politics of democratic dialogue (p. 135). Therefore the development of more nearly democratic societies is not a matter of indifference, particularly if such developments do not forget in the name of progress that they must take the time necessary to listen to the weakest member.

To see history doxologically means we must learn to test our behavior by identifying our life with those descriptions we call "the beatitudes." Such an identification makes clear that what we do is to be judged not by the result of what we claim to bring about but by the shape of the

Kingdom Jesus has announced is now present. This does not mean that consequential reasoning does not have its uses, but such reasoning is inadequate if it is assumed that the future is a closed choice. In particular, such reasoning is inadequate when, in the name of the "human values at stake," the good of our enemies is excluded from consideration (p. 138). To refuse to exclude the enemy, a refusal at the heart of Martin Luther King Jr.'s witness, is to see history doxologically, requiring as it must the patience that the Lamb's victory has made possible (p. 137) — a reminder that progress in history is borne by the underdogs.

Perhaps the most demanding stance required if we are to see history doxologically is the refusal to rejoice that "somebody got what they had coming. Since Eden God is busy protecting people from what they have coming. God's glory transcends human confusion but neither needs it nor rejoices in it" (p. 138). Dietrich Bonhoeffer was right to warn us against "Methodism," that is, our desire to rejoice in people's humiliation because we perversely believe that their pain will further their salvation because God exalts the humble (p. 139).

Yoder ends his account of what it means to see history doxologically by reminding us that it is not Christian ethicists who rule the church or set the conditions for the meaningfulness of moral discourse. We do not determine the terms of sense-making. Rather, our vocation is vigilance against the abuse of words. Our task is not to determine, validate, or define what it means to say "Jesus is Lord." That is what we, as members of Christ's body, celebrate "as we participate in his priestly role and kingly rule by watching our words" (p. 140).

Yoder's account of what it means to see history doxologically is an expression of his claim in *The Politics of Jesus* that "the triumph of the right, although it is assured, is sure because of the power of the resurrection and not because of any calculation of causes and effects, nor because of the inherently greater strength of the good guys. The relationship between the obedience of God's people and the triumph of God's cause is not a relationship of cause and effect but one of cross and resurrection."[27] This is a powerful claim, one that some may think far too powerful just to

---

27. John Howard Yoder, *The Politics of Jesus: Vicit Agnus Noster*, 2nd ed. (Grand Rapids: Eerdmans, 1995), p. 232.

the extent that those making the claim may think a world so redeemed is no longer beset by "the difficulty of reality."

No one has made this challenge more forcefully than Alex Sider. Sider asks if "interpreting history as praise risks generating tremendous complacency in the face of injustice, violence, suffering, and death."[28] He worries that construing doxology as the definitive form of Christian participation in history may drown out the place of other voices in Scripture. Does praise threaten to make us ignore the voice of penitence, intercession, and lament? Does praise silence the cry for justice?

Sider does not deny that Yoder may not have always sufficiently guarded against these results. Yet he also argues that to so read Yoder, a reading that too often isolates Yoder's pacifism from his ecclesiology, fails to acknowledge Yoder's subordination of nonviolence to his attempt "to think the church as a *kenotic* politics and way of being in time that destabilized the borders between church and world, nevertheless without abolishing them."[29] Accordingly, Sider argues that Yoder's historical method, his understanding of the centrality of forgiveness for giving us a useable past when what was done was so wrong that it cannot be put right, means patience is always in jeopardy. He acknowledges that "the human capacity for misrecognizing the other, or of expatriating the other onto one's own terrain, and thus for potentially damaging relations of power and knowledge" always remains a risk for a church learning to see history doxologically.[30] To see history doxologically makes it possible to acknowledge "the difficulty of reality" without such an acknowledgment becoming a justification for violence.

Sider calls attention to Gillian Rose's epigraph in *Love's Work*, "Keep your mind in hell and despair not." Rose used this epigraph to counsel patience, yet it turned out to be a patience we cannot use. For Rose, our lives are broken in ways that threaten to call up inhuman responses that would repair our brokenness without leaving scars. Rose sought a politics that could produce a holiness in which the boundaries between self and other are erased. In contrast, Yoder's ecclesiology is an attempt to envision an

---

28. Sider, *To See History Doxologically*, p. 138.
29. Sider, *To See History Doxologically*, p. 12.
30. Sider, *To See History Doxologically*, p. 201.

ethics that necessarily involves corrigible institutions, but through social processes such as open meetings, forgiveness, and economic sharing, through sacramental processes, and through a real but difficult politics is made possible. The choice is not between difficulty and holiness; rather, the choice is to be a community in which holiness is difficulty.[31]

Bearing Reality

If I could choose any epigraph that might summarize what my work has been about, it would be "Keep your mind in hell and despair not." What I learned from Yoder, what I learned from Yoder learning from Barth, is that being Christian requires the recognition of "the difficulty of reality." We are suffering creatures whose suffering tempts us to be more than we are, which insures that we will be less than we were created to be. We create hells for ourselves and for others fueled by false hopes anchored in the presumption of our significance. We are wounded by sin, we are wounded by our illusions of control, we are wounded by our inability to acknowledge the wounds our desperate loves inflict on ourselves and on others.

One may well wonder if the language "the difficulty of reality" is, as my use of the phrase suggests, another way to talk about sin. Elizabeth Costello even resorts to the language of sin as she reflects on the guilt of the average German for Hitler's wars. She observes, "In Germany, we say, a certain line was crossed which took people beyond the ordinary murderousness and cruelty of warfare into a state we can only call sin. The signing of the articles of capitulation and the payment of reparations did not put an end to that state of sin. On the contrary, we said, a sickness of soul continued to mark that generation. . . . Only those in the camps were innocent."[32]

We, that is, those of us schooled by Reinhold Niebuhr, know Costello should not restrict the attribution of sin to the Germans. All are, to employ Niebuhr's compelling but confused claim, equally sinful but not all

31. Sider, *To See History Doxologically*, p. 205.
32. Coetzee, *Elizabeth Costello*, p. 64.

are equally guilty. I have no reason to think the language of sin may be appropriate to account for "the difficulty of reality," but I think the recourse to sin can give the impression that sin provides some kind of explanation for what Diamond understands to be "the difficulty of reality." If sin does function as an explanation then a mistake has been made, because that reality Diamond describes defies explanation.[33] That is why her account of Costello is so haunting.

Yet we should not despair. We are Christians. We believe we have been redeemed. We believe history can be seen doxologically. These are bold words used boldly in the hope that so used we will not be tempted to recognize that we are unsure what we say. We fear that the very claims we make about our redemption cannot help but give us a sense of unreality. Given the reality of the world in which we find ourselves, such language can easily be seen to do no work. If ever there was a language that seems to be on a holiday, "to see history doxologically" seems a ready candidate.

Yet Yoder's parsing of what it means to see history doxologically, I believe, makes it possible for us to recognize realistically the difficulty of reality and yet be able to go on. For Yoder never promised us a rose garden. Rather, he calls attention to what God has made possible by calling us to acknowledge our wounds and the wounds of others without that acknowledgment becoming justification for our attempts to make ourselves invulnerable.

It is true that humankind cannot bear much reality, but too often "humankind" is the name we give to our assumption that we must bear the burden of our self-inflicted wounds alone.

But we are not alone. That we are able to see history doxologically, as Yoder suggests, reflects our discovery that we have been called into a

---

33. Jason Mahn puts this better than I have when he observes, "Against all efforts to contextualize and moralize sin — to situate it within a closed economy of salvation — Kierkegaard has sin contextualize us. Unable to say what he or she means about sin, the reader is left only to confess it. And even if the confession that 'I am a sinner' would then seem to comprise the most primary and transparent (Derrida would say logocentric) of theological speech . . . Kierkegaard makes clear that it too is thoroughly ironic. . . . At its most basic linguistic level, *felix culpa* marks the incommensurability between Christian salvation and moral innocence, deconstructing the modern moralization of sin." *Fortunate Fallibility: Kierkegaard and the Power of Sin* (New York: Oxford University Press, 2011), p. 209.

community unimaginable if Christ has not been raised from the dead. We do not bear reality alone, but rather we share the load by being called to participate in the body of Christ.

I am obviously trying to avoid saying "church." I am trying to avoid saying "church" because to say "church" can sound like a "solution" to the challenge "the difficulty of reality" presents. Toward the end of a year-long course in which Wittgenstein was read as well as philosophical and theological responses to Wittgenstein, a student, influenced by Cavell's arguments that it is a philosophical mistake to think that skepticism can be defeated philosophically, asked me if by analogy to Cavell's understanding of philosophy I thought there is something the church cannot do. I answered that there is indeed something the church cannot do. The church cannot make the difficulty of reality less difficult. What I hope the church can do, a hope that I think is the heart of Yoder's work, is help us bear the difficulty without engaging in false hopes.

To be a Christian has never meant that we cease to be human beings. To be a Christian does not mean we are endowed with virtues that empower us to bear the terrors of this life without difficulty. We are human beings. We are inheritors of histories that involve cruelties so horrible there can be no way to make what was done undone. For those of us who have survived without being too scarred by the past, the temptation is to relieve our guilt for so surviving by identifying with those who have paid the price for our survival. Yet too often such tactics fail to acknowledge that those more injured than we are also face the difficulty of reality.

What, if anything, does any of this have to do with the work of the Society of Christian Ethics? I think this. Let us be a society that refuses to give easy answers to the difficulty of reality. Let us be a society that does not fear questions to which we do not know the answer. Let us be a society that would listen to the challenge raised by people like Elizabeth Costello. In short, let us be a society whose members strive to tell one another the truth about the difficulties of reality. For I believe if we do so we may discover we have something to say to a world that no longer believes that anyone can speak the truth.

Habit Matters:
The Bodily Character of the Virtues

Why Habits Matter according to Aristotle

I am a theologian and an ethicist. I have never liked the "and" because I think theology done well is a discipline of practical reason. I also do not like to be known as an ethicist. To be so identified invites questions that can drive you mad. For example, some think that if you teach "ethics" you must be able to answer questions such as "Why should I be moral?" That kind of question seems equivalent to the response offered by many when they discover the person they have just met is a minister. Such a discovery often elicits the confession, "I have been meaning to go to church again, but I find that walking in the woods is how I really connect with God."

This confession is meant to be a challenge to those in the ministry to show why this sensitive soul should go to church. But people who present such challenges fail to understand that any minister who knows what he or she is about would find any attempt to answer them on their own terms uninteresting. How could you even begin to help people understand that the god they find in the woods is probably not the God the church worships? In a similar way, I find the question "Why should I be moral?" not only uninteresting but misleading. Any attempt to answer the question cannot help but confirm the presumption that morality is a clearly identifiable set of principles about right or wrong acts.

It took me some years, but I finally learned to respond to those who wanted me to convince them of why they should be moral with the question "Do you like to eat?" To ask that question challenges the presumption, a presumption legitimated by Kantian-inspired ethical theory, that a clear distinction can be drawn between ethics and, for example, manners at the dinner table. I also think "Do you like to eat?" is a good response because it reminds my questioner that we are bodily creatures whose desires pull us into the significant engagements that constitute our lives.

Of course, "significance" may be a description of those aspects of our lives rightly associated with being moral. In other words, the attempt to distinguish morality from other aspects of our lives may entail judgments about what we take to be significant. I have no objection to such a suggestion as long as those who make it remember that eating is one of the most significant things we do.

I should like to think that the response "Do you like to eat?" owes something to my early attempt to develop an account of character that would help us better understand what it might mean to live well. *Character and the Christian Life* was published in 1975.[1] I made many mistakes in the book, but I had at least begun to grasp that the dualism between body and agency, so characteristic of much of moral theory at the time, could not be sustained if you attended to character and the virtues. Influenced by Ludwig Wittgenstein, G. E. M. Anscombe, and Gilbert Ryle, I was trying to avoid accounts of agency that presumed that our ability to act requires an account of autonomy or the will that was not bodily determined.

Yet as I acknowledged in the introduction to a later edition of *Character and the Christian Life*, the account of agency I developed in that book, an account I thought necessary to avoid behaviorism, came close to reproducing the dualism between body and agency I was trying to avoid.[2] I had tried to develop an account of agency by presuming that conceptual primitive notion was "action," rather than, as I later learned from Alasdair MacIntyre's account in *After Virtue*, that "intelligible action," not action, is the determinative notion if we are to properly understand agency.[3] Though I think

1. Stanley Hauerwas, *Character and the Christian Life* (San Antonio: Trinity University Press, 1975).
2. Stanley Hauerwas, *Character and the Christian Life* (Notre Dame: University of Notre Dame Press, 1985).
3. For my discussion of this issue see the introduction of *Character and the Christian Life* (1985), pp. xix-xxi.

that was a step in the right direction, I find it interesting that one of the mistakes I did not acknowledge in the 1985 edition of the book, and I think it is a mistake that was implicated in my understanding of agency, was my failure to develop the significance of habit for any account of the virtues.

To be sure, I had a brief account of habit in which I tried to suggest that Aristotle and Aquinas had a richer account of habit than the modern relegation of habit to the unreflective aspects of our lives.[4] I even footnoted George Klubertanz's still very important book *Habits and Virtues*, in which he had drawn on then recent work in psychology to develop an account of habit that distinguished complex from simple habits.[5] But it is still the case that in my early work on character and the virtues I did not develop an account of habit that is surely necessary for an adequate account of the virtues.

At least, such an account is required for anyone who would draw upon the work of Aristotle and Aquinas. For I should like to think that a question such as "Do you like to eat?" is one Aristotle might have appreciated, given the way he explores happiness in Book One of the *Nicomachean Ethics*. There Aristotle observes that, even though many — that is, those whom he calls the uncultivated — may associate happiness with pleasure, wealth, or honor, such goods cannot make us happy because they are so easily lost.[6] To begin by asking people if they like to eat is a way to remind us that our desire to eat pulls us into life in such a manner that we cannot fail to discover there is more to life than eating.[7]

---

4. Hauerwas, *Character and the Christian Life* (1985), p. 69. Of course, that way of stating the problem, that is, how to distinguish the kind of habituation the virtues name from the unreflective aspects of our lives, reproduces presumptions that need to be challenged for a proper understanding of habituation. It is no accident that baseball players must "unreflectively" throw and catch the ball numerous times in order to respond "without thinking" to a ball hit to them or to a throw from another fielder. Such habits are skills that make possible complex forms of action that require equally complex retrospective descriptions if we are to say what "happened."

5. George Klubertanz, *Habits and Virtues: A Philosophical Analysis* (New York: Appleton, Century, Crofts, 1965).

6. Aristotle, *Nicomachean Ethics*, trans. Terence Irwin (Indianapolis: Hackett Publishing Company, 1999), 1095a15-1095b10. Hereafter references to the *Nicomachean Ethics* will appear in the text.

7. I use the language of "pull" to resist the presumption that "habits" are "efficient

It is, therefore, never a question whether we will or will not develop habits and virtues, but what kinds of habits and virtues we will develop. We are complex creatures constituted, according to Aristotle, by non-rational as well as rational capacities. The non-rational, however, in some way "shares in reason" just to the extent that the non-rational is capable of being habituated (1102b15-1103a10). We eat by necessity, but how we eat is determined by habits that the necessity of our eating requires if we are to eat as human beings.

For Aristotle, our nature requires that we acquire a second nature that is constituted by habits. Habits come, moreover, in all shapes and sizes, requiring that we develop some habits that make possible our acquisition of other habits. Aristotle often directed attention to how one learned to ride a horse or wrestle to suggest how, through repetition, our bodies acquire the habits that make complex activities seem "effortless."[8] Indeed, Aristotle not only thought learning to ride or to wrestle to be a good way to begin to acquire habits necessary for the moral life; he thought such activities *were* what taught the young to become virtuous.[9]

Aristotle also thought how one becomes proficient in a craft to be quite similar to how one acquires the habits necessary to become a person of virtue. Just as we learn a craft by repetitively producing the same product that was produced when we first were learning the craft, so we become virtuous by performing actions that are virtuous. But the analogy with the crafts can be misleading because the relation between the actions that produce the habits that make us virtuous are constitutive of the habit in the way the product produced by the craftsman is not (1105a25-35). According to Aristotle, like actions produce like virtues, but to determine "likeness" is a complex process that presumes common judgments.

That is why Aristotle argues that legislators must attend to the training of citizens in the virtues by instilling good habits. A good politic, according to Aristotle, must aim through the law to instill in citizens the

causes." For Aristotle and Aquinas, we are purposive beings capable of acquiring a history through the acquisition of habits.

8. For an insightful account of habit as effortless see Samuel Wells, *Improvisation: The Drama of Christian Ethics* (Grand Rapids: Brazos, 2004), pp. 73-82.

9. There is obviously a hierarchy that should determine the acquisition of habits in order that we become what we do. How such a hierarchy is to be understood, however, may well vary from one tradition to another. I suspect such a hierarchy, in order to be spelled out, will require a narrative display.

habits necessary for the development of the virtues. For it is crucial that the young acquire early in their lives the right habits. That they do so is not just very important; it is all-important. It is so because if we fail to acquire the right habits rightly, we will have a character that is incapable of acting in a manner that makes us virtuous (1103b1-25).

Jennifer Herdt observes that Aristotle's insistence on the significance of early formation of a virtuous person is wrapped in what she characterizes as "the mystery of habituation."[10] The "mystery," Herdt identifies, is how the habits children acquire are at once necessary but not sufficient for their becoming virtuous. For children often learn what they should or should not do for reasons that are not the morally compelling reasons for why they should or should not do what they do. They are, for example, told not to be unkind to their brother or sister because "I said so."

Herdt observes, however, that the transition from obeying authority to the acquisition of the habits of virtue is aided by our instinctual desire to imitate our elders. She does not think our instinct for imitation is sufficient to make us virtuous, but by imitating those who act virtuously we can at least begin to acquire the habits that will produce a firm and unchanging character. Such a character is required if we are to be the kind of person who can act in such a manner that what we do is not different than what we are.[11]

The problem is, how do we make the transition from habits acquired by imitation to the habits necessary for us to be virtuous, that is, habits that are formed by our having chosen what we have done in the manner in which a just or temperate person would act? Herdt suggests that if one's desires are to be transformed into those of a virtuous person, then not only must the person acting enjoy what he or she does but also the enjoyment that accompanies the act must be elicited by the love of the one the person imitates.[12] I feel quite sure that there is great wisdom in

10. Jennifer Herdt, *Putting on Virtue: The Legacy of the Splendid Vices* (Chicago: University of Chicago Press, 2008), p. 25.

11. Herdt, *Putting on Virtue*, p. 26. Aristotle suggests that persons who would act in such a manner that, so acting, they become virtuous must act in such a manner that they know what they do as well as acting from a "firm and unchanging state" (1105a-10).

12. Herdt, *Putting on Virtue*, p. 28.

Herdt's suggestion that the relations in which the habits are formed make a great deal of difference, but that still does not seem sufficient to understand how the acquisition of habits is sufficient for making the transition to being a person of virtue.[13]

In order to explore how we might think further about the "mystery of habituation," I want to direct our attention to Aquinas's development of Aristotle on habit. I do so because I think Aquinas provides a richer account of the kinds of habits necessary for our becoming persons of virtue. Aquinas's understanding of habituation does not "solve" all the questions associated with a stress on the kinds of habits necessary for the development of the virtues, but I hope to show that in drawing on Aristotle's work he helps us better understand the process of habituation.

Aquinas on Habituation

Aquinas develops his account of habit in the appropriately entitled "Treatise on Habits" in the Prima Secundae of the *Summa Theologica*.[14] I call attention to the title because the "Treatise on Habits" includes not only Aquinas's account of the habits but also his initial account of the virtues: his understanding of how the virtues are individuated as well as inter-

13. In an essay responding to the second edition of *The Blackwell Companion to Christian Ethics* entitled "The Virtue of the Liturgy," Herdt observes that a focus on the virtues does not play a prominent role in most of the essays in the *Blackwell Companion*. She argues that this is appropriate because we have come to recognize that the virtues are not individual achievements but can be sustained only in the context of a community. Accordingly, the task of Christian ethics is not to promote a virtue ethic but to show how the virtues are in service to growth in human friendship with God. Therefore the virtues are not ends in themselves but are constitutive of the life we are called to live with one another and with God. The focus on the liturgy is one way to suggest how an "imaginative grasp of the whole form of life in which one's own activity participates" is required if we are to have the capacity to extrapolate from one situation to another what we must do if we are to act, for example, with courage. Jennifer Herdt, "The Virtue of the Liturgy," in *The Blackwell Companion to Christian Ethics*, ed. Stanley Hauerwas and Samuel Wells, 2nd ed. (Oxford: Wiley-Blackwell, 2011), pp. 536-37.

14. Thomas Aquinas, *Summa Theologica*, trans. the Fathers of the English Province (Westminster, MD: Christian Classics, 1981). Hereafter references to the *Summa Theologica* will appear in the text.

connected, the role of the gifts of the Spirit, and the nature of sin and the vices. The latter is particularly important to insure that we not forget that the vices are also habits. That the "Treatise on Habits" includes what in effect is the outline of Aquinas's understanding of the Christian moral life indicates how important habituation was for Aquinas.

Yet it is equally important to recognize that the "Treatise on the Last End" had preceded the "Treatise on Habits." The "Treatise on the Last End" begins with the claim that humans differ from the irrational animals because as creatures who possess will and reason we can be masters of our actions (I-II, 1). "Mastery" is Aquinas's description of what it means for us to be able to act in such a manner that what we do and who we are are inseparable. It is this ability that enables us to acquire the habits necessary for the virtuous life. Aquinas will distinguish between the intellectual and moral virtues, but it is crucial to note that both the intellectual and moral virtues must be habituated in such a manner that they cannot be separated from one another (I-II, 58, 2).

Aquinas develops his account of our ability to act in such a manner that habits are formed which make us virtuous by introducing a concept unknown to Aristotle, that is, the will. The will is a rational appetite that makes possible our ability to act in such a manner that our actions, by being directed by reason, become our own (I-II, 8, 1). It is extremely important that he not be read, as he is often read, to suggest that the will and reason are independent capacities. The exact opposite is the case. For example, in his fine-grained account of what makes an act an act Aquinas observes, "acts of the reason and of the will can be brought to bear on one another, insofar as the reason reasons about willing and the will wills to reason so that the result is that the act of the reason precedes the act of the will, and conversely. And since the power of the preceding act continues in the act that follows, it happens sometimes that there is an act of the will insofar as it retains in itself something of the act of reason; and conversely, that there is an act of the reason insofar as it retains in itself something of the act of the will" (I-II, 1).

For Aquinas, the will and reason are interdependent because every act of the will is preceded by an act of the intellect, but it is also the case that an act of the intellect is preceded by an act of the will (I-II, 4, 4, ad 2). Accordingly, Aquinas does not invite the presumption that habit is the result of the will being tamed by reason. Rather, as Herdt suggests, for Aquinas reason and will are "formed in tandem through habituation; the will must learn to conform reliably to reason's grasp of the good."[15] But reason's grasp of the good depends on the will being disposed to the good through habit.[16]

Aquinas uses the language of the soul, but it should be clear, given his account of the will and reason, that the soul and the body are inseparable. The soul names for Aquinas that we are bodies destined by our desires to be befriended by God. Accordingly, he understands reason to be rational desire and will to be desiring reason. We are creatures shaped by our desires, desires as basic as our desire to eat, to have a last end. By being so determined we necessarily acquire habits through our actions shaped by our desires.

Aquinas does not think, therefore, that we are souls who happen to have a body, nor that we are bodies who have a soul. Rather, Aquinas thinks we are ensouled bodies.[17] That is why he says that a living body is of a different species than a dead body (I-II, 18, 5 ad l).[18] Aquinas under-

---

15. Herdt, *Putting on Virtue*, p. 83. Herdt supports her interpretation by calling attention to I-II, 56, 3.

16. In his book *The Soul of the Person: A Contemporary Philosophical Psychology* (Washington, DC: Catholic University of America Press, 2006), Adrian J. Reimers draws on C. S. Peirce to develop an account of habit, and in particular, the habituation of will and reason through act, quite similar to my account of Aquinas on will and reason. Reimers emphasizes the bodily character of all action but observes, "because the act falls under a general description, it admits of development into or subsumption under a habit. We may say that every act, every purposeful motion is at least a nascent habit. It is precisely because of this that the development of habits is even possible" (p. 166). Accordingly, reasoning itself is a set of habits "by which human beings represent things to themselves as possibly true or false" (p. 111). Though the will is infinite in scope, it must be habituated if we are to be capable of self-determination (p. 161). Reimers's book is a gold mine for anyone who would reflect on these matters.

17. Fergus Kerr suggests that Aquinas's understanding of the body as the form of the soul is quite close to Wittgenstein's remark in the *Philosophical Investigations* (2, 152) that "the human body is the best picture of the human soul." See Kerr's *"Work on Oneself": Wittgenstein's Philosophical Psychology* (Arlington, VA: Institute for the Psychological Sciences Press, 2008), p. 94.

18. Alasdair MacIntyre, without referencing Aquinas, argues that "a corpse is not a human body, just because it no longer has the unity of a human body. The unity of a human body is evidenced on the one hand in the coordination of its voluntary and directed movements, in a way in which different series of movements by eye and hand are directed to one and the same end and in the ways in which movement towards a

stands the soul as the animating principle of the body; but, following Aristotle, the soul is also the form of the body. Dana Dillon nicely characterizes Aquinas's view this way: "the soul is the principle of life in the body, and the organizing principle or form of the whole person" (I, 76, 5).[19]

The significance of our bodies for how we understand the habituation of our desires is particularly evident in Aquinas's account of the role of the passions. Aristotle had suggested that virtue is about pleasure and pain (1104b15-1105a15), but Aquinas provides an extended account of the passions that enriches how pleasure and pain are understood.[20] In the process we are better able to appreciate how the passions at once make the habituation of our bodies not only possible but necessary. For, in the words of Kent Dunnington, habits turn out to be "strategies of desire."[21]

---

range of different ends is directed, and on the other in the coordination of its nonvoluntary and nonintentional movements. No such teleology, no such directedness, and certainly no voluntariness characterizes the movements of a corpse." "What Is a Human Body?" in Alasdair MacIntyre, *The Tasks of Philosophy: Selected Essays*, vol. 1 (Cambridge: Cambridge University Press, 2006), p. 88.

19. Dana Dillon, "As Soul to Body: The Interior Act of the Will in Thomas Aquinas and the Importance of First-Person Perspective in Accounts of Moral Action" (Ph.D. diss., Duke University, 2008), p. 20.

20. For the best contemporary treatment of Aquinas's account of the passions see Robert Miner, *Thomas Aquinas on the Passions* (Cambridge: Cambridge University Press, 2009). Miner notes that even though Aquinas dedicates Questions 22-48 of the Prima Secundae of the *Summa* to the passions, his "Treatise on the Passions" remains the most neglected of his corpus. This neglect, Miner suggests, may well be due to the Kantian reading habits so dominant in our time. See for example John Milbank, "Hume versus Kant: Faith, Reason, and Feeling," *Modern Theology* 27, no. 2 (April 2011): 276-97. Milbank observes that "Hume broke with rationalism by empirically observing that reflection cannot seriously separate itself from habit and that even the most basic assumed stabilities (substance, the self, causation) depend upon habit and not upon sheer intuited 'givenness.' But he also began to break with empiricism by allowing (albeit in a highly reserved fashion) that, in being slaves to habit, human beings must acknowledge the workings of a natural power that exceeds our capacity to observe it" (p. 281). This issue of *Modern Theology* consists of papers written for a conference put together by Sarah Coakley, dedicated to exploring the role of the passions for our understanding of faith and reason. Other papers from the same conference appear in *Faith and Philosophy* 28, no. 1 (January 2011). Together these papers are extremely important for the development of issues raised in this essay.

21. Kent Dunnington, *Addiction and Virtue: Beyond the Models of Disease and Choice* (Downers Grove, IL: InterVarsity, 2011). Dunnington credits this way of putting the matter to Paul Wadell.

Aquinas provides a more nuanced account of the passions than Aristotle does. The passions for Aquinas are movements of the sensitive appetite and are therefore to be distinguished from the desires that constitute our animal and rational appetites. Sensitive appetites are quite simply inclinations toward some good that is perceived as pleasant. Aquinas further distinguishes the concupiscible passions from the irascible passions. The passions that "regard good or evil absolutely, belong to the concupiscible power; for instance, joy, sorrow, love, hatred and such like: whereas those passions which regard good or bad as arduous, through being difficult to obtain or avoid, belong to the irascible faculty; such are daring, fear, hope and the like" (I-II, 23, 1). The concupiscible and irascible passions are, so to speak, the engine that pulls the body into engagements by which the acquisition of habits is not only necessary but possible, befitting a being who is destined to have a history.[22]

Given his account of the passions, we can say that to be human for Aquinas is to be a body destined by love. We are created to be creatures of desire for goods known through reason and will, making us agents through the acquisition of habits. Aquinas observes that the very word "passion" "implies that the patient is drawn to that which belongs to the agent" (I-II, 2). We are moved movers because we are creatures created to be capable of love made evident by our capacity for joy, sorrow, and hatred. That we are beings constituted by such desires, such hopes, means, for example, that courage requires that we will need to be daring, given the fears that our loves create (I-II, 23, 1).

The passions so understood are the condition of the possibility for

---

22. MacIntyre puts it this way: "Agency is exercised through time. To be an agent is not to engage in a series of discrete, unconnected actions. It is to pursue ends, some closer at hand in time, some more remote, some to be achieved for their own sake, some for the sake of furthering some end, and some for both. And to pass from youth through middle age toward death characteristically involves changes in and revisions of one's ends. Furthermore the ends that one pursues through sometimes extended periods of time are often not only one's own, but are ends shared with others, ends to be achieved only through the continuing cooperation of others, ends to be achieved only through the continuing cooperation of others or ends that are constituted by the ongoing participation of others. And so the exercise of the powers of the body through time in the exercise of agency requires a variety of types of engagements with others." "What Is a Human Body?" p. 100.

the habitual perfection of a power.[23] Thus Aquinas's contention that the moral virtues such as temperance and courage, that is, the virtues that form the concupiscent and irascible passions, do so by drawing on movements that constitute those passions (I-II, 59, 5).[24] This claim may seem too obvious to mention unless one remembers that such an understanding of actions that instill the habits necessary for our acquiring the virtues stands in marked contrast with the Stoic contention that the passions are to be if possible suppressed.[25] In contrast to the Stoics, Aquinas argues that the presence of the passions is a sign of the "intensity of the will," indicating a greater moral goodness than would be the case if the passions were absent (I-II, 24, 3).

Aquinas, drawing on Aristotle, describes habit as "a disposition whereby that which is disposed is disposed well or ill, and this, either in regard to itself or in regard to another: thus health is a habit" (I-II, 49, 1). In particular, habits are those qualities that are not easily changed, for the very word "habit" suggests a lastingness that the word "disposition" does not.[26] The enduring quality of habits is the result of their relation to acts

23. Miner, *Thomas Aquinas on the Passions*, p. 289.

24. Aquinas observes that the body is ruled by the soul just as the irascible and concupiscible powers are ruled by reason, but he notes that the irascible and concupiscible powers do not obey reason blindly because "they have their own proper movements" (I-II, 56, 4, ad 3).

25. Martha Nussbaum has argued that the Stoics did not think all passions are to be eliminated but only those that are "subrational stirrings coming from our animal nature," which can be "cured" by a philosophical therapy. See her *The Therapy of Desire: Theory and Practice in Hellenistic Ethics* (Princeton: Princeton University Press, 1994), pp. 366-72.

26. It would be a fascinating study to compare how William James and Aquinas understand the nature and significance of habit. Some might think James's account of habit too "biological" compared to Aquinas, but I hope I have at least suggested that habits for Aquinas are rooted at least initially in our most basic desires. I do not think Aquinas would dispute James's understanding of habit "from the physiological point of view" as "but a new pathway of discharge formed in the brain, but which certain incoming currents ever after tend to escape." James, "Habit," in *The Heart of William James*, ed. Robert Richardson (Cambridge, MA: Harvard University Press, 2010), p. 102. Aquinas would have also been in agreement with James's observation that we are born with a tendency to do more things than the ready-made arrangements of our nerve centers can handle; thus the need for habits. Aquinas might, however, have challenged James's suggestion that habit diminishes the conscious attention by which our actions are performed. It all depends on what you might mean by "conscious."

that are done in such a manner that they make the agent good as well as the act good.

Aquinas follows Aristotle in suggesting that like habits are formed by like acts (I-II, 50, 1). Aquinas provides, however, an account of actions that enriches Aristotle's understanding of choice and the voluntary. In particular, Aquinas introduces the notion of intention, which is crucial for him to make clear how the means used to achieve an end are constitutive of the end that is pursued. Thus the "intention of the end is the same movement as the willing of the means" (I-II, 12, 4). The reason this is so important is that it helps us see how, at least if we are to act in such a manner that our actions form habits that are virtuous, the very description of the act and the character of the agent are mutually implicated. Thus Aquinas's argument that "consent" is crucial for an act to be an act, that is, the necessity of persons "to approve and embrace the judgment of their counsel" (I-II, 15, 3).

Our habituation is necessary because our appetitive powers, our desires, are underdetermined. Aquinas observes that the will by its very nature is inclined to the good of reason, but because this good is varied the will needs to be inclined by habit to some good fixed by reason so that the action may follow more readily (I-II, 50, 5, ad 3). We are beings who need habituation because, as we have seen, we are composed of potentiality and act, making it necessary to be one thing rather than another. We need habits. God does not.[27]

---

27. Félix Ravaisson in his extraordinary book *Of Habit* (London: Continuum, 2008) provides an account of the metaphysics of habit. Ravaisson's book was written in 1838 in French, but only recently translated. That may account for why this important book has been so overlooked. Ravaisson observes, for example, "that habit is not an external necessity of constraint, but a necessity of attraction and desire. It is, indeed, a *law of the limbs*, which follows on from the freedom of the spirit. But this law is a *law of grace*. It is the final cause that increasingly predominates over efficient causality and which absorbs the latter into itself. And at that point, indeed, the end and the principle, the fact and the law, are fused together within necessity" (p. 57). Though the language is foreign to Aquinas, I suspect the fundamental intuition to be quite similar to Aquinas's understanding of grace. Later Ravaisson suggests that "Nature lies wholly in desire, and desire, in turn, lies in the good that attracts it. In this way the profound words of a profound theologian might be confirmed: 'Nature is prevenient grace.' It is God within us. God hidden solely by being so far within us in this intimate source of ourselves, to whose depths we do not descend" (p. 71; quoting Fénelon).

Habits are the result of repeated actions because the appetitive faculty can oppose the formation of settled dispositions. But a habit can be directed to a good act in two ways. In the first sense, a person can acquire, for example, the habit of grammar to speak correctly, but grammar does not ensure that the person will always speak correctly, which means the person may sometimes be guilty of a barbarism. But a habit in the second sense may confer not only aptness to act but also the right use of that aptness. Thus the virtue of justice not only gives a person a ready will to do just actions but also makes the person just by the ability to act justly.[28]

Therefore to have the habits of the second kind means that a person not only does the good but is good. Moreover, "since virtue is that which makes its possessor good, and his work good likewise, the latter habits are called virtuous simply; because they make the work to be actually good, and the subject good simply" (I-II, 56, 3). Such is the character of what Aquinas identifies as the acquired moral virtues, that is, the cardinal virtues of courage, temperance, justice, and prudence. These virtues dispose us to act for our end insofar as that end can be known by reason, but we have an ultimate end, friendship with God, that exceeds our nature (I-II, 51, 4). To be put on the road to that end we need the infused theological virtues of faith, hope, and charity.

Just as the moral virtues cannot be without prudence and prudence cannot be without the moral virtues, it is also true that the acquired moral virtues cannot be fully virtues without charity. Thus Aquinas's claim that only the infused virtues are perfect since they direct us to our ultimate end, but the acquired virtues are virtues in a restricted sense because they direct us to some particular end (I-II, 65, 2). Aquinas therefore claims that with charity all the virtues are given to us, including what he calls the "infused moral virtues" (I-II, 65, 3). That Aquinas makes this turn may seem to make unclear why he had spent so much time developing his account

---

28. Justice, according to Aquinas, is an operative virtue. He uses that language because justice is not clearly correlative to a passion, but rather suggests the habitual formation of the will. Justice, like friendship, is the qualification of a relation. Such a "qualification" is surely habitual, but what the habit qualifies is not clearly named by Aquinas. The "qualification" entails the formation of practical reason, but surely more needs to be said.

of habit. Given his account of the infused moral virtues, one can only wonder what to make of the acquired moral virtues.[29] Does the introduction of the infused moral virtues make Aquinas's account of habituation irrelevant?

These are complex matters of interpretation of Aquinas's understanding of the Christian life. But I think Sheryl Overmyer is right to suggest that, in introducing the infused moral virtues, Aquinas does not leave behind the importance of habit and the acquired virtues. Rather, the infused moral virtues lack what only the acquired virtues can supply, that is, the pleasure that comes from acting well.[30] The infused moral virtues — that is, the virtues formed by charity — provide the habits that make us capable of living lives of joy.

John Milbank, in a manner not unlike Overmyer's, suggests that Aquinas sees that our acquired "natural" habits are approximations of supernatural infused habits. All habits in order to be habits require ongoing development, but in order to become a habit the acquired habits must, so to speak, be made more than they can be on their own by the gift of the Holy Spirit. Accordingly, "habit as fundamental is only explicable as grace, and . . . for this reason the grace of eternal life which we receive again through Christ — a supernatural infused habit as Aquinas puts it — is, although superadded, paradoxically the most fundamental ontological reality in the universe: the undying force of life itself."[31]

To rightly interpret Aquinas on these matters requires that we not forget that he assumes we are always on the way to being virtuous. Thus his favorite metaphor for the moral life is that we are wayfarers who are on a journey of the soul to God. Accordingly, the distinction that most determinatively informs his account of the virtues is that between the

---

29. For a good account of these issues see Bonnie Kent, *Virtues of the Will: The Transformation of Ethics in the Late Thirteenth Century* (Washington, DC: Catholic University of America Press, 1995), pp. 24-38.

30. Sheryl Overmyer, *The Wayfarer's Way and Two Guides for the Journey: The Summa Theologiae and Piers Plowman* (Durham, NC: Duke University Press, 2010), p. 91. Aquinas says, "acts produced by an infused habit do not cause a habit, but strengthen the habit already existing, just as medicinal treatment given to a man who is naturally healthy does not cause a healthy condition, but invigorates the health he already has" (I-II, 51, 4).

31. Milbank, "Hume versus Kant," p. 288.

imperfect and perfect virtues.[32] That we are "on the way" to being virtuous means, therefore, that though we may have acquired the habits to be, for example, temperate, unless those habits are shaped by a more determinative way of life they may be a semblance of virtue rather than the virtue itself.

Aquinas observes, for example, that a miser may appear to be prudent and even to have the virtue of temperance. For the miser may think the satisfaction of lust costs too much. But to have the habits of prudence and temperance determined by the fear of losing control of our wealth cannot be what it means to be virtuous (II-II, 23, 7). Accordingly, we must acquire the habits necessary for us to be virtuous in such a manner that the virtues "qualify one another by a kind of overflow." For just as prudence overflows into all the other virtues, each of the virtues overflows to the others in such a manner that one who can curb his desires for pleasure of touch, which is a very hard thing to do, will also be more able to check his daring in dangers of death so he will not go too far. In this way "temperance is said to be brave, by reason of fortitude overflowing into temperance; in so far, to wit, as he whose mind is strengthened by fortitude against dangers of death, which is a matter of very great difficulty, is more able to remain firm against the onslaught of pleasures" (I-II, 61, 5).

I am painfully aware that I have not done justice to the complexities of Aquinas's understanding of how habit is fundamental for any account of how we are drawn by God into a life of beatitude. But hopefully I have at least provided a sufficient account that helps us see that Aquinas would have no reasons to resist what we might learn from the neurosciences about the bodily character of our becoming more than we are through the habituation of our desires. Indeed, it seems that recent developments in neurobiology that draw on dual-process models of thought and activity may well provide an account quite compatible with Aquinas's understanding of how our complex habits become "second nature."[33]

---

32. I am in debt to Overmyer for this important interpretive point about Aquinas's understanding of the virtues.

33. I am thinking of Michael Spezio's article "The Neuroscience of Emotion and Reasoning in Social Contexts: Implications for Moral Theology," *Modern Theology* 27, no. 2 (April 2011): 339-56. That said, I am sympathetic to Stephen Mulhall's argument in the same issue of *Modern Theology*, which suggests that if Wittgenstein is rightly

Putting on Virtue

Kwame Anthony Appiah, however, in *Experiment in Ethics*, calls attention to work in psychology that seems to challenge the approach to the moral life Aristotle and Aquinas represent.[34] He notes that psychologists have called into question what many take to be the core claim of those who make character central to our understanding of morality — that is, that we are consistent in what we do and do not do. Psychologists have found that what most of us do is not best accounted for by traits of character but by systematic human tendencies to respond to situations, tendencies that no one previously thought to be crucial. In other words, someone who may be honest in one situation will often be reliably dishonest in other situations.[35]

Appiah calls attention to experiments by psychologists such as Alice Isen and Paula Levin, who found that if you dropped your papers in a phone booth you were far more likely to have them returned if those who found the papers had just had the good fortune of finding a dime in the coin-return slot. John Darley and Daniel Batson followed up Isen's and Levin's study by showing that someone slumped in a doorway in distress was less likely to be helped by seminarians if they were told they were late for an appointment. In a similar kind of experiment, Robert Baron and Jill Thomley have shown that you are more likely to get change for a dollar outside a fragrant bakery than outside a dry-goods store.[36]

Such studies, Appiah suggests, challenge the perspective of the virtues, that is, the view that through the acquisition of virtuous habits we can be counted on to act in a manner consistent with those habits. In

---

understood then brain sciences may have little to add to the philosophy of mind. For a fascinating account of the work of Gary Lynch, a neuroscientist whose research attempts to determine how communication between brain cells works to make memory possible, see Terry McDermott, *101 Theory Drive: A Neuroscientist's Quest for Memory* (New York: Pantheon, 2010). Lynch's work could be the kind of biology we need to sustain the account of habit I have tried to develop in this essay, but it is equally clear that this kind of research is anything but conclusive.

34. Kwame Anthony Appiah, *Experiment in Ethics* (Cambridge, MA: Harvard University Press, 2008), pp. 33-72.

35. Appiah, *Experiment in Ethics*, p. 39.

36. Appiah, *Experiment in Ethics*, p. 41.

short, human beings are just not "built that way." Appiah quotes this maxim from Owen Flanagan, whom he describes as having long worked at the intersection of psychology and moral theory: "Make sure when constructing a moral theory or projecting a moral ideal that the character, decision processing, and behavior described are possible, or are perceived to be possible, for creatures like us."[37] Appiah comments on Flanagan's maxim by noting that the deep epistemological challenge for a virtue ethic is that no actual virtuous people exist.

Appiah, however, does not think this is a decisive challenge to an understanding of the moral life understood as a life of virtue. According to Appiah, a life of virtue is good because of what a virtuous person is, not because of what he or she does. So a distinction is possible between having a virtue and being disposed to do the virtuous act over a wide range of circumstances.[38] He thinks, therefore, that it is a mistake to think virtue ethics to be a rival to deontological or consequential approaches to ethics. For a virtue approach is one in response to the question of how we should live our lives rather than a cluster of duties or calculations about what to do in X or Y circumstance.[39]

Needless to say, I am deeply sympathetic with Appiah's attempt to

---

37. Appiah, *Experiment in Ethics*, p. 46.

38. Appiah, *Experiment in Ethics*, p. 61.

39. Appiah, *Experiment in Ethics*, p. 63. I am extremely sympathetic with Appiah's general approach to ethics and, in particular, the stress on exemplification in his most recent book, *The Honor Code: How Moral Revolutions Happen* (Princeton: Princeton University Press, 2010). He observes that he has spent a good deal of his life trying to get his fellow philosophers to recognize the importance of aspects of our lives about which they may take too little notice, such as race and ethnicity, gender and sexuality, and nationality and religion. In particular, he thinks honor a crucial topic that philosophers have neglected; but honor is crucial for our social identities because it connects our lives. Attending to honor helps us to treat others as we should, as well as making the best of our own lives. His book is a series of studies dealing with such matters as the end of dueling, how the binding of women's feet was ended, the suppressing of transatlantic slavery, the recognition of the full humanity of women — all of which turned on the extrapolation of some to discover what honor requires. He argues that we need to reckon with honor because our desire for respect "draws on fundamental tendencies in human psychology. And it is surely better to understand our nature and manage it than to announce that we would rather we were different or worse, pretend we don't have a nature at all. We may think we have finished with honor, but honor isn't finished with us" (p. xix).

defend a virtue perspective, but I find it odd that he seems to have forgotten that the virtues are habits. Of course, the habitual character of our lives does not "solve" the problem of our moral inconsistencies. Indeed, I should think calling attention to the role of habit should help us better understand why we are so often inconsistent. We are inconsistent because we have not sufficiently acquired the habits that make certain decisions non-decisions.

The inconsistencies identified by psychologists would not have made Aristotle or Aquinas rethink their positions. Indeed, they would have expected the kinds of behaviors identified by the psychologists because they were acutely aware that often we possess the semblance of a virtue rather than the true virtue. That is why Aquinas thought it so important that the virtues are interconnected. It is not enough that we are courageous, but we must be courageous in a manner that the temperate person is courageous. If courage determines all our actions, we may well live disordered lives. Accordingly, the moral life is never finished, requiring as it does retrospective judgments about what we may have thought we rightly did but later discover we were self-deceived.

A sobering conclusion, but one I think also quite hopeful. For it may be that, as creatures who must acquire habits to be able to act, we are not thereby condemned to be determined by our past. We dare not forget that hope is also a habit. Hope is that which requires the development of habits that make hope pull us into life. We are hardwired by our bodies to be people of hope. After all, we do like to eat.

Suffering Presence: Twenty-five Years Later

Looking Back

The title of this essay intentionally mimics an essay I wrote some time ago entitled "The Narrative Turn: Thirty Years Later."[1] In the essay on narrative I revisited the general theme so determinative for how I think, that is, that knowledge of God and knowledge of the self are best displayed through narratives. I used the opportunity to assess the "turn to narrative" in order to distance myself from what I thought were some of the doubtful apologetic and popular uses of "story theology." In particular, I worried that the emphasis on story could reproduce habits associated with foundational theological projects that too often result in anthropological reductive accounts of theological claims. I was not then, nor am I now, suggesting that I think the attention to narrative for displaying the grammar of theological work to be a mistake, but rather I meant only to remind myself and those influenced by what I had said about narrative that theological appeal to narrative is not an end in itself.

Suffering Presence: Theological Reflections on Medicine, the Mentally Handicapped, and the Church was published in 1986. I am going to use this opportunity to write about the relation of theology and medicine to look again at what I was trying to do in that book. I wish I could say that

---

1. In Stanley Hauerwas, *Performing the Faith: Bonhoeffer and the Practice of Nonviolence* (Grand Rapids: Brazos, 2004), pp. 135-50.

this retrospective look back to the publication of that book was meant to serve the same purpose as my essay about narrative theology, that is, to counter some of the enthusiasm engendered by the publication of that book twenty-five years ago.[2] But *Suffering Presence* is a book that, as far as I can judge, fell stillborn from the press.[3] That it did so is not surprising. After all, I was trying to challenge some of the dominant paradigms associated with the development of medical ethics. From my perspective the development of medical ethics was but a legitimating discourse to underwrite, as Joel Shuman would later argue in a more sustained way, the transformation of medicine into an "industry that is in the business of selling an especially desirable product, namely health."[4]

I risk being self-indulgent by directing attention to my past work, but by doing so I hope to suggest that there is a connection between "the narrative turn" and how the relation of theology and medicine should be understood. By making explicit some of the intuitions that informed what I was trying to do in *Suffering Presence,* I hope I can say better now what I had tried to say then about how the body that is the subject of illness and death is a storied body. That it is so, moreover, means that any attempt to care for the body that fails to so recognize the storied character of our bodies cannot help but distort the gesture of presence called medicine.

By developing this understanding of the body I hope it may help us say better what role a person's faith makes for responding to illness and the care and healing of the ill, but that is not my primary interest. I am sure the religious convictions patients and physicians bring to their encounters can and sometimes do make a difference for the character of those interactions. I have no doubt that prayer can and does make a difference when we are ill. I worry, however, that to emphasize the difference that prayer makes may lead to our forgetting that prayer has been given to us, not to make a difference even when we are sick, but in order

2. Stanley Hauerwas, *Suffering Presence: Theological Reflections on Medicine, the Mentally Handicapped, and the Church* (Notre Dame: University of Notre Dame Press, 1986).

3. I am, however, particularly grateful to Gerald McKenny for his insightful account and critique of my work in his book *To Relieve the Human Condition: Bioethics, Technology, and the Body* (Albany: State University of New York, 1997), pp. 147-83.

4. Joel Shuman, *The Body of Compassion: Ethics, Medicine, and the Church* (Boulder: Westview, 1999), p. 10.

that we might acknowledge the difference God has made by choosing to be our God. My subject, therefore, is not the difference "religion" can make for the recovery from illness. Rather, I understand my task to be a normative one, that is, I want to try to say how Christians should care for one another through the office of medicine.

My argument assumes, using the title of Wendell Berry's wonderful chapter "Health Is Membership" in *Another Turn of the Crank*, that health is just that, namely, membership in a community.[5] Berry's insight about health as membership may seem, like much he has to say, a commonplace, but I hope to show that it is a commonplace that is a deep challenge to the practice of contemporary medicine. For medicine as a practice in advanced societies like the United States cannot acknowledge that it reflects the material conditions of any particular community.

The irony, of course, is that medicine does reflect the material conditions of a particular community, but it is a community dominated by economic and political ideologies that claim to be first and foremost about securing the freedom of the individual. As a consequence anonymity becomes a way of life and as a result many of our interactions with one another cannot help but be manipulative.[6] In a world in which it is assumed that we share no goods in common, medicine cannot help but seem to be merely another impersonal institution that delivers services to consumers. Ironically, a medicine so determined cannot acknowledge that the body, which allegedly is the subject of the medical arts, is a storied body. For a storied body is not the body of "anyone," but the body determined by a particular history of a particular community.

If the body is appropriately understood as a storied body, Berry argues that no hard and fast distinction can be drawn between the physical and the spiritual. That we currently make that distinction, according to Berry, only reflects how an understanding of the body as a machine has come to

---

5. Wendell Berry, *Another Turn of the Crank* (Washington, DC: Counterpoint, 1995), pp. 86-109.

6. Alasdair MacIntyre's account of the relationship of bureaucracy and the manipulative character of human relationship in a liberal culture remains unsurpassed but unfortunately not sufficiently acknowledged for the significance of his insights. See his *After Virtue*, 3rd ed. (Notre Dame: University of Notre Dame Press, 2007), pp. 23-35.

dominate our lives and, in particular, medical care. As a result Berry describes the contemporary hospital as a place where the world of love meets the world of efficiency, that is, the world of specialization, machinery, and abstract procedures, in such a manner that those worlds are relegated to separate spheres.[7] At best love can be expressed in such a context primarily as the attempt to get the "best medical care available," but the "best medical care available" is not determined by a community of love.

These are complex matters that easily invite misunderstanding. *Suffering Presence* was written before I had read Berry, but I think it is quite compatible with Berry's understanding of health as membership. For example, in *Suffering Presence* I argued that medicine is an office of a community in which some are set aside to be present to the sick even when they cannot cure the person who is sick. I should like to think that understanding of the role of medicine to be quite similar to the way Berry depicts the mutual responsibilities of the physician and patient.

I have been criticized for allegedly assuming a far too idealized account of medicine. I understand the worry, because such a view of medicine seems to have little relation to the reality of the medical care currently practiced. I was not, however, trying to suggest that we must find a way to recover the medicine practiced by the "small town doctor." The medicine we have is the medicine we have. Modern medicine can be quite brutal, but so could the medicine of the past. It is my judgment, however, that the actual practice of medicine, even a medicine determined by the demands of efficiency, is often more "humane" than it is given credit for.

That Berry understands health to be a concept that draws on a more determinative sense of community, however, is the reason his reflections on illness are formed by stories. Berry remains far too close to the ground to forget that no matter what we may say about who we "really are," who we "really are" is most determinatively indicated by our bodies in relation to other bodies. For Berry, when our bodies are abstracted from the communities that constitute the trust and love that give life, we have an exemplification of an abstract understanding of the body that can only be destructive.[8]

---

7. Berry, *Another Turn of the Crank*, p. 102.

8. For a wonderful overview of Berry's work see Fritz Oehlschlaeger, *The Achievement of Wendell Berry: The Hard History of Love* (Lexington: University Press of Kentucky, 2011).

A body so determined may invite a concern about "spirituality" when that body needs to be healed. But a spirituality (and religion) divorced from the actual practices that shape the body threatens to be far too generic to do any serious work if serious work is understood to be the work of Christian theology.[9] "Health" may even be a more ambiguous term than "spirituality." When "health" is thought to name "total well-being," as it often is in modernity, and medicine becomes the agent of health, this threatens to make medicine the institution of a secular salvation.[10] I suspect that is why for many today medicine has become an alternative church.

This assessment formed the background for the case I tried to develop in *Suffering Presence*, where I called for a practice of medicine that subordinated medical care to the determinative ends of a community. Of course, the community with which I was principally concerned is called "church." The emphasis on the body as the proper subject of medical care in *Suffering Presence* was an attempt to suggest why a church must exist if the care we provide to one another through the office of medicine is to be kept within appropriate limits. While I think that emphasis is needed, in my attempt to highlight the hubris of modern medicine I failed to say enough about the body that is the proper subject of medicine.

That hubris — that is, the presumption that through medicine we can get out of life alive — is not the fault of physicians. Rather, that expectation, admittedly an expectation that physicians and researchers have encouraged and from which they have benefited, is carried by patients who

9. For my worries about "religion" see the chapter "The End of 'Religious Pluralism': A Tribute to David Burrell, C.S.C.," in my *The State of the University: Academic Knowledges and the Knowledge of God* (Oxford: Blackwell, 2007), pp. 58-75. More significant is William Cavanaugh's argument in *The Myth of Religious Violence: Secular Ideology and the Roots of Modern Conflict* (Oxford: Oxford University Press, 2009) to the effect that the very creation of the category of religion went hand in hand with the attempt to legitimate the modern nation-state as the necessary alternative to the alleged wars of religion.

10. In 1948 the newly founded World Health Organization defined health as "a state of complete physical, mental, and social well-being and not merely the absence of disease or infirmity." The list has been expanded to include as aspects of health emotional, intellectual, physical, environmental, social, occupational, and spiritual. I am indebted to Melanie Dobson Hughes for calling my attention to the WHO account of health.

are anything but patient.[11] Ironically, the spiritualization of the body, a denial of the finite character that is our body, a denial often legitimated by Christian "beliefs," means that the body patients ask physicians to care for is not the body shaped by the body of Christ.[12]

I wrote *Suffering Presence*, therefore, in an effort to remind us that medical ethics is not a disciplined mode of reflection concerning how physicians should act toward patients. For I take it that medicine does not only name what physicians do but rather is a determinative interaction between doctor and patient. The focus on patients for determining how we should think about the ends of medicine, therefore, was at the heart of the fundamental perspective I tried to develop in *Suffering Presence*. We will not get a more modest medicine in service to the body until we recognize that as patients, for good or ill, we get the medicine we deserve. Let me try to explain this last remark by suggesting some of the problems that currently seem to bedevil communication between patients and physicians in our day.

Barriers to Communication between Doctors and Patients

It is often forgotten that physicians are human beings. Because physicians are human beings, they — like their patients — would like to be liked. Translated into the grammar of medicine, this desire to be liked means physicians would like to help those who are sick and seek their help. This desire becomes problematic when the patient has been formed to expect "cures" that the physician cannot honestly provide. The sick seek out physicians because they rightly think a physician knows what needs to be known to help them and can do what needs to be done to make what is threatening them less threatening. The problem is quite simply that, given the reality physicians confront on a daily basis, they know what their patients know but do not want to acknowledge, that is, when it is all

---

11. See my "Practicing Patience: How Christians Should Be Sick," in Charles Pinches and Stanley Hauerwas, *Christians among the Virtues: Theological Conversations with Ancient and Modern Ethics* (Notre Dame: University of Notre Dame Press, 1997), pp. 166-78.

12. I am indebted to Keith Meador for this point.

said and done we are all going to die. Patients, however, often do not or cannot acknowledge that reality, and as a result they subject physicians to expectations that cannot be met.

The tension between what the patient expects and what the physician can do is complicated by the recognition that at least one aspect of the therapy a physician represents is the trust the patient has in the physician. If physicians seem to be in doubt about what is wrong with their patients — even more, in doubt about what might be an appropriate intervention — patients can feel betrayed, making it even more difficult for physicians to speak truthfully to their patients. This is complicated by the vast differences that education, class, gender, and race present for communication between physician and patient. Essays like this one are written by highly educated people who assume that most patients physicians deal with are like them, that is, highly educated. But physicians do not care only for the highly educated. They also care for people who do not know what blood pressure names.

Yet the physician, at least in theory, is obligated to care for a patient no matter what his or her educational level or race may be. Medicine, for all of its problems, remains an extraordinary morally formed practice. That is why in *Suffering Presence* I suggested that the very idea that physicians needed to be taught "ethics" to sustain their work only leads to a distortion of the ethics that is constitutive of the physicians' work. Fundamental to that ethic is the presumption that physicians are to care for the patients before them in a manner that makes all other considerations irrelevant. That commitment I take to be at the heart of the trust that should characterize the relation between physicians and their patients. Patients must have confidence that the care they are receiving will not be subject to considerations of what they can pay, what another patient may need, or whether the physician does or does not like them. So physicians are caught. They must care for patients in a manner commensurate with their training and skills, but the patients may well not appreciate the limits of what the physicians can do.

The account of medicine I provided in *Suffering Presence* was meant to be a response to this unhappy state of affairs by developing an account of authority that legitimates the physician's care of another human being even when that care cannot "cure." I developed that suggestion by calling attention to the "authority of the body." I even suggested that by focusing on the body I was exploring a kind of natural law reasoning shaped by our bodily character. For at least one of the aspects we share as human beings is that we are bodies. Moreover, that we are bodies makes possible the interactions necessary to discover the goods we have in common. To be sure, those goods are mediated by traditions that are diverse and often in conflict, but to the extent that we share in having bodies we have some basis for mutual recognition.

Accordingly, I argued that "medicine is the name for a tradition of wisdom concerning good care of the body. As such it is not a 'means' to health, but rather is part of the activity of health — an activity that involves as much participation of the patient as the physician."[13] The body sets a norm for medicine because the body is classically understood as the artist of its own healing. The task of those in medicine is to aid us in living through our bodies, because it is a mistake — a mistake, I fear, that may ironically be characteristic of the celebration of the body in modernity — to try to live beyond our bodies.

In *Suffering Presence* I argued that, in contrast to such an understanding of the body, medicine is therefore best understood as an ongoing tradition of wisdom and practices through which physicians acquire the responsibility to remember, learn, and pass on the skills of learning to live with a body that is destined to death.[14] To sustain medicine so understood would require a community that was capable of resisting the seduction of what I can only characterize as the Gnosticism of modernity.

The focus on the body, a body that is not simply a physical body but a lived body, was my attempt to show how physician and patient alike share a common good that could at once limit as well as legitimate physician intervention. By calling attention to how the body can act as an "authority" I sought a way to help physician and patient to discover a common language making communication possible. In particular, I commended Eric Cassell's account of the physician's task to be first and foremost to educate patients to acknowledge their bodies.[15]

13. Hauerwas, *Suffering Presence*, p. 47.
14. Hauerwas, *Suffering Presence*, p. 48.
15. Hauerwas, *Suffering Presence*, p. 49. Eric Cassell's book is *The Healer's Art: A New Approach to the Doctor-Patient Relationship* (Philadelphia: Lippincott, 1976).

Body Matters

I continue to think I was on the right track in directing attention to the body as the locus for the kind of discourse necessary to legitimate the work of medicine. But I confess I was trying to have my cake and eat it too. I was trying to show how the body can provide a necessary limit to our desires for escaping finitude while also suggesting the difference Christian formation makes for the care we provide for one another through the office of medicine. Because I believe that to be a Christian is the fullest expression of what it means to be a human being, I do not think these two emphases necessarily to be in tension. But given the imperative of the Baconian project, we cannot assume the body Christians believe is a gift from God is the same body that shapes modern medicine.[16]

Jeffrey Bishop, for example, argues in his book *The Anticipatory Corpse: Medicine, Power, and the Care of the Dying* that the body that determines the care provided by modern medicine is the corpse. That a medical student's encounter with his or her first patient is an encounter with a corpse Bishop takes to be a sign of how the body is generally understood in modern medicine. According to Bishop, at least since Bacon, it has been assumed that the body, like the world itself, is essentially without purpose other than our ability to impose on it our arbitrary desires. The body is therefore understood as a malleable object subject only to instrumental causation.

Given this mechanistic understanding of life, Bishop argues that the care, particularly of the dying, provided by modern medicine is built on a metaphysics of efficient causation made possible by the epistemological assumption that true knowledge of the body is knowledge of the dead body. In contrast, knowledge of a lived body, a body that to be sure is transitory, makes a science of medicine difficult because a lived body is an unpredictable body.

That is why Bishop suggests that the body presupposed by research medicine is the dead body, because a dead body makes possible predictable knowledge. Bishop concludes that "the dead body is the measure of medicine, creating the sense that life is primarily a matter of moving effi-

16. For an account of the Baconian project see Gerald McKenny, *To Relieve the Human Condition*, pp. 25-38.

ciently within a space. Such movement is not only within the space of the body itself but also within space of the body politic."[17]

I am sure many may think Bishop has overstated his argument. Surely the body that is at the center of medical care is the lived body. After all, the subject of medical art is not the body but a bodily patient. The body that the patient presents to the physician, moreover, is a storied body that physicians soon learn they must listen to if they are to care for the patient. Yet it is surely the case that there is a tension between the science of the body presumed by research medicine and the everyday practice of medicine. Jerome Groopman illustrates that tension by calling attention to Dr. Myron Falchuk's observation that patients come to him as a specialist who is able to perform a procedure using a specialized technology. The technology is vital for caring for the patient, but Falchuk observes, "I believe that this technology also has taken us away from the patient's story. And once you remove yourself from the patient's story, you no longer are truly a doctor."[18]

Increasing medical specialization may be an indication that the body that shapes medical care is, as Bishop maintains, a dead body. For a lived body means there is no way to avoid judgments about patients that may prove to be mistaken.[19] The uncertainty associated with primary care may well be one of the reasons many physicians try to avoid that "specialty." But specialization serves only to give those in the diverse specializations of medicine a false sense of certainty, because specialization can result in a failure to "see" the patient.[20] To be able to see the patient one has to listen to the patient.

17. Jeffrey P. Bishop, *The Anticipatory Corpse: Medicine, Power, and the Care of the Dying* (Notre Dame: University of Notre Dame Press, 2011), pp. 27-28.

18. Jerome Groopman, M.D., *How Doctors Think* (Boston: Houghton Mifflin, 2007), pp. 16-17.

19. Atul Gawande observes, "We look for medicine to be an orderly field of knowledge and procedure. But it is not. It is an imperfect science, an enterprise of constantly changing knowledge, uncertain information, fallible individuals, and at the same time lives on the line. There is science in what we do, yes, but also habit, intuition, and sometimes plain old guessing. The gap between what we know and what we aim for persists. And this gap complicates everything we do." *Complications: A Surgeon's Notes on an Imperfect Science* (New York: Picador, 2002), p. 7.

20. Groopman, *How Doctors Think*, pp. 152-55.

As specializations increasingly correspond to technological developments, specializations also occasion both critical and constructive reflections on the physician-patient relationship as it is affected by technology. Many fear that technology contributes to a further distancing between doctor and patient. But Atul Gawande observes that compassion and technology are not incompatible and may even be mutually reinforcing. The machine may make mistakes less likely, and, he notes, nothing is more disruptive of the relation between a patient and a doctor than a mistake.

Of course, as Gawande acknowledges, machines can and do make mistakes, but as "systems" take on the more technical work of medicine technologies can free physicians to embrace dimensions of care that mattered prior to the development of technology, such as talking to their patients. To talk to patients is necessary because, as he puts it, "medical care is about our life and death, and we have always needed doctors to help us understand what is happening and why, and what is possible and what is not. In the increasingly tangled web of experts and expert systems, a doctor has an even greater obligation to serve as a knowledgeable guide and confidant. Maybe machines can decide, but we still need doctors to heal."[21]

Gawande is right: we do need doctors to heal. But if Bishop is also right, then the "healing" that physicians provide may be determined by an understanding of the body that is in tension with the lived body of the patient. Therefore, I think it important to say explicitly what I only hinted at in *Suffering Presence*. If the Christian body is first and foremost a body meant to glorify God, then Christians must begin to contemplate that the kind of medicine that should characterize the Christian body may be quite different from the kind of medicine that does not share the practices of the church. In short, I think Christians may well find that they will need to develop a medicine that reflects the Christian difference. For the body the church presents to be cared for is not the isolated body of strangers but the baptized body of the people of God. That body, the baptized body, is shaped by practices carried by the story of God in which illness, suffering, and death are not regarded as the ultimate enemy. They cannot be regarded as the ultimate enemy because Christians believe that

---

21. Gawande, *Complications*, pp. 45-46.

even our suffering can be a gift that makes more intimate our relation with God and with one another.[22]

The Christian Body

I indicated above that the body that presents itself to a physician is a lived body. A "lived" body is a storied body. This is why my earlier essay on narrative is relevant to the case I tried to make in *Suffering Presence*. Our bodies demand habituation through which we acquire, as Aristotle argued, "a second nature."[23] If brought up rightly, that "nature" makes possible the acquisition of the habits we call the virtues. How the virtues and their interrelation are understood reflects the stories that shape the fundamental practices of the communities in which we live. For Christians, health itself is a virtue that makes possible our presence to one another in health, sickness, and suffering. Health, like all the virtues, is a reflection of the love of God.[24]

Indeed, a Christian view of health does not deny that some among us are sick and will need care. Rather, a Christian view of health requires that the community recognize illness so that the one who is sick may be restored to health, but also, more importantly, so that the one who is sick remains part of the community even if his or her health is not restored. This means that the Christian view of health forms patients who want to be cured but are not seeking that cure at all costs. In other words, the Christian view of health entails the understanding that the Christian difference means being at peace with human finitude — and even seeing human finitude as gift.

---

22. For a defense of this understanding of suffering see Eleonore Stump, *Wandering in Darkness: Narrative and the Problem of Suffering* (New York: Oxford University Press, 2010).

23. Aristotle, *Nicomachean Ethics*, trans. Terence Irwin (Indianapolis: Hackett, 1999), 1103a15-35.

24. Aquinas understands health to be a virtue, but he provides an extremely sensitive account, noting that the measure of health is not the same in all or even in one individual. Accordingly, a person may be sick but still embody the virtue of health. Health is a habit, and like all habits health can be greater or less. *Summa Theologica*, I-II, 52, 1, trans. the Fathers of the English Dominican Province (Westminster, MD: Christian Classics, 1948).

Conversely, Christian health also means that it may be appropriate for Christians to hold one another accountable when choices are being made that negatively affect one's health such that one is inhibited from participating fully in service to God and world. From this perspective, Christian health does not mean the absence of illness but the reliance on Christ and his community, the church, even while facing the realities of illness and death. It is this faithfulness to Christ that marks the difference of Christian suffering, and it is but a response to Christ's faithfulness to us — even in the midst of his own suffering. Like Christ, Christians must learn how to suffer without losing hope. We must learn to pray for our physicians, not only that they might have the knowledge to help us, but also that they might have the courage to tell us when they cannot. Even more, we must learn to forgive them when they lack the courage. And, finally, we must learn to sit with one another in the valley of the shadow of death.

By suggesting that we need to attend to the Christian difference I am not trying to argue that difference as an end in itself. Rather, I am suggesting that the Christian difference should determine how Christians understand the role and office of medicine. As I argued in *Suffering Presence*, for a community to set aside some to be with the sick is an extraordinary gesture that draws on a profound sense of the significance of presence to one another as a defining mark of the church. That presence, moreover, is made possible through a shared language, a language of the body, that makes communication between the doctor and patient possible.

I do not mean to suggest that the formation of physicians by the church would restrict them to caring only for Christians. But if Christian doctors believe they must speak truthfully to their patients, non-Christians might begin to worry whether they want a doctor who is a Christian. This is not simply because a physician who is a Christian will not perform an abortion or entertain the possibility of euthanasia. Those kinds of concerns certainly matter, but I am suggesting more than this. If "health is membership," the very isolation that the doctor-patient relation too often enacts has to be reconsidered.

Formed by the presumptions of modern medicine as we are, I fear that the way Christians pray indicates that there is too often very little difference between how Christians approach illness and how non-

Christians approach it. The god to whom we pray when we are ill, I fear, is too often a "god of the gaps"; that is, the god to whom we pray is a deistic god whose existence seems to be an insurance policy to protect us from the unknown. But that god cannot be the One who came in the flesh so that we should not despise our flesh that beacons our deaths.

The God we worship as Christians taught us to pray "Thy will be done." We even believe that the Holy Spirit prays on our behalf when, in the face of suffering, we are unable to pray for ourselves. I am suggesting that the Christian difference means our prayers are not determined by the valley of the shadow of death; rather, they are determined by the presence of the One who walks with us. The story that determines the Christian body is the story of Emmanuel, God with us. This is the story we were baptized into, which means we have already died. Therefore, the hope we share is ultimately not a hope to get through life unscathed, but a hope to remain faithful until the end. It is the hope of the resurrection.

A medicine understood as an office of that community called church means the "and" between theology and medicine cannot represent two quite distinct activities that must now be related. Rather, the "and" indicates the task of the church to be the kind of community that can sustain the care of the bodies we share through the office of medicine.

Illness usually comes as an unexpected guest, threatening to disorder our routines and make our lives incoherent. The stories that constitute our lives are meant to give us a sense of control and to assure us that we know where we are and in what time we live. Yet the stories that we may actually be living may not be the ones we think we are living, but our illusions are dear to us. Illness often destroys our illusions as well as our confidence that we are in control. To be a Christian is to undergo the training necessary to know how to live out of control. Accordingly, to suffer those who suffer bonds those who are currently not sick to those who are sick through a common story, making possible the acknowledgment that even the suffering of those we love cannot separate us from the love of God.

A medical care shaped by such a people does not need to promise "cure" to have authority or legitimacy. The care of one another in the name of medicine does not even need to promise "restoration." Rather, what such a medicine promises, the trust it instills, is to reflect through its care of the sick the story into which we were baptized. Such a community must be capable of supporting physicians who can tell us that they have no idea what may be wrong with us, but they will continue to care for us. Such a community must be capable of sustaining physicians who are able to acknowledge that practicing the best medicine they know will sometimes entail making a mistake. Such a community is able to sustain a practice of medicine so conceived because patient and physician alike have been made participants in a common story.

For many what I am calling for will seem unrealistic, given the character of the contemporary church as well as the power of modern medicine. However, I think the way I am trying to help us think about our care of one another through the office of medicine as Christians can be in continuity with the everyday reality of church life. For the everyday reality of church life is to participate in the worship of God and in the process to discover the storied character of our lives. We have been given what we need, but we can lose what we have been given because we have been captured by other narratives that tempt us to describe our lives in terms foreign to the gospel.

In his memoir, *The Pastor*, Eugene Peterson provides an account of the formation of a congregation that suggests that what I am trying to imagine can be possible.[25] Peterson, who had not intended to be a "pastor," found himself in the process of starting a new church. He soon discovered he had no idea who would show up from one Sunday to another Sunday. Not all who came stayed, but as the church grew, he observes, something like a story began to develop that shaped the self-understanding of those who shared the worship of God. Reflecting on this development, Peterson observes that when we get caught up in a story, if it is a truthful story, we do not know how it might end and/or who else will become part of the story.[26] The storied character of a congregation and the storied character of our lives are inextricably interrelated as they involve discoveries we had not anticipated — discoveries that occur through our living together.

Peterson is candid that the church that was coming into being was not

---

25. Eugene Peterson, *The Pastor: A Memoir* (New York: HarperCollins, 2011), pp. 118-19.

26. Peterson, *The Pastor: A Memoir*, p. 118.

an ideal church, but a church made up of human beings. They were people who became ill and died. And those illnesses and deaths became part of the story that made Christ Our King Church the body of Christ. Peterson observes that this reality was made possible because the stories that constitute Christ Our King Church provide a language in which everyone is organically related through the discoveries of "patterns and meanings — beauty and truth and goodness: Father, Son, and Holy Spirit. In the seemingly random and disconnected pieces of experience and dream, tasks and songs, promises and betrayals that make up daily life, words and sentences detect and fashion stories in places of hospitality."[27]

I should like to think the church Peterson describes is one I was trying to imagine twenty-five years ago in *Suffering Presence.* Physicians and patients, whether Christian or not, find that we are increasingly trapped in a medical system that is not sustainable and may well be self-destructing. So we have little to lose if Christians begin to try to imagine what it might mean to form our care of one another through a medicine that respects the body that is storied by Christ.

27. Peterson, *The Pastor: A Memoir,* p. 309.

Cloning the Human Body

With Joel Shuman

> *. . . now we are children of God, and what we will be has not yet been made known. But we know that when he appears, we shall be like him, for we shall see him as he is.*
>
> 1 JOHN 3:2

> *We know that the whole creation has been groaning as in the pains of childbirth right up to the present time. Not only so, but we ourselves, who have the firstfruits of the Spirit, groan inwardly as we wait for our adoption as sons, the redemption of our bodies. For in this hope we were saved. But hope that is seen is no hope at all. Who hopes for what he already has? But if we hope for what we do not yet have, we wait for it patiently.*
>
> ROMANS 8:22-25

> *In the circle of the human we are weary with striving, and are without rest. Order is the only possibility of rest.*
>
> WENDELL BERRY

Cloning — the nonsexual reproduction of an organism using the genetic material of another organism — has been a theoretical possibility

---

In this essay, all scriptural references are taken from the New International Version of the Bible.

for some time. As such, it seems to have elicited very little in the way of moral argument. Recent laboratory developments in mammalian cloning indicate, however, that we soon may have the capacity for human cloning, the nonsexual reproduction of the human body, using the genetic material of another human being. This prospect has evoked a loud and somewhat alarmed call for public moral debate, ostensibly to be led by "experts" in the field of bioethics. Our imaginations, however, do not seem ready for such challenges. As a result, the first question we ask of them always seems to be, "Should we do what we now can do?"

We do not think we should do what we now can do. Christians, we believe, should resist the technological imperative that gives rise to such questions. However, we also think it a mistake to begin arguments about cloning with questions about whether we should do what we now can do. To begin in this way presupposes that we know who is asking such questions and why they are being asked. As a result, the politics producing the technologies that give rise to the questions are hidden from view.

For example, consider this sentence: "Our imaginations do not seem ready for such challenges." Who is indicated by the "our" in that sentence? Confronted by such an "our," Christians assume that we are included in the "our." As a result we — that is, we Christians — think we must then say what, if any, particular insights we have about these matters correlative to our convictions about God's created order or some other relatively benign set of beliefs. This is particularly challenging to Christians living in modernity who are afraid of appearing to be against human progress. After all, does not cloning promise to cure genetically carried diseases or even to eliminate hunger? Surely Christians cannot be against technology that promises such results simply in the name of not messing around in God's creation. Christians, especially given our relatively insignificant status in modernity, simply cannot afford another Galileo affair.

Such challenges certainly may need to be addressed, but we think to begin with such statements of the "problem" is to rob ourselves of the resources of the Christian imagination. In short, the question for us is not whether cloning is a good or a bad thing, but rather how Christians, given the character of the Christian community and in particular the way that community understands the human body, are to understand cloning. "Cloning" is not a new thing for Christians, since we believe we have been made part of Christ's body. But because the promised redemption of our bodies seems so slow in coming, we may be tempted to compromise the body we have in Christ by subjecting that body to biomedical technologies promising immediate relief from all forms of human suffering. Ironically, from the standpoint of the Christian body, biological cloning then becomes but another Gnostic technique designed to avoid or to overcome our bodies as Christians.

This very way of putting the matter in fact challenges the presumption that what makes Christians Christians is the beliefs they hold. The same practices that have reduced Christianity to a set of beliefs freely chosen by the individual make cloning seem like such a humane technology. The modern presumption, formed by the practices of capitalism, that the "I" names a self apart from and reigning over my body also produces a Christianity that is mainly about satisfying my "I." In contrast to this view, we assume that what makes Christians Christians is that through baptism they are made part of Christ's body.

We believe, accordingly, that the question Christians must ask about nonsexual reproduction of the body is not whether it should be done, but whose body, exactly, should we be nonsexually producing? For Christians have for nearly two thousand years been about the business of nonsexually reproducing the one body that matters most, and indeed the only one that must be reproduced in pursuit of the human good, and that is Christ's body. We are part of a community of people comprised of many very diverse members that is itself that body, and we understand that it is our baptism and our discipleship as members of that body, and not the information encoded in our genes, that finally determines our lives.

The apostle Paul, though he was never tempted by the possibility of cloning, nonetheless saw the reproduction of his body as being essential to his life as a minister of the gospel. The body matters to Paul; he knew no spirit, no soul, and no self that existed apart from the body. It is in and through the bodies of Christians, he claimed, "whether by life or by death" (Phil. 1:20), that Christ would be made redemptively present to the world. This presence, moreover, was to be transmitted — or reproduced — in a very particular way, through a particular kind of pedagogy that is perhaps best understood as a profound friendship. "Whatever you have learned or received or heard from me, or seen in me," Paul wrote, "put into practice. And the God of peace will be with you" (Phil. 4:9). Therefore Paul did not hesitate to exhort those in the young churches under his guidance to imitate him. For in that imitation he understood that the disciples were being formed into a body determined by something far more substantial than a DNA sequence. This is evidenced by the language he uses in corresponding with those troublesome Christians in Corinth, to whom he wrote:

> Even though you have ten thousand guardians in Christ, you do not have many fathers, for in Christ Jesus I became your father through the gospel. Therefore I urge you to imitate me. For this reason I am sending you Timothy, my son whom I love, who is faithful in the Lord. He will remind you of the way of life in Christ Jesus, which agrees with what I teach everywhere in every church. (1 Cor. 4:15-17)

This passage suggests not only that Paul expected his life to be imitated by those converted in response to his witness, but also that he understood that this imitation would constitute their lives in a way so substantial that he freely used frankly "biological" language — the language of father and child — to express the relationship between himself and Timothy and himself and the Corinthian Christians. Our tendency as moderns is to make light of such language, to say that it is a "mere" metaphor for what Paul understood to be occurring in the "spiritual" realm — the realm of "belief." But to understand Paul's writing in this way is to weaken his understanding of the church by imposing upon him an incorporeal dualism he probably would have rejected.

Dale Martin argues that when we read Paul we need to leave behind distinctions between the physiological and psychological that we in modernity have come to accept as obvious.[1] Paul assumes the church is Christ's body in such a way that immorality is not *like* the body becoming ill or polluted; it *is* the body becoming ill or polluted. So questions of a man having sexual relations with his stepmother (1 Cor. 5:1), of Christian men visiting prostitutes (6:12-20), of eating meat sacrificed to idols (chaps. 8–10), and of the proper eating of the Lord's Supper (11:17-34) are

---

1. Dale Martin, *The Corinthian Body* (New Haven: Yale University Press, 1995).

all connected. For Paul, all of these are questions of the purity of the body and consequently of the avoidance of pollution. A Christian man visiting a prostitute is the exact equivalent of the body being invaded by a disease that threatens all its members, since in fact every member is the body.

Paul understood that in this life there is no genuine spirituality that does not take the body seriously. Speaking as if things were otherwise, suggests Wendell Berry, tends to "imply that the Creation is divided into 'levels' that can readily be peeled apart and judged by human beings." Some version or another of this very compartmentalized view seems to prevail in modernity, and we typically understand the spiritual as another means of escape from the banality of the everyday. Against this perspective, Berry posits an alternative that clearly derives from his Christianity: "I believe that the Creation is one continuous fabric comprehending simultaneously what we mean by 'spirit' and what we mean by 'matter.' "[2]

Only when Paul is read in this manner do we understand the radical challenge he presents to the assumption that what makes us Christian and/or human is our "self-understanding." Paul really expected those converted by his preaching to display in their bodies the same way of life he displayed in his own. This expectation was rooted not in any sort of megalomania but in Paul's faith that his body had been transformed by his baptism in so profound and so mysterious a way that he could not speak of that transformation except paradoxically: "I no longer live, but Christ lives in me. This life I live in the body, I live by faith in the Son of God, who loved me and gave himself for me" (Gal. 2:20).

Paul's expectation that his body would be reproduced in the bodies of others was based on his understanding that "all of us who were baptized into Christ Jesus were baptized into his death. We were therefore buried with him through baptism into death in order that, just as Christ was raised from the dead through the glory of the Father, we too may live a new life" (Rom. 6:3-4). This is to say that Paul understood baptism into the church as the beginning of a process of transformative reproduction through which the Christian body would be "conformed to the likeness of his Son, that he would be the firstborn among many brothers" (Rom.

---

2. Wendell Berry, *Another Turn of the Crank* (Washington, DC: Counterpoint, 1995), pp. 91-92.

8:29). Paul knew that the body being reproduced in those he baptized and taught was not his own, but Christ's. In this sense Paul understood the body more thoroughly than those who see genetic cloning as being a sufficient means of reproducing the body. Really being a body, he understood, requires certain kinds of relationships with others. Berry makes a similar point in arguing:

> the body is not so formally self-contained; its boundaries and outlines are not so exactly fixed. The body alone is not, properly speaking, a body. Divided from its sources of air, food, drink, clothing, shelter, and companionship, a body is, properly speaking, a cadaver. . . . Merely as an organism (leaving aside issues of mind and spirit) the body lives and moves and has its being, minute by minute, by an interinvolvement with other bodies and other creatures, living and unloving, that is too complex a diagram to describe.[3]

We believe that we are speaking here, lest anyone think otherwise, of the very moral issues that surround technologies of cloning. Berry's broad point is that our bodies are constituted by an extraordinary web of contingencies on a multitude of levels. What Christians should believe about the way these contingencies, especially baptism and discipleship, constitute the body seems not only consistent with what Wendell Berry is saying, but also analogous with the point the philosopher of science Michael Polanyi was trying to make in his critique of modern science's strong tendency toward mechanistic reductionism. Polanyi opposed the insistence of certain scientists that a thing's ontology lay, not in its being a comprehensive structure functioning in a given environment toward a particular end, but in an analysis of its constituent parts. This view, he argued, although valuable in its place, is finally inadequate:

> Indeed, nothing is relevant to biology, even at the lowest level of life, unless it bears on the achievements of living beings — achievements such as their perfection of form, their morphogenesis, or the proper functioning of their organs — and the very conception of such achieve-

3. Berry, *Another Turn of the Crank*, pp. 94-95.

ments implies a distinction between success and failure — a distinction unknown to physics and chemistry.[4]

How this point is analogous to Berry's becomes clear when restated in explicitly theological terms: any theological discussion of the human body, at any level, must include a consideration of the body's goods and the relationship of those goods to the highest Good — its ultimate purpose — which is eternal friendship with God in the new creation. Such friendship is attained through the process of baptism into the life, death, and resurrection of Jesus of Nazareth, through which the body is transformed and made part of Christ's body, which is itself at once both an organism and a network of friendships that make Christ redemptively present to the world.

We cannot then speak of the body's goods — including the physical health of any one individual body — apart from its Good; for to do so is to attenuate the body's health, which cannot be properly considered apart from its relationship with other bodies. As Christians, we find our bodies taken up — "cloned," if you will — through baptism and discipleship into the one body whose presence the world cannot do without, a presence that affords the possibility of finally bringing order to chaos and giving rest from our striving in God's new creation. It is thus imperative that we continue first of all to reproduce that body — a reproduction that cannot be effected genetically — and to wait patiently for the final redemption of our individual bodies.

From this perspective biological cloning represents but another attempt at perfection in a world that no longer acknowledges God. No longer trusting in our ability to make sense of our sufferings through the sharing of our bodies with one another, we now seek to perfect our isolated bodies as if such bodies were intelligible in themselves. In the name of eradicating suffering, we use technological power to avoid being with one another in illness and death. Cloning thus becomes simply another means to escape the knowledge that, when all is said and done, we will have to die alone.

4. Michael Polanyi, "Scientific Outlook: Its Sickness and Cure," *Science* 125 (1957): 480-84, at 482.

Ironically, the high humanism used to justify cloning as a means to overcome the limits of our condition as creatures reproduces the very presumptions that are at the heart of the environmental crisis. When all life is seen to exist for the sole purpose of serving *human* life, then humans presume that we can instrumentally subject all life to our purposes. The widespread assumption is thus that human cloning is wrong because it violates the uniqueness and the autonomy of the individual, but that cloning animals is a fundamentally good thing insofar as it contributes to the elimination of human suffering. But this assumption is highly questionable from the perspective we have developed in this chapter.

The redemption Paul says has begun in our bodies is cosmic. Animals and humans are equally creatures of a good Creator, and the ultimate purpose of both is nothing less than to praise God. The idea that animals exist for no other purpose than to supply human needs and desires cannot be justified theologically. Given the practices of the Christian community with regard to the body, we can see no reason why Christians might think animals — much less humans — can be cloned in the name of human progress. Any "progress" that is not found in the joining of our bodies into the one body of Christ we suspect to be an idolatrous attempt to perfect the created order in a manner that denies that our lives have already been perfected in Christ.

Doing Nothing Gallantly

With Gerald McKenny

The Way We Live Now

In the Book of Common Prayer, in the section titled "Prayers for Use by a Sick Person," we are given this prayer:

> This is another day, O Lord. I know not what it will bring forth, but make me ready, Lord, for whatever it may be. If I am to stand up, help me to stand bravely. If I am to sit still, help me to sit quietly. If I am to lie low, help me do it patiently. If I am to do nothing, let me do it gallantly. Make these words more than words, and give me the Spirit of Jesus. Amen.

That prayer says everything we want to say about what it would mean to set the practice of medicine in the context of the good life. It does so, first of all, because the prayer is not prayed by a physician but by the sick. Too often, by focusing on the physician we underwrite the presumption that the profession of medicine is separable from those whom physicians serve. That presumption, we fear, underwrites the autonomy of medicine and as a result separates the hands that practice medicine from the moral presuppositions of those they serve.

So rather than beginning with the medical profession, we think we need to begin by asking what kind of virtues those who come to physicians as patients should have in a way that does not distort the kind of care a physician is capable of giving. This prayer provides a list of the virtues we think are crucial for patients. It begins by indicating that the patient will be surprised by what the day brings. The surprise may be positive or negative. Accordingly, the patient is not expected to act but to be willing to sit quietly. This will require patience. And even more, the patient may be asked to do nothing, but to do nothing gallantly. Finally, this prayer clearly acknowledges that in praying we may not be able to believe the words we are praying. So we will need the Spirit to make the words we say true.

To prepare physicians to serve people who can pray such a prayer we suspect is the condition necessary if physicians are to be trained to talk with patients in a truthful manner. We take it that one of the great problems we confront is the lack of communication between physician and patient. This lack of communication is often because the patient and physician share no common moral world. A moral anonymity that characterizes our lives and in particular the relationship between physician and patient makes it impossible for physicians to know for whom it is they are caring, and for patients to know who it is that is caring for them. The result is that the physician and patient are locked in a desperate embrace to defeat death. That embrace makes it close to impossible to pray asking for the ability to do nothing gallantly and to understand what the practice of medicine would mean in light of that prayer.

We do not mean the last comment to be a counsel of despair. Rather, we believe that physicians and patients often discover greater commonality than they had anticipated through the kind of care they give one another in the face of illness. The problem is how to make articulate those discoveries so that we learn how to go on in the face of suffering. We believe that medicine is fundamentally a teaching art that requires physicians not to limit their work only to those who present illnesses but also to serve those who are allegedly well.

In his book *How Doctors Think*, Jerome Groopman makes the interesting observation that though modern medicine has at its disposal a dazzling array of technologies such as high-resolution MRI scans and pinpoint DNA analysis, "language is still the bedrock of clinical practice."[1] Therapy be-

---

1. Jerome Groopman, M.D., *How Doctors Think* (Boston: Houghton Mifflin, 2007), p. 8.

gins, Groopman observes, with patients telling doctors what is bothering them, how the way they feel is different from the way they usually feel, followed by the responses patients give to the doctors' questions. Groopman suggests that often misdiagnosis is caused by miscommunication. So a doctor who is providing the appropriate care will return to language: "Tell me your story again as if I'd never heard it — what you felt, how it happened, when it happened."[2] Telling the story again can help us recall a detail that we have forgotten yet that is crucial if the physician is to make a judgment about what is wrong.

Groopman is surely right to call attention to the importance of language for patient care. For if we are right that communication is at the heart of medical care then it is crucial that we share a common language. Yet it is by no means clear that we do so. Of course, it may be that technological developments mean that communication between doctor and patient is not as important as it once was. But the very technologies that we think protect us from false diagnoses, Groopman suggests, may well tempt doctors away from taking the histories that are crucial if the results of certain tests are not to mislead. Thus his wry comment that radiologists are not usually characterized as people capable of nuanced communication.[3]

The story of how modern medicine has tended to substitute technologies for communication between doctors and patients is a familiar one.[4] Steven Shapin argues, however, that the problem of communication between physicians and patients does not begin with the development of modern technologies. According to Shapin, the physician has always occupied a precarious position between expertise and common sense. Insofar as physicians presented themselves as having the authority of an expert, what they had to say about the causes as well as cure of our illnesses had to be different from mere common sense. Physicians were assumed to have specialized knowledge about how the body works derived from the experience acquired from caring for sick people.[5]

2. Groopman, *How Doctors Think*, p. 261.
3. Groopman, *How Doctors Think*, p. 194.
4. See Stanley Reiser, *Medicine and the Reign of Technology* (New York: Cambridge University Press, 1978).
5. Steven Shapin, *Never Pure: Historical Studies of Science As If It Was Produced by*

Yet Shapin observes that the authority of physicians, their medical expertise, was tempered by their knowledge of the people who paid them for their services. "At any time from Antiquity through at least the early twentieth century, much of the basic conceptual vocabulary of medical science and art was held in common by medical experts and laity, and it is not easy in many cases to say to whom such vocabulary authentically 'belonged.' "[6] Accordingly, physicians acknowledged that their patients were experts on themselves as medical objects, leading some such as Montaigne to believe that after the age of thirty every man should be his own physician.[7]

This understanding of the relation between medical expertise and common sense shared by physician and patient underwent a radical change in the late seventeenth and eighteenth centuries. Shapin suggests that the micromechanism of René Descartes, Pierre Gassendi, Robert Boyle, Giovanni Borelli, and, above all, Isaac Newton suggested that an invisible realm existed that was radically different from that posited by commonsense actors. The body could now be understood mathematically, giving physicians the authority to speak from an invisible realm that was declared to be more securely founded than that which it supplanted. Francis Bacon became the standard-bearer of this revolution, arguing that progress in medicine depended on the reform of medical practice by placing it on natural-philosophical foundations. Now that physicians could know the microstructures and micromechanisms of the body's ailments, they could intervene effectively. "Micromechanism ambitiously promised the maintenance of health, the cure of disease, and the prolongation of human life."[8]

Shapin's account helps us say more clearly what is at stake in our own theme. The problem of communication is not just that doctors rely too much on technology and pay too little heed to what their patients are telling them. It is rather that a practice of medicine centered on a shared vocabulary of the body and its capabilities, limitations, and pathologies

---

People with Bodies, Situated in Time, Space, Culture, and Society, and Struggling for Credibility and Authority (Baltimore: Johns Hopkins University Press, 2010), p. 289.

6. Shapin, *Never Pure*, p. 289.

7. Shapin, *Never Pure*, p. 290.

8. Shapin, *Never Pure*, p. 293.

gave way to a practice of medicine based on a specialized vocabulary of scientific expertise with its promise of effective control, a vocabulary that stood at a lofty (and for the vast majority of patients inaccessible) distance from the commonsense vocabulary of patients. The common moral world that is necessary for the ethical practice of medicine could no longer rely on a shared vocabulary regarding the body but now had to be cobbled together by combining standards of professional competence of the physician, who employs a highly technical knowledge of the body, with respect for the autonomy of the patient, whose preferences regarding the uses of medical knowledge and competence must not be violated.

Of course, some would argue that the dissemination of health information made possible by information technology has somewhat narrowed the gap between the medical expert and the autonomous patient. Increasingly, patients no longer wait for their doctors to offer a diagnosis or propose an intervention but come to them with their own ideas of what these might be. But health information is not medical knowledge, and in any case its possession by patients only means that they have assimilated the understanding of the body as micromechanism, albeit in a partial and fragmentary way. Broad accessibility to health information, then, does not bring about a shared vocabulary in any but the most superficial sense. The Baconian revolution is still under way.

In *To Relieve the Human Condition: Bioethics, Technology, and the Body*, McKenny elaborated the significance of the Baconian revolution by drawing on the work of Michel Foucault. We see no reason to go over that ground again, other than to call attention to what McKenny characterizes as his "modest" argument, namely, "that modern moral discourse provides no vocabulary with which to deliberate about the meaning of corporality, what moral purposes the body serves, what goods health should serve, or what limits the control of our bodies by technology should observe. Hence it allows for no discussion of what kinds of suffering should be eliminated, what kinds of choices human beings should make, and what role technology should play in all this."[9]

What seems to be missing is a vocabulary, a way of speaking, that will

---

9. Gerald McKenny, *To Relieve the Human Condition: Bioethics, Technology, and the Body* (Albany: State University of New York Press, 1997), p. 21.

let us deliberate about the meaning of corporality and suffering. Such a vocabulary, according to McKenny, will require an account of the virtues and skills necessary to live out the double alterity of the body (namely, the "otherness" with which it both resists our aims and ideals and opens us to the vulnerability of others) as well as being capable of making judgments about the possibilities as well as the limits of technology.[10] It is our contention that if Christians are to provide such a vocabulary, a vocabulary suggested by the prayer with which we began, a concrete community will be required capable of forming subjects with attitudes and practices that are an alternative to the Baconian project. But if such a community does not exist, writing another book cannot do what needs to be done.

Hauerwas has made quite similar arguments about the centrality of language for medical care, calling attention to problematic ways of speaking that distort the profession and practice of medicine and giving voice to an alternative idiom.[11] But neither of us has developed the kind of constructive alternative we say we need. Surely more can be said. Some suggestions about the vocabulary that it seems we need to sustain the care of one another through the office of medicine can be made. We should like to think the attempt by some of us to reclaim Aristotle's account of the virtues and correlative politics, to be sure in a theological key, is the beginning of a constructive alternative. At least we thought that until we read Jonathan Lear's account of Aristotle in *Happiness, Death, and the Remainder of Life.*[12] For Lear issues a profound challenge to any attempt to use Aristotle's account of the virtues to sustain our care of one another through the office of medicine.

---

10. McKenny, *To Relieve the Human Condition*, p. 226.

11. See especially Stanley Hauerwas, *Suffering Presence: Theological Reflections on Medicine, the Mentally Handicapped, and the Church* (Notre Dame: University of Notre Dame Press, 1986); and *God, Medicine, and Suffering* (Grand Rapids: Eerdmans, 1994).

12. Jonathan Lear, *Happiness, Death, and the Remainder of Life* (Cambridge, MA: Harvard University Press, 2000).

Lear's Seduction

Drawing on psychoanalytic insights, Lear argues that Aristotle's *Nicomachean Ethics* is a great seduction that issues in a fantasy that is bound to leave us discontented. The seduction begins with the declaration that there is something, namely, *"the* good," that is the ultimate aim of all our actions. This declaration, Lear argues, is a performative speech-act designed to seduce us into a way of life, one in which we must imagine our lives as a whole. Lear is not suggesting that Aristotle's seductive project is manipulative, because seduction is, from a psychoanalytic point of view, inevitable. "Seduction is constitutive of our entry into language" because we cannot help but be susceptible to enigmatic signifiers whose content we do not understand.[13] The concept of *"the* good" is an enigmatic signifier, one that draws us into the inquiry Aristotle is conducting as we begin to wonder what this concept is that we currently lack but that we now are led to believe is necessary to make sense of our lives as a whole. Aristotle seduces us by tempting us to think that we have "chosen" to believe that we desire to live a life that is a coherent whole from "the inside," but in truth such a choice is necessary so that our lives have an inside.[14] Drawing on Socrates and Plato, Aristotle thus creates "ethics," changing our lives by changing our concepts.[15]

Aristotle, according to Lear, continues his seduction by claiming that according to general agreement *"the* good" of a "whole human life" is "happiness." But this suggestion, that is, that we can consider happiness as an adequate concept to describe what it means for our lives taken as a whole to be well lived, exerts pressure on us. For as soon as it is made then we must try to find out what happiness is.[16] Aristotle's critique of all forms of happiness that are less than self-sufficient is but the further development of his strategy of seduction. The claim that happiness is that

---

13. Lear, *Happiness, Death, and the Remainder of Life*, pp. 20-21.

14. Lear, *Happiness, Death, and the Remainder of Life*, p. 26.

15. Lear, *Happiness, Death, and the Remainder of Life*, p. 8. Lear acknowledges that this reading of Aristotle reflects the influence of Ludwig Wittgenstein and Martin Heidegger, who have taught us that there can be no viable distinction between the existence of concepts and the lives we live with them.

16. Lear, *Happiness, Death, and the Remainder of Life*, pp. 22-23.

which makes life desirable and lacking in nothing is a tautology shaped by our deepest fantasies. It is a fantasy, moreover, that turns out to be deadly, for a life that lacks nothing is a life beyond desire, that is, a life that is equivalent to a living death.[17]

Such a life, a life that is deathlike, Lear suggests, accounts for why Aristotle culminates his inquiry with the claim that contemplation must be the mode of life that realizes happiness. Up to that point Aristotle had given every indication that happiness consists in the ethical life, the life of virtue, but now he tells us that this life, the life of political activity, is itself for the sake of contemplation. "At the beginning of the inquiry we were invited to agree that 'happiness' was 'complete' and 'self-sufficient' though we had little understanding of what any of these terms might mean. . . . But now a new conception of happiness is introduced in relation to which the political life, even at its best, is now revealed as 'incomplete,' as not *really* 'self-sufficient.'"[18] Many commentators have found this move anomalous, but from Lear's psychoanalytical perspective it is not at all puzzling.

> Aristotle's inquiry "induces a kind of being-unto-death. It creates a fantasy of a release from the ordinary pressures of ethical life, a fantasy of sharing with the gods the greatest, stressless pleasure. . . . It is a fantasy of release which helps us organize and direct our ordinary practical lives. . . . What is best about being human is the opportunity to break out of being human. Or: to be most human is to break out of the ordinary conditions of human life.[19]

According to Lear, then, Aristotle's identification of happiness with the contemplative life is a powerful organizing fantasy that hides from those who so understand their lives its fantastic status. From Lear's perspective the crucial lesson is that any account of the good of human life as a whole will generate a fantasy of what lies beyond the life that is described. We will return to this point. For the moment, though, it is im-

17. Lear, *Happiness, Death, and the Remainder of Life*, p. 27.
18. Lear, *Happiness, Death, and the Remainder of Life*, p. 43.
19. Lear, *Happiness, Death, and the Remainder of Life*, pp. 54-55.

portant to summarize why, if Lear's account is correct, we cannot turn to Aristotle for the vocabulary we are looking for. For Aristotle, in spite of his account of friendship, presumes that our good is most fully realized by not having to regard our neighbors as having any role in the satisfaction of our happiness. Even more disturbing, depending on your point of view, is Lear's suggestion that Aristotle has provided an account of the moral life that makes contemplation the closest we can come to the activity of the gods, that is, a "deathlike form of life."[20] These implications of Aristotle's concept of happiness are only to be expected if the conditions for the good of human life are completeness and self-sufficiency. We suggested above that we need a vocabulary to understand better the care we provide for one another through the office of medicine. Without such a vocabulary physician and patient cannot communicate, and communication, it turns out, is at the heart of the care medicine provides. But a vocabulary that describes the good life in this way is certainly not a vocabulary that can resist the Baconian revolution.

Lear's account is not only an interpretation of Aristotle from a psychoanalytical perspective. It is a challenge to the idea that we can come up with a better moral psychology by hitching psychoanalysis with its exploration of unconscious motives to an Aristotelian account of character formation and thereby arriving at a form of ethical life that does justice to the full range of our motivations. The reason this kind of project cannot succeed, Lear argues, is that unconscious motives are too disruptive to be contained by any teleological principle.[21]

We cannot begin to do justice to Lear's nuanced articulation of this idea through the failures of Aristotle and Sigmund Freud, even if we have grasped it at some level, to fully accept its implications. Nor can we do justice to Lear's suggestion that an ethical life that is adequate to our awareness of the unconscious must be one that shows us how to live without the attempt to subsume our lives under an overarching principle. Rather, what we find significant for our purposes is his persistence, in *Happiness, Death, and the Remainder of Life* and even more poignantly in *Radical Hope*, in understanding ethics as consideration of the question

---

20. Lear, *Happiness, Death, and the Remainder of Life*, pp. 53-54.
21. Lear, *Happiness, Death, and the Remainder of Life*, p. 3.

of what it means to go on in the face of radical disruption. Surely, the vocabulary we need in order to make sense of the prayer with which we began these reflections will be one that is capable of answering the question of how to go on in the face of illness and death. For that is exactly what the prayer exhorts and helps us to do.

What is the disruption? Obviously it is the illness of the one who prays the prayer. But it is also the disruption that every illness and, even more, the persistence of disease, death, and suffering visit on the project envisioned by Bacon and others described by Shapin: the expectation that biomedical progress will "solve" the "problem" of suffering and finitude. Again, both of us have written about how this expectation distorts the ethics of medicine, and we will not repeat it here. What we want to do instead is to say more about what this prayer teaches us about how to go on in the face of radical disruption, with the hope that we can begin to form the vocabulary Christians need in order to understand medicine as a practice and profession.

In *Radical Hope* Lear contrasts the responses of Plenty Coups and Sitting Bull to the radical disruption of their ways of life, and in so doing he argues against the messianic fervor that determined the response of the Sioux to the loss of their way of life. Here is Lear's conclusion: "In a sense, Plenty Coups and Sitting Bull had the same vision, but they interpreted it in opposite ways. Both saw the ghosts of buffalo, but for Plenty Coups the vision signified they were going away forever; for Sitting Bull and his Sioux followers, it signified that they were coming back. This is the danger for all forms of messianic religions: a wish can easily be mistaken for reality."[22]

We do not wish to defend Sitting Bull's form of messianic religion. And while there is always the danger of confusing a fantasy with reality in religions shaped by messianic hopes, we do not think some amount of danger can be or should be avoided, given the eschatological character of existence. In fact, we believe that Christian eschatological convictions, rightly understood, offer a vocabulary for going on in the face of radical disruption. Indeed, without these convictions the prayer we have been

---

22. Jonathan Lear, *Radical Hope: Ethics in the Face of Cultural Devastation* (Cambridge, MA: Harvard University Press, 2006), p. 151.

considering makes no sense. In what follows, by drawing on the work of that great apocalyptic mind, Karl Barth, we will suggest how the Christian understanding of the practice and profession of medicine presumes an eschatological perspective, one that makes sense of the prayer that opens this essay and rightly situates the profession and practice of medicine in the good life.

Barth on Life, Death, and Medicine

Dogmatics and ethics are not only inseparable for Barth; they are indistinguishable.[23] They are indistinguishable because at the heart of Barth's theology is the presumption that God and humanity are mutually implicated as covenant partners. In Christ, the Father from all eternity has freely elected to be God with and for us and has elected us to be those whom God is with and for (election). Ethics has to do with God's "command," which summons, directs, and empowers us to live as those who truly are God's covenant partner, whom God is with and for (sanctification). Creation is the external ground of this covenant, the particular form in which God has chosen to bring it about, while its consummation is realized through the redemption wrought in Christ. That story — that is, that all that is, is due to God's eternal decree in Christ and the Holy Spirit — determines how life itself is to be understood.

Thus Barth begins his treatment of "Freedom for Life" in volume III/4 of the *Church Dogmatics* with the claim: "As God the Creator calls man to Himself and turns him to his fellow-man, He orders him to honor his own life and that of every other man as a loan, and to secure it against all caprice, in order that it may be used in this service and in preparation for this service."[24] The radical character of Barth's position can and often

23. For a full account of Barth's "method" see Gerald McKenny, *The Analogy of Grace in Karl Barth's Moral Theology* (Oxford: Oxford University Press, 2010), pp. 1-21.

24. Karl Barth, *Church Dogmatics*, III/4 (Edinburgh: T&T Clark, 1961), p. 324. Hereafter, page references to this volume of the *Dogmatics* will appear in the text. McKenny calls attention to the problematic translation of *Ehrfurcht* by the English word "respect" just to the extent that the latter fails to suggest how Barth's understanding of life is one that entails that our conception of life is intelligible only as divine property. See *The Analogy of Grace*, p. 256.

is missed because we are so tempted to read him as confirming our everyday assumptions.[25] But Barth immediately challenges one of our most cherished assumptions, that is, that we have a natural desire to live.

So it is not surprising that Barth begins his account of respect for life by distinguishing his understanding of life in response to God's command from Albert Schweitzer's "mystical" understanding of life as the supreme good (p. 324). From Barth's perspective, such a view of life cannot help but result in a vitalistic or naturalistic ethics in which life assumes a tyrannical or totalitarian role, as Barth thinks it does in philosophers such as Auguste Comte, John Stuart Mill, Herbert Spencer, and Ernst Haeckel (p. 326). No doubt Barth has in mind the horrific form vitalism took in Nazi ideology and practice, but the problem he sees with this view extends beyond that extreme instance. The problem is that in this view life is taken as a "given" and must be simply accepted in its "givenness" rather than regarded as a matter in which we are explicitly responsible before God. But life as such, however understood, is not its own imperative. It is not even to be accepted without question as the condition for everything we do. It is rather the object of an explicit command of God, and by treating it as such Barth makes life a matter of human responsibility before God rather than leaving it as "the ethical lord, teacher and master of man" (p. 326).

This point is an important one for Barth's discussion of health. As we will see, he insists that health is not just a physiological condition that can be more or less left to itself until we lose it but a condition that involves our ongoing activity. On this basis Barth will emphasize that responsibility for health is something that falls on each of us, even to the extent that (as we will also see) it becomes a significant question whether it is legitimate to rely on a physician.

We are responsible for life, but we are responsible to God for it, and that is because life, even our own life, is not something we possess. That

---

25. McKenny makes clear that Barth's rejection of the modern presumption — a paradigmatic presumption of bourgeois humanism that the moral world is one of our own making — means Barth must point us away from "the factual reality of our moral lives to a moral reality which, precisely as an eschatological reality in Christ, makes available to us a freedom and power for the good which would otherwise be inaccessible to us." *The Analogy of Grace*, p. 200.

brings us to another cherished assumption Barth challenges, namely, the assumption that our life belongs to us. According to Barth:

> Life as such means to live for the One to whom it belongs and from whom it has been received as a loan. Life, human life, thus hastens as such towards freedom before God and only *per nefas*, and never according to its own nature, can it depart from this direction or take the opposite one. We must accept the fact that in respect of this natural direction of his life towards God, man is not its owner and lord. Together with everything else which determines and characterizes his life, the fact that it is orientated on God is also and particularly God's creation and loan. (pp. 330-31)

Our life is a loan from God. We do not dispose of it. Thus the respect for life that is required of us always comes in the framework of presuppositions and intentions that God determines for life.

That framework makes possible and requires respect for life. We respect life because in Christ the living God has unmistakably differentiated human life from all other life. Accordingly, life is to be regarded as a mystery made possible by God's willingness to be identified with us. That identification means we cannot tire of life, but rather we must live in affirmation of what we have been given. Respect for life thus begins with awe or reverence for life but must also take the form of a will to life.

Moreover, because our existence as God's covenant partner is also existence in fellowship with others, this framework requires respect for our neighbor's life as well as our own. Our will to life encompasses the life of our neighbor as well as our life, a point that is especially relevant when it comes to health. As with Wendell Berry's understanding of health as membership, Barth argues that the will for health of each of us must finally take the form of the will to improve the living conditions of all people.[26] For sooner or later illness will threaten each of us, isolating

---

26. Berry observes that you can tell from our increasing concern about health how diseased we are. From Berry's perspective, health is a kind of unconsciousness whereas disease makes us conscious by creating a division of our bodies and world into parts. He notes that "health" comes from the root for "heal," "whole," and "holy." To be healthy is to literally be made whole, but Berry does not think "mortal healers

us from ourselves and from one another. But such isolation can only be partly successful if we recognize that when one person is ill we are all ill. Therefore in the battle against sickness the final human word cannot be isolation but fellowship (p. 363).

Yet the reverence for life commanded of us is not without limit. The limit is the very will of God whose command sets the horizon that determines the character of our existence. It is first of all a creaturely limit. As created by God, our life is loaned to us for the service of God, and we may be required to surrender it in service to God. But as temporal, our life also has an eschatological limit. Unlike eternal life, temporal life is bounded. Eternal life is given to us not only as a loan but as a gift we possess inalienably. But temporal life is given to us in the form of a loan; it is not our possession (p. 338). For both of these reasons respect for life cannot consist in an absolute will to live, "but in a will to live which by God's decree and command, and by *meditatio futurae vitae,* may perhaps in many ways be weakened, broken, relativised and finally destroyed" (p. 342).

Once again, what Barth says of our life in general also applies to that aspect of it that involves our health or sickness. "It does not belong to [man] to be and to live as God. Rather, he may see the goodness of God the Creator in the fact that to his life and strength and powers a specific space is allotted, i.e., a limited span" (p. 372). The point is that we are to see in this limit to our life the goodness of God and not just a cruel fate, a point we return to below.

With these fundamental features of respect for life in mind, we can turn our attention to the specific topic of health. Barth begins by telling us that we should not think of health in terms of physiological and psychological functions (that is, as the absence of pathology). "Health is the strength to be as man." In other words, it is "the capacity, vitality and freedom to exercise the psychical and physical functions, just as these themselves are only functions of human existence" (p. 357). Health is a state, but it is a state in which we actively exercise our functions. It is

---

should be credited with the power to make holy." Wendell Berry, *Another Turn of the Crank* (Washington, DC: Counterpoint, 1995), pp. 86-87. Berry finds it extraordinary that some now think medicine should be in service of making death a curable illness, with the result that the modern medical industry increasingly imitates disease in the way it isolates us from ourselves and from others.

therefore an object of the will, and respect for life in this instance takes the form of the will to be healthy.

Sickness hinders the exercise of those functions and thus is a negative impact on the "strength to be as man," but it is not the negation of health, since "the strength to be this . . . can also be the strength and therefore the health of the sick person" (p. 357). Thus, even those who are seriously ill can and should will to be healthy, but without any illusions about their condition. "The sick person should not cease to let himself be addressed, and to address himself, in terms of health and the will which it requires rather than sickness" (p. 358). By the same token a person whose physiological and psychological functions are free of pathology may lack the "strength to be as man" and therefore may be sick (p. 358). In short, health is inseparable from our physiological and psychological functioning, but it is not reducible to it. In all cases "the question to be answered is: 'Wilt thou be made whole?' (Jn. 5:6), and not: 'Wilt thou have healthy limbs or be free of their sickness?' " (p. 359).

While this conception of health is elusive, falling somewhere between physiology and agency, it is not unfamiliar. Doctors and family members both understand what it means to say, for example, "she's still fighting" even when her prognosis is bad or to know that "he's given up" even when objective indicators show no deterioration in his condition. Barth's purpose in any case is to get us to see the whole order of physiological and psychological function as something to be brought into the domain of our activity, something for which we must take explicit responsibility rather than leave it to itself or simply trust the workings of a natural desire. So it is no surprise that when it is a question of what the will to health concretely requires us to do he quite readily commends hygienics, that is, the measures one takes on one's own to maintain one's psychical and physical well-being and prevent disease.

But if health is a matter of our own active responsibility, what is to be said about turning to the physician to promote or restore it? "The more a man understands the question of health and sickness correctly, i.e., the question of his own strength to be as man and therefore of the continuation of his own life history," the more wary he will be of "the objectivity of the knowledge, diagnosis and therapy of a stranger to whom we are required to give place and confidence at the very heart of our own history, handing over to him far-reaching powers of authority and instruction" (p. 361). What can a stranger, particularly a stranger whose way of seeing is determined by the categories of a general science, know of my strength or weakness to be human? To consult the physician would seem to be an abdication of one's responsibility and the surrender of one's unique humanity to the generality of objectifying knowledge.

The wariness is appropriate, but Barth thinks the refusal to consult the physician rests on a misunderstanding. It is worth noting that he suspects the misunderstanding is more prevalent among patients than among doctors (which is one good reason for beginning the answer to the question of medicine and the good life with patients rather than doctors). The misunderstanding has to do with the limits of medicine. "There exists . . . a medical and especially in our own day a psychological totalitarianism and imperialism which would have it that the doctor is the one who really heals." But this is a mistake because the strength to be human "is something which each can only will, desire and strive for, but not procure nor attain of himself" (p. 361). What medicine can legitimately do, however, is to assist the strength to be human "by giving free play, and removing the obstacles, to the will for real health" through the application of the physician's knowledge of the physiological and psychological functions (p. 362). The physician has no power or authority over health as such but does have knowledge of and authority over the psychical and physical conditions that affect health for better or worse. In the exercise of this role the famous exhortation of Ecclesiasticus 38:12 is sound: "Give place to the physician, for the Lord has created him; let him not go from thee, for thou hast need of him." Medical art and science are part of the gifts given to humankind. Barth, no doubt with a sly smile, suggests, "If the history of medicine has been as little free from error, negligence, one-sidedness and exaggeration as any other science, in its main development it has been and still is, to lay eyes at least, as impressive, honourable, and promising as, for instance, theology" (p. 362).

It is important to recognize that Barth rejects the familiar humanist critique of the practice of medicine formed by the Baconian revolution, namely, that medical knowledge and intervention objectify the patient, annihilating the irreducible particularity of the patient's illness as part of his or her life story. He rightly reminds us that medicine, when practiced well, is the application of general knowledge to the patient in his or her singularity. The problem instead is that we are tempted by the Baconian revolution to expect medicine to do too much. Taken with the promise of control over the body, we look to medicine to deliver us from the vexing struggle with the possibilities and limitations of our corporal existence, to absolve us of the obligation to affirm our life in its full and unique humanity, before God and with others, whatever our physiological or psychological condition. The result of looking in this way to medicine to secure our humanity in the face of threats to it is that we are likely to distort the benefits medicine really can confer.

What are these benefits? Barth begins with the pedagogical role of the physician, who instructs us concerning "what possibilities of movement and action still remain in spite of the present injury, and within what limits one may still will to be healthy." Medicine may also provide a cure, though Barth seems determined to keep expectations modest: "The doctor goes on to treat the patient with a view to arresting at least the damage, to weakening its power and effect, perhaps even to tackling its causes and thus removing it altogether, so that the patient is well again at least in the medical sphere." Finally, medicine may offer palliative care: "And even if the doctor cannot extend the limits of life available, he can at least make the restrictive ailment tolerable, or at worst, if there is no remedy and the limits become progressively narrower, he can do everything possible to make them relatively bearable" (p. 362). In these modest yet profound ways the physician serves the will to be healthy, assisting without replacing the struggle to affirm our corporal life under all its conditions. But "having done this to the best of his ability he should withdraw. He has no power in the crucial issue of the strength or weakness of the patient to be as man" (pp. 362-63). Of course, it is a matter of casuistry to know when the doctor should withdraw, but it is clear from all Barth has said that such a discernment draws not only on medical knowledge but also on the shared convictions of patient and doctor.

What do we actually will when we will to be healthy? This question brings us to the eschatological framework of respect for life we mentioned above. Drawing broadly on Scripture, Barth argues that "sickness is a forerunner and messenger of death, and indeed of death as the judgment of God and the merited subjection of man to the power of nothingness in virtue of his sin" (p. 366). Sickness is thus "an element and sign" of the chaos threatening creation as well as the judgment of God, and so it is rightly understood in the Psalms, Job, and the synoptic Gospels as the encroachment of the realm of death on the living space God has created for us. But if this is so, can the will to health commanded by God have any force? What is our will in comparison with the power of chaos unleashed by our sin and the divine judgment on it? Should we not let chaos take its course and succumb to sickness in pious resignation?

That would be a mistake. The power of chaos is opposed by God, who has defeated it and exercised judgment in Christ, making possible and necessary our hatred of sickness and death. "In harmony with the will of God," then, "what man ought to will . . . in face of sickness, can only be final resistance" (pp. 367-68). Therefore, as powerful as sickness remains, the command of God to live remains in effect, and those who struggle against sickness are obediently healthy by the very fact that they struggle (p. 369). Barth has no use for a false humility that passively accepts the lot cast by our sinfulness. Just as sickness itself is an element and sign of the destructiveness brought about by human sinfulness, our resolute will to health in the face of sickness is the proper response to God's eschatological triumph in Christ over that destructiveness.

At the same time, "health, like life in general, is not an eternal but a temporal and therefore a limited possession" (p. 371). We have seen that for Barth this limitation is an expression of the goodness of God. In what sense is this so? It is worth quoting Barth's answer at length:

> Just because it is limited, it is a kind of natural and normal confirmation of the fact that by God's free grace man may live through Him and for Him, with the commission to be as man in accordance with the measure of his strength and powers, but not under the intolerable destiny of having to give sense, duration, and completeness to his existence by his own exertions and achievements, and therefore in obvious exclusion of the view that he must and may and can by his own strength and powers eternally maintain, assert, and confirm himself, attaining for himself his own dignity and honor. (pp. 372-73)

The temporal limit of life indicates the limit to our responsibility. As we live in and by God's grace it is not up to us to make our lives complete, self-sufficient, and whole by our own power and exertion, making them a substitute for the eternal life that, like our temporal life, is God's gift. There is a limit to what is demanded of human beings, and the temporal limit of human life reminds us of this truth. Thus, Barth asks, what if sickness "is not only the forerunner and messenger of death and judgment, but also, concealed under this form, . . . the forerunner and messenger of the eternal life which God has allotted and promised to the man who is graciously preserved and guided by Him within the confines of his time?" (p. 373).

It is significant that Barth poses this as a question, for "there is no question of giving up the will for health and the fight against sickness." However, "if this fight is to be fought rightly and finally, it will not exclude but include patience." Insofar as it remains present, sickness will have to be "borne." That it can be borne is made possible by the recognition that even in sickness we are being drawn to God (p. 374). Accordingly, illness and pain can be, indeed they must be, borne in joy (p. 374).

We believe it is significant that Barth's last word on the will to health (quite literally the last word in the English translation) speaks of the joy we may have in sickness. But before we discuss that significance we will summarize our argument to this point. We began our answer to the question of what it would mean to situate the practice of medicine in the context of the good life with one of the "Prayers for Use by a Sick Person" from the Book of Common Prayer. The points we wanted to make are that the answer to this question must begin with the patients whom medicine serves rather than with the profession of medicine itself, that this prayer gives us an indication of the virtues patients must have if we are to situate medicine in the good life as Christians understand it, and that the problem is that doctors and patients lack the common moral vocabulary to sustain the practice of medicine that is implied in these virtues.

After showing why we do not think Aristotle's vocabulary is suitable for this task, we turned to Karl Barth's discussion of the will to health. Here we found a vocabulary that focuses on those whom medicine serves, describing the ethical stance toward the possibilities and limitations of the body we must have if we are to make proper use of medicine. Like the prayer we began with, Barth knows that our fundamental responsibility before God and our neighbor regarding health is not something medicine can accomplish for us. Yet he also knows that medicine can assist us in exercising this responsibility, and it is in this role that medicine is to be received as God's gift (as Ecclesiasticus 38 rightly stresses). Finally, Barth places sickness and health in their eschatological dimension, which is necessary if we are to understand the prayer as a truthful one. Sickness is an element and sign of the world threatened by destruction due to sin, and our fight against sickness is our response to God's opposition to sin and its destruction. Yet within this same context, and without overriding the required will to health, sickness may be received as a concealed sign of the enclosure of our lives by God's grace and thus borne in joy.

On Being Seduced

Sickness can be borne in joy because to will life, that is, to obey the command of God to live, is also to will joy, delight, and happiness. Lear insightfully shows how Aristotle's account of happiness is a seduction that can only result in discontent with our ordinary lives and what amounts to the living of a deadly life. We think it is instructive, therefore, to contrast Barth's understanding of joy with Aristotle's understanding of happiness. For Aristotle, happiness must be complete and self-sufficient and must finally be under our control. For Barth, as we will now see, the joy that makes our lives worth living comes as a gift not under our control. "To be out of control" is what it means to learn to live eschatologically.[27]

---

27. At this point a comparison with Lear is instructive. For Lear the problem with Aristotle, and also with Plato and Freud, is that by constructing an "inside" (for Aristotle, the ethical life) in relation to which the true good is "outside" they perpetuate the problem of human life they are trying to solve. "For the idea is that ordinary life, restricted as it is by fantasy, is necessarily limited, but that if only we could break through all these limitations we would arrive at absolute knowledge and absolute happiness" (Lear, *Happiness, Death, and the Remainder of Life*, p. 163). For Lear the solution is to stop thinking of life in this way, namely, in terms of the fantasy of an outside into which we might escape the limitations of life as we experience it. From this perspective Barth might seem to be offering another such fantasy. But his eschatological theology breaks with the fantasy of an outside into which we might escape the

Barth describes joy as an interruption of the movement of continual striving that characterizes our lives as temporal, a point where that movement is momentarily arrested.

> [Man's] life as movement in time has led him to a point where it gives him no more trouble but presents and offers itself as a gift. . . . Joy is really the simplest form of gratitude. When we are joyful, time stands still for a moment or moments because it has fulfilled its meaning as the space of our life-movement and, engaged in this movement, we have attained in one respect at least the goal of our striving. . . . In so far and for so long as we know true joy, we desire only the duration of this fulfillment, of life in the form of a gift, and therefore of the joyful moment. . . . The desire for duration, even if realized only in a single case, is an essential characteristic of all joy as such. (pp. 376-77)

Thus, unlike Aristotle, and like Lear, Barth locates joy in moments of interruption rather than in one's life envisioned as a complete whole, or what Lear calls "our teleologically organized strivings."[28] At the same time, Barth observes, joy is not pure interruption without relation to the rest of our life; it is "an intensification, strengthening, deepening and elevation of the whole awareness of life which as such is necessarily more than joy" (p. 382).

Neither is joy self-sufficient. This point brings us to the key to Barth's concept of joy and indeed to his understanding of life as such: joy is the gift of God's grace. "To be joyful is to expect that life will reveal itself as God's gift of grace, that it will present and offer itself in provisional fulfillments of its meaning and intention as movement. To be joyful means to look out for opportunities for gratitude." Although respect for life re-

---

limitations of life as we experience it. For, as the gift of grace, life as he understands it is what it is precisely by virtue of its interruption from outside. That is why it can only be lived eschatologically.

28. Lear, *Happiness, Death, and the Remainder of Life*, p. 129. Lear's concept of happiness as living without a principle, in openness to the wealth of possibilities life offers (pp. 164-65), superficially resembles Barth's concept of joy. Yet the resemblance is superficial in the end, for while Barth's moments of joy are eschatological interruptions of grace (see the previous footnote), Lear's moments of happiness are purely chance occasions.

quires the "will to joy," that is, the ready anticipation that life will reveal itself as God's gift, joy is not "an event to be enacted and established by ourselves" (p. 378).

Finally, because joy is the gift of God and because we have rebelled against his gift and live only by his mercy, it is not in our power to discover what constitutes the fulfillment that gratitude evokes. But we should not limit that fulfillment by excluding suffering from it. Barth's language for this reality is that all that is, including our lives, stands under the shadow of the cross. Accordingly, the "real test of our joy of life as a commanded and therefore a true and good joy is that we do not evade the shadow of the cross of Jesus Christ and are not unwilling to be genuinely joyful as we bear the sorrows laid upon us" (p. 383).

This last point is not a matter of limiting joy by scaling back expectations of it, as the Stoics sometimes did. Rather, it is how Christians are formed to be joyful even in suffering. For it turns out that our capacity for joy is but a correlative of our capacity for suffering. The Christian, therefore, must accept "with reverence and gratitude the mystery and wonder of the life given to us by God, its beauty and radiance, and the blessing, refreshment, consolation and encouragement which it radiates as the gift of God, even where it presents itself to us in its alien form" (p. 384). It is, of course, in this alien form that sickness may be an occasion of joy.

For a Nietzsche, of course, all Barth (or rather, God!) has done is seduced us into affirming life by giving a meaning to our suffering. Yet for Nietzsche, to be seduced into affirming life is not a bad thing, and in this sense he understood to some degree what Barth's entire discussion of respect for life is meant to convey, namely, that temporal life is an incomparable gift of God, even with all its limitations and afflictions, and that it is an incomparable loss when life is not received as the gift it is. Respect for life requires that we live in the expectation of joy even as we stand (or lie) in the shadow of the cross. At its worst, medicine (or at least our expectations of medicine) cuts us off from the joy we may have on such occasions by fueling our fantasies of control. But at its best, as Barth realized, medicine is a great help to us in fulfilling that requirement. And when it does play this role medicine speaks, in its own idiom, the language of the prayer we began with.

Disability: An Attempt to Think With

The Challenge

The challenge for anyone who would try to reflect on the suffering of those who are described as disabled is that they must do so from the presumption that they are not disabled. As a result, it is hard to avoid appearing pretentious and arrogant to those who are disabled as well as those who care for the disabled. It is always a dangerous practice to write about others, to try to characterize the life of others, because it is too easy to project on their lives our fears and fantasies. Such projections become particularly dangerous when someone, often with the best will in the world, tries to say what it means to be disabled as well as how those who are disabled should command our attention.

Note how the challenge that I am suggesting is entailed by attempts to think about disabilities is implicated by the grammar of the preceding sentence. To suggest, as that sentence does, that the disabled have no way to protect themselves from the power of those who try to say why and how the disabled should be understood and cared for presumes that those who are disabled are "helpless." That, of course, is not the case, as anyone who has learned to live with someone whom we identify as disabled can testify. I will have more to say about what it means for us to live with one another, but I must first try to develop some categories for better understanding the challenge of the "with."

The problem is manifest in the presumption that the very category "disability" is a useful way to describe anyone. What it means to be deaf, blind, intellectually disabled, young, and old is so different that it seems to make little sense to lump these various conditions under a general category called "disability." It turns out that there is such variety in each of these designations, and more could easily be added, that it is by no means clear that we have learned anything useful by characterizing someone as deaf or intellectually disabled. That we learn little from such categorizations makes the use of the general description "disabled" all the more problematic.

That I have included in the list the young and the old is, of course, a gesture to help us think again about our tendency to use the language of disability to create a world of "us" and "them." Xavier Le Pichon, in a powerful reflection on the significant work of Jean Vanier and Fr. Thomas Philippe, observes that they considered infancy and old age, with their proximity of death and its suffering, as the two golden ages of our lives. Vanier and Philippe did so because they thought a common characteristic of being young or old was a vulnerability that is forgotten or denied in the more active periods of our lives. Our experience of vulnerability, they think, is a resource for helping us understand the vulnerability of persons with disabilities.

According to Le Pichon, Vanier and Philippe identify these ages as golden because they think the vulnerability we experience by being young or old creates the condition that makes the work of the Holy Spirit possible. To be young or old is to lack the means, as the disabled do, to disguise our desire to be loved. Yet that "weakness" enables the Holy Spirit to act toward the young, the old, and the disabled in a special way. Le Pichon observes that the Holy Spirit makes "the immense love of God" present to those who suffer the lack of tenderness that only love can provide.[1]

To call attention to vulnerability to characterize the commonalities between those who suffer from intellectual disabilities, the old, and the young can threaten, however, to make the general category of disability meaningless. To be human is to be vulnerable — this sounds not only true but wise. Such an observation, however, can be the kind of generalization

---

1. Xavier Le Pichon, "The Sign of Contradiction," in *The Paradox of Disability*, ed. Hans Reinders (Grand Rapids: Eerdmans, 2010), p. 96.

that hides from us the different kinds of vulnerabilities that characterize particular lives. Le Pichon, however, is surely right to direct attention to the times in our lives when we find it difficult to hide from ourselves or others that we need help. In truth, we are bodily creatures subject to illness and accidents at any time of our lives, but we are quite capable of suppressing knowledge of our finitude — a suppression that I suspect is one of the reasons we are so intent to distance ourselves from those who are disabled.

I think Le Pichon is right to suggest that our desire to love and to be loved is the heart of the matter. In her recent book, *Wandering in Darkness: Narrative and the Problem of Suffering*, Eleonore Stump, drawing on Aquinas, develops an account very much like Le Pichon's understanding of the relation between our desire to be loved and our vulnerabilty.[2] For example, Stump calls attention to Vanier's account of the loneliness engendered by shame, a shame that often pervades the lives of those described as intellectually disabled, which can only be overwhelmed by the love Vanier has learned to receive and give by living with his friends in L'Arche.[3]

Such love is constituted by narratives that make it possible for Vanier to know that his friend is mentally handicapped but without that knowledge becoming a form of domination. Thus for Vanier the name of his friend is more determinative for their relation than what may characterize the friend's "disability." To know the name of someone who is also mentally disabled I take to be what it means to risk wanting to be loved even when we may think we suffer from a disability that makes it difficult for us to be loved.[4]

I do not pretend, however, that the vulnerability created by our desire to love and be loved "solves" what I regard as the insolvable and acute problem of labeling. Licia Carlson helpfully calls attention to the differ-

---

2. Eleonore Stump, *Wandering in Darkness: Narrative and the Problem of Suffering* (New York: Oxford University Press, 2010), pp. 90-97.

3. Stump, *Wandering in Darkness*, pp. 146-47.

4. Hans Reinders has developed a compelling account of the significance of friendship for understanding the relationship between the profoundly disabled and those who are not, in his book *Receiving the Gift of Friendship: Profound Disability, Theological Anthropology, and Ethics* (Grand Rapids: Eerdmans, 2008).

ence between the clinical and the social systems approach to describing and labeling intellectual disability. The clinical or medical model views intellectual disability as a condition of an individual that has pathological characteristics that transcend socio-cultural groups. In contrast, the social systems approach sees intellectual disability as a status entailed by a social system and the role played by a person in that system.[5]

Advocates of the social systems approach generally maintain that disability is a social construction. Applied to the deaf, those who assume a systems approach argue, for example, that deafness should not be considered to be a category of disability, but rather the deaf are to be understood as a linguistic minority. Yet even if it is acknowledged that various categories of disability are socially constructed, it nonetheless remains the case that some categories of disability must continue to be used so that persons with severe intellectual and physical disabilities receive the care and support they need.[6] The challenge is how that is to be done without the categories becoming self-fulfilling or self-legitimating forms of discrimination.

Carlson helpfully suggests that a category like "intellectual disability" is best understood as a contingent classification, which means that it is not in the philosophical sense a natural kind; that is, it is not a name for an inevitable necessity. Accordingly, the description "intellectual disability" rightly is a category that must change over time, not only in reference to a class, but also for individuals. It is quite possible, for example, that, given a radical change in the environment, an individual might no longer be thought to be "disabled."[7] What must always be kept in mind, however, is that the categories used to characterize disabilities are "interactive," which means that they "are applied to self-conscious individuals who are aware of these labels and may act and react in such a way that in turn affects the nature of the classification itself; and they are affected by the discursive practices and institutions in which these labels are defined and maintained."[8]

---

5. Licia Carlson, *The Faces of Intellectual Disability: Philosophical Reflections* (Bloomington: Indiana University Press, 2010), p. 87.

6. Carlson, *The Faces of Intellectual Disability,* pp. 88-89.

7. Carlson, *The Faces of Intellectual Disability,* p. 93.

8. Carlson, *The Faces of Intellectual Disability,* p. 95.

"Interactive" is, I hope to show, but another name for why it matters that the most compelling accounts we have concerning disabilities take the form of stories. For example, Ellen Painter Dollar, in her book *No Easy Choice: A Story of Disability, Parenthood, and Faith in an Age of Advanced Reproduction,* provides a well-informed account of the moral ambiguities surrounding the use of the technology of preimplantation genetic diagnosis (PGD). She used this technology once to try to avoid having another child who might suffer as she and her daughter do from a brittle bone disease. That disease makes those who suffer from it extremely susceptible to broken bones. Dollar, however, decided after further reflection to abandon the attempt to use PGD, but she nonetheless chose to have two more children who might have been born suffering from the same disease. Happily they were born free of the disease.

In her book Dollar reports on the ethical issues surrounding the use of PGD by drawing on the philosophical and theological resources available. Yet she is quite explicit that she does not regard that aspect of her book to constitute the primary argument of the book. Rather, it is the story she has to tell of how she came to the decision not to use PGD that is the heart of her book. That is why her book is in the form of a memoir. It is so because she hopes that by telling her story she might be of help to others in a similar situation. But, equally important, she argues that the narrative of her life is a form of moral deliberation that is particularly significant in the face of a life like her own.[9]

Some time ago I wrote a book on the suffering and death of children entitled *Naming the Silences: God, Medicine, and the Problem of Suffering.* I did not think of the book as "my book" because the book consists primarily of stories I tell that are not unlike Dollar's story of her struggle with her and her daughter's illness.[10] I argued that without such stories medicine threatens to be a technology shaped to no purpose other than the elimination of suffering and death. Yet Christians believe we are de-

9. Ellen Painter Dollar, *No Easy Choice: A Story of Disability, Parenthood, and Faith in an Age of Advanced Reproduction* (Louisville: Westminster/John Knox, 2012), pp. 144-47.

10. Stanley Hauerwas, *Naming the Silences: God, Medicine, and the Problem of Suffering* (Grand Rapids: Eerdmans, 1990). The second edition of the book used only the subtitle as the title for the book.

termined by a narrative that can make what we suffer purposeful. Note that I did not say the fact that our lives can be narrated makes it possible to explain suffering. Rather, I tried to show, and show is the operative word, in *Naming the Silences* that in the absence of explanations for suffering the story that makes us Christian provides a way to go on. It is that contention I now want to develop by drawing on Eleonore Stump's argument that the knowledge we gain through narratives is crucial if we are to know how to be with those we label as disabled. Such knowledge, moreover, is a knowledge made possible by love.

Why Stories Matter

Stump begins her account of narrative by quoting Isak Dinesen's statement, "All sorrows can be borne if you . . . tell a story about them." Stump confesses that she is not sure Dinesen's claim is true, but Stump is sure that reflection on suffering is better with the help of a story.[11] Crucial to Stump's argument is the contention that there are things to be known by way of a narrative that cannot be known by more analytical modes of reasoning. The latter way of intending the world Stump characterizes as Dominican because it thrives on abstract properties and designations. In contrast, a Franciscan mode of knowledge divides up and describes the world on the basis of typologies that require an acquaintance with stories and persons (pp. 40-41). Of course, to distinguish between ways of knowing by naming the alternatives Dominican and Franciscan is an exemplification of a Franciscan way to think.

According to Stump, the Dominican way of knowledge consists in having an attitude toward a proposition. It is to know *that*. Such knowledge is not to be dismissed because it is extremely important for sustaining our lives. It is knowledge that draws on first- and third-person avowals (pp. 49-50). In contrast, Stump claims that there is a kind of knowledge of persons that is not reducible to knowledge *that*. This is second-person knowledge, which requires that we actually have interaction with another person to have the knowledge we say we possess (p. 53).

---

11. Stump, *Wandering in Darkness*, p. 26. Hereafter references to *Wandering in Darkness* will appear in the text.

Stump helpfully illustrates the variety of this latter kind of knowledge by calling attention to its expression in sentences such as, "Joseph knew that the men he saw in front of him in the crowd were his brothers," or "Thomas Aquinas knew the presence of God in the Eucharist" (pp. 53-55). Stump observes that such sentences make clear that one could not hope to characterize the knowledge implied without the narratives that make those sentences make sense. Thus to "know" why it is significant that Joseph recognized his brothers we need to know that they had tried to kill him. That Aquinas knew God is present in the Eucharist entails the story of God in Christ.

Moreover, it is within such narrative contexts that we begin to understand that the problem with the assumption that there is something called *the* problem of suffering is the singular *the*.[12] The stories we tell and stories we are told identify different kinds of suffering and raise different kinds of questions and beg for different kinds of responses. So the narratives that constitute the lives of those who suffer matter for determining the kind of challenge raised by stories such as those of Job, Samson, Abraham, and Mary of Bethany. Different though they may be, however, Stump helps us see how each of these stories in quite different ways involves our desire to be loved and to love.[13]

Accordingly, Stump argues that any account of the challenges suffering raises entails narratives of our relations with one another. To develop this point she calls attention to the challenge of those who suffer from autism. She does so because those who suffer from autism seem to be unable to sustain second-person interactions that make the kind of knowledge that narratives constitute possible. The social isolation, the lack of eye contact, and the absence of empathy so often associated with autism are the conditions that make their knowledge of the world and other persons problematic.

---

12. This way of putting the matter reflects more my understanding of Stump. I should like to think she might be in agreement, but I do not want to attribute to her my interpretation. Though Stump sometimes suggests that *Wandering in Darkness* is a book dealing with "the problem of evil," I do not think in fact that is the primary subject of the book. Suffering, not evil, is her primary theme.

13. The heart of Stump's book is a close reading of the stories of Job, Samson, Abraham, and Mary of Bethany. She refuses, for example, to separate the prologue and epilogue of the Book of Job from the poetic parts of the book on the grounds that the epilogue and prologue manifest God's desire to redeem through love even Satan.

Moreover, autism, Stump suggests, is rooted in our biology. She is impressed by recent findings involving the significance of the mirror neurons in the brain that are crucial for our knowledge of other persons. These neurons fire in the brain both when "one does some action one-self *and also* when one sees the same action being performed by someone else" (p. 68). Mirror neurons, therefore, seem to be the biological conditions that make it possible for babies to experience someone else as a person. To the extent that autistic children are deficient in their knowledge of the mental states of other people, that deficiency is not because they lack knowledge of the *that;* rather, they are impaired because they lack the capacity for the kind of knowledge that is not reducible to the *that* (p. 67).

Stump even suggests that the discovery of mirror neurons confirms Wittgenstein's remark, "We *see* emotion — As opposed to what? — We do not see facial contortions and *make the inference* that he is feeling joy, grief, boredom" (p. 67). The mirror neuron system, while capable of being described in first- and third-person perspectives, is generated by second-person experiences. Accordingly, second-person experience cannot be reduced to first- or third-person experience without remainder (p. 78).

That is why second-person expressions take the form of a story, which makes second-person experiences available to us in such a manner that they can be shared by a wider audience. Stump puts it this way: "a story gives a person some of what she would have had if she had had un-mediated personal interaction with the characters in the story while they were conscious and interacting with each other, without actually making her part of the story itself. The re-presenting of a second-person experience in a story thus constitutes a second-person account. It is a report of a set of second-person experiences that does not lose the distinctively second-person character of the experiences" (p. 78).

To be a person is to find through others the possibility of a life that can be storied. There is therefore an interrelation between the storied character of our lives and the character of love. Drawing on Niko Kolodny's account of love, Stump suggests that our love for another is not without reason, but the reason is constituted by the lover's relationship with the beloved. Such a relationship, moreover, is historical because whatever relationship in which I may stand with someone at any given time depends on our pasts. Therefore one of the reasons for loving another is the ongoing history one shares with that person (p. 88).

Stump enriches this account of love by calling attention to Aquinas's understanding of love as requiring the interconnected desires of the good of the beloved as well as the desire for union with the beloved (p. 91). These two desires are not independent of one another, particularly when the ultimate good that binds those who love one another is the desire for union with God. To be capable of such love requires that we desire the good for ourselves and thus that we be in union with ourselves. Therefore the good requires internal integration because without the ability to rightly love ourselves we cannot love another rightly (pp. 100-101).

According to Stump, the worst thing that can happen to a person from Aquinas's perspective is to become permanently psychically fragmented, making possible alienation from oneself, from others, and from God. God has through Christ made himself known in history in a manner that makes God's desire to be close to us sure. So nothing can separate us from the love of God even when we will to pursue that which is not our good, with the result that we are divided against ourselves. Such a "willed loneliness" is unfortunately the condition in which we find ourselves, making our lives incoherent narratives of distorted loves (pp. 129-50). But we are not without hope because through forgiveness regeneration is possible, making possible lives with the capacity to love and be loved, that is, to share a common story.

We suffer from our determination to love and be loved on our terms rather than desiring that which is our true good; but no matter how alienated we may be from God, "to one degree or another God is always present to every sufferer. No sufferer is isolated from the love of the omnipresent God; and to the extent to which the sufferer is open to it, the presence of God to the sufferer comes with shared attention and closeness, for the consolation of the sufferer" (p. 411). Given our sin, therefore, that world, a world in which the mystery of individual suffering must remain unexplained, is governed by God who has not abandoned us.

Therefore, for Aquinas, even the worst and apparently hopeless suffering has a point. It is a mistake to think the point will be or can be made apparent at the time. Nor does the claim that suffering has a point justify indifference in the face of suffering. Stump argues that, though God can use suffering for our good, it does not follow that this gives us permission to remain indifferent to our suffering or to the suffering of others (p. 477). Our suffering, the suffering of others, can be the occasion for interaction that makes possible the impossibility of telling the stories of our lives independent of one another. Such interdependence, moreover, is the reality love names.

Stump uses Claiborne Park's story of her care of Jessy, her fourth child, who suffered from autism, to illumine the relation between love and the storied character of our lives. Claiborne Park, who confesses to having no faith in God, describes herself as an intelligent and intuitive person who was proud of the three lovely children she had raised. Her pride, however, was challenged by the suffering, pain, and sheer exhaustion that came with the birth of her fourth child, Jessy, who is autistic. Yet Park writes that it is true "that one grows by suffering. And that too is Jessy's gift. I write now what fifteen years past I would still not have thought possible to write: that if today I were given the choice, to accept the experience, with everything that it entails, or to refuse the bitter largesse, I would have to stretch out my hands — because out of it has come, for all of us, an unimaginable life. And I will not change the last word of the story. It is still love" (p. 470).

Stump wisely does not try to use Park's story to suggest that Park *really* believes in God. But she does observe that Park has grown through suffering just to the extent that her life has been integrated by her goodness through love. Park came to see "even the suffering of her life as gift." By writing her book, Park gives voice to how, through the "alteration affected in her by suffering, by her heartbreak over her daughter's autism, she found her heart's desire anyway, only in a way much different from that in which she had originally sought it. As she herself testifies, in the bitter largesse of that gift — from her daughter, from a giver unacknowledged by a breather of thin, faithless air — she found something she cared to have more than she cared to have what she lost in the suffering" (p. 471).

Yet Stump's account of Park's love story seems to ignore the question, "But what about Jessy?" Jessy suffers from autism. Jessy does not seem to have a life that can be storied as she has made possible for her mother's life to be storied. Stump acknowledges that her account of the relation of love and narrative, which she develops as a response to suffering, is one limited to "fully functioning adult human beings." It is not meant to apply to human beings who are not adult, who are not fully functional mentally, or to non-human animals. One cannot help but think, however, that more needs to be said.

For example, Alex Sider in a paper on disabilities calls attention to his godson, Martin, who is autistic and has a hard time communicating the world in which he lives with words, making difficult his interaction with others. Sider quotes from Martin's mother's blog about Martin's being appointed "leader of the day" in his class at school. His mother writes that "Martin's willingness to compromise so that he can be the leader reminds me that the poor kid is just trying to feel in control of at least one thing in his life. A world with established routines and people. But that world can't be so predictable and established by adults that he feels no sense of freedom."

Sider observes that it is a good thing that Martin's appointment as class leader may help him develop a sense of belonging and acceptance, but it is also a vivid reminder of how out-of-control Martin's life remains. Sider confesses, therefore, that though he wants Martin to be Martin, the fact that he wants him to be free and competitive with typically developing children means that Sider does not "want him to have his disability." Sider suggests, moreover, that the thought that he does not want Martin to have his disability rightly challenges some of the romantic reflections on disability legitimated by some theological accounts of disability. How are we to rightly regard the Martins of our world as precious creatures of God and yet wish they might not suffer from their disability? That question I take to be an intensification of questions surrounding the labeling of the disabled.

On Being With

Sam Wells and Marcia Owen, in a book that deals with the development of liturgies for families and friends of murder victims in neighborhoods of Durham, North Carolina, develop categories that I think can help us think how at least some response to Sider's challenge is possible. The book is entitled *Living without Enemies: Being Present in the Midst of Violence*. The book tells the story of how Marcia Owen found a way to respond to the murders through gatherings shaped by prayer. She recognized that there was nothing that could be done to make those who had been murdered return to life, but a response was possible even when it seemed that any response could not help but seem inadequate.

Wells begins their book, therefore, by characterizing four responses to the question elicited in such circumstances, that is, "How can I help?" The first response is that of the professionals with well-trained skills who think of themselves as "working for" those who need help. With the best will in the world, these professionals, who are often philanthropists, can unintentionally, by the way they intervene, rob those they desire to "help" of any voice.

A second way to think about how one might help Wells identifies with those who seek to "work with" those identified as disadvantaged. In contrast to those who work for those in need, people who work with those needing help abandon any pretension of "expertise" in order to help others discover their own solutions based on their understanding of the "problem."[14]

A third way in which one might help, "being with," describes a way not orientated to providing solutions because it is assumed that more important is the formation of companionship amid struggle and distress. Wells identifies Jean Vanier's work with L'Arche and the hospice movement as paradigmatic forms of "being with." For example, Jean Vanier's discovery of his vulnerability in the process of being with the vulnerable is the kind of insight Wells expects "being with" to make possible. In a similar fashion, learning to be with the dying turns out to be a reminder of our common humanity.

Wells thinks there is a fourth way to respond to the question of how we can be of help when it seems that there is nothing that can be done to help. He calls this "being for" those in need. This way of responding Wells suggests may seem to be "a poor relation" to the other three approaches

14. Samuel Wells and Marcia Owen, *Living without Enemies: Being Present in the Midst of Violence* (Downers Grove: InterVarsity, 2011), pp. 26-30.

because it may seem to "do nothing." Wells argues, however, that those who teach in universities, whose work may not address explicitly issues of justice, nonetheless can rightly hope that their work as well as their lives make a difference to those who are disadvantaged. In a similar fashion, the prayers of monastics for the poor may be a singular way of being of service to the poor.[15]

Wells explores each of these four responses to expose their strengths and weaknesses. The "working for" model tends to dominate the imagination of many who seek to be of service, and no doubt much good is done by those who undertake the task of trying to help those less fortunate. The problem with those who work for others, however, is that a relationship of inequality is assumed that can be humiliating, making friendship impossible. "Working with" the disadvantaged has the advantage of trusting the disadvantaged, recognizing that how one achieves a goal is as important as the goal itself.[16]

To "be with" may seem indistinguishable from "working with," but to be with the disadvantaged means that you must experience in your own life the disempowerment associated with the disadvantaged. To "be with" requires that the experience of poverty in its many forms shapes your body in such a manner that a commonality of trust is made possible. For those shaped by the strategies of "working for" and "working with," the stance of "being with" seems hopeless because those who are so determined do not see those for whom they care as a problem to be solved. To "be for" runs the risk of being so sensitive and knowledgeable about the issues that it can end by leaving those who are disadvantaged alone.[17]

Wells suggests that these alternative ways of engagement can be used to display the character of Jesus' life and ministry. Jesus certainly worked for and with Israel, but Wells argues that it is a mistake to fail to remember that before his ministry in Galilee Jesus spent thirty years in Nazareth. That he did so, Wells suggests, makes clear that Jesus' work for and with us was made possible because he spent the years in Nazareth being with us. Wells asks what difference that might make for how we approach

---

15. Wells and Owen, *Living without Enemies*, pp. 30-32.
16. Wells and Owen, *Living without Enemies*, pp. 34-36.
17. Wells and Owen, *Living without Enemies*, pp. 38-40.

engagement with the socially disadvantaged. He answers by suggesting that the work of Christ has made it possible for those who would follow him to work with and to be with those we care for because we believe that is the way God is with us.[18]

Put in terms identified by Stump, what Wells's account of being with and for helps us see is that we have the time to discover that through Christ we share a common story with those we mistakenly assume do not have the ability to narrate their lives. For in truth none of us has the ability to know what stories we are living out until our lives are connected with other lives, our bodies are touched by other bodies, making possible a common story rightly called a love story. The presence of those identified as the disabled is but a prismatic exemplification of how we learn to be human beings by learning one another's name.

I noted above that I know of no satisfactory way to deal with the problem of labeling the disabled. But I hope by calling attention to Stump's account of narrative and Wells's understanding of modes of intervention we can at least imagine how to be of "help" without the way we try to help only contributing to the problem. Labeling is a strategy that seems necessary if we are to "work for" the disadvantaged. Much that needs to be done is made possible by the labels that legitimate interventions meant to aid those in need. But working for can make us forget that we must know how to work with and be with those whom we would aid.

I suspect we are tempted to take the stance of working for the disadvantaged because too often those we would help at once frighten and frustrate us. They frighten us because we fear the acknowledgment of a common humanity. They frustrate us because too often there does not seem to be anything that can be done to "make things better." But that is to fail to see that there is always something that can be done. What can be done is, as Stump suggests, to love and be loved, making possible a common story. Such a love may be difficult and hard, but that is how we know it is of God.

Sider was right to wish that Martin was not autistic. Dollar was right to wish her daughter had not been born with brittle bone disease. Dollar was right to rejoice that her other children did not suffer from her dis-

18. Wells and Owen, *Living without Enemies*, p. 43.

ease. But let us rejoice that Sider and Martin have one another, that the Dollar family exists, for without stories like theirs we would not know what love looks like.

Index

narrative logic of, 84; redemption
of, 82
To Relieve the Human Condition
(McKenny), 204
"To Serve Our God and to Rule the
World" (Yoder), 25, 150
Tolstoy, Leo, 20, 128
Tradition-constituted rationality,
114-15
Traditions, 101, 115n43
"Treatise on Habits" (Aquinas),
163-64
"Treatise on the Last End" (Aquinas),
164
"Treatise on the Passions" (Aquinas),
166n20
Trinity, 10, 20-21, 110
Trust, 182, 189-90
Truth, 37-38

Unintended Reformation (Gregory),
79n34, 107n22
Unity: as aim of ecumenism, 96-97;
and catholicity, 113-19; as challenge
for Protestantism, 91, 119; and
conflict, 109, 117; denominational,
104, 105; of government, 106; and
locality, 110-12, 116-17; of love, 117;
through worship, 110; and truth
of the gospel, 114. *See also* Catholicity; Ecumenical movement;
Ecumenism
University, ix-x

Vanier, Jean, 223, 224, 233
Vatican II, 101-2
Vices, 164
Violence, 21n53, 26-27, 85
Virtues: acquired moral virtues, 170-
71; and habituation, 160-63; health
as, 187; infused moral virtues, 170-
71; and liturgy, 163n13; of medical

patients, 200-201, 218; operative,
170n28; produced by catholicity,
118; as reflection of God's love, 187;
semblance of, 172, 175
*Vital Ministry in the Small-
Membership Church* (Mather), 94
Vitalism, 211
Vogel, Jeffrey, 6n14
Voltaire, 130
Vulnerability, 223-24

Wainwright, Geoffrey, 99n2
Wandering in Darkness (Stump), 224
War: "blank check" stance toward,
135n35; characterizing, 120-24; and
difficulty of reality, 149; as idolatry,
85n49; in Iraq, 89; justification of,
122, 132-34; Kant's view of, 124-29;
and mass murder, 85; religious,
129-32; as sacrifice, xivn9, 34-35,
36, 70
"War and Peace" (Hauerwas), xiv, 120
War and the American Difference
(Hauerwas), xiv, xivn9, 85n49
War and the Christian Conscience
(Ramsey), 133
"Wars of religion," 129-30
Wealth, 90
Webster, John, 4n4
Wells, Sam, 117n48, 232-35
Wesley, John, 93
Western culture: civil religion in, 69;
martyrdom as threat to, 70; politics
of, 35; role of church in, 71; and
witness, 54, 62
"Which Church? Whose Unity?"
(Hauerwas), 98
Whitfield, Joshua, 61n49
"Why Gays (as a Group) Are Mor-
ally Superior to Christians (as a
Group)" (Hauerwas), 89
Wilken, Robert, 3-4, 5-6